GREAT BRITAIN AND THE UNITED STATES

Special Relations since World War II

TWAYNE'S INTERNATIONAL HISTORY SERIES

Akira Iriye, editor
Harvard University

GREAT BRITAIN AND THE UNITED STATES

Special Relations since World War II

Robert M. Hathaway

TWAYNE PUBLISHERS • BOSTON
A DIVISION OF G.K. HALL & CO.

Published by Twayne Publishers
A division of G. K. Hall & Co.
70 Lincoln Street, Boston, Massachusetts 02111

Twayne's International History Series, no. 4

Designed by Barbara Anderson
Produced by Gabrielle B. McDonald
Copyediting supervised by Barbara Sutton

Printed on permanent/durable acid-free paper
and bound in the United States of America

First Printing, 1990

Library of Congress Cataloging-in-Publication Data

Hathaway, Robert M., 1947–
    Great Britain and the United States : special relations since
World War II / Robert M. Hathaway.
        p.   cm.—(Twayne's international history series ; no. 4)
    Includes bibliographical references.
    ISBN 0-8057-7909-4 (alk. paper).—ISBN 0-8057-9206-6 (pbk. :
alk. paper)
    1. United States—Foreign relations—Great Britain. 2. Great
Britain—Foreign relations—United States. 3. United States—
Foreign relations—1945–   4. Great Britain—Foreign
relations—1945–   I. Title. II. Series.
E183.8.G7H36 1990
327.73041—dc20

ISBN 0-8057-7909-4 (alk. paper). 10 9 8 7 6 5 4 3 2 1
ISBN 0-805-9206-6 (pbk.: alk. paper). 10 9 8 7 6 5 4 3 2 1

For
Susie
Amy, Kristin, Kelly
with love

Lord Palmerston once said that Britain has no permanent friends—she has only permanent interests. With due respect to that illustrious British statesman, I must disagree. For Americans, Britain is a permanent friend, and the unbreakable link between our two nations is our permanent interest.

—Lyndon Johnson, 1966

In pursuit of the will-o'-the-wisp of Anglo-American partnership, the British have succeeded in castrating themselves intellectually, politically and morally.

—British historian Robert Skidelsky, 1971

CONTENTS

LIST OF ILLUSTRATIONS

The following illustrations are found between pages 69 and 70.

FOREWORD

Twayne's International History Series seeks to publish reliable and readable accounts of post–World War II international affairs. Today, nearly fifty years after the end of the war, the time seems opportune for a critical assessment of world affairs in the second half of the twentieth century. What have been the major themes and trends in international relations since 1945? How have they evolved and changed over time? What have been the connections between international and domestic affairs? How have states and peoples defined and pursued their objectives and what have they contributed to the world at large? How have conceptions of warfare and visions of peace changed in the last fifty years?

These questions must be raised in any attempt to understand the contemporary world. That understanding must be both international—with an awareness of the linkages among different parts of the world—and historical—with a keen sense of what the immediate past has brought to human civilization. Hence the *International History* Series. It is hoped that the volumes in this series will help the reader in exploring important events and decisions since 1945 and in developing the global awareness and historical sensitivity required for confronting today's problems.

The first volumes in the series examine the United States' relations with other countries, groups of countries, or regions. The stress on the United States is justified in part because of the nation's predominant position in postwar international relations, and also because far more extensive documentation is available on American foreign affairs than is the case with other countries. The series addresses not only those interested in international relations, but also those studying American and other countries' histories, who will find here useful guides and fresh insights into the recent past. Now more than ever it is imperative to understand the linkages between national and international history.

This volume offers a comprehensive account of postwar U.S.–British relations. Based on a great deal of archival research in the two countries, the book carefully and methodically looks at strategic, political, economic, and other aspects of the "special relationship" as it has developed, become sidetracked, or been reaffirmed over the years. Robert M. Hathaway, a specialist in postwar American and British history, has taken pains to look at both the United States and Britain to understand their mutual perceptions, expectations, and misgivings. The emphasis on personalities as well as on domestic politics makes for very lively reading. The book is an excellent introduction to the study of recent international history.

Akira Iriye

INTRODUCTION

The people of the United Kingdom, a leading British statesman warned in 1987, must guard against assuming that "Americans see their international interests and objectives as always identical with ours. . . . We should never take it for granted that the Americans always see what we see."[1] Coming at a time when virtually every measure of British popular opinion indicated a widespread uneasiness with the policies of the United States, David Owen's statement was remarkable. Indeed, it would have been a remarkable statement at any time; one's countrymen do not customarily need to be cautioned that their interests seldom correspond exactly with those of another country. But it was all the more extraordinary to hear such a warning at this particular moment. In 1987, poll after poll suggested that the average Briton believed that the United States could not be counted upon to look after British interests. In 1987, Britons still smarted over American use of British bases to launch an air raid against Libya. In 1987, the Iran–contra hearings daily reinforced the prevalent British skepticism about the judgment and competence in Ronald Reagan's Washington. And yet in 1987, a former British foreign secretary felt compelled to remind his countrymen not to postulate an automatic identity of interests with the United States. Why? Was this simply an exercise in redundancy? Or did Owen's injunction hint at something more fundamental about ties between the United States and the United Kingdom?

The answer to these questions lies in a history that reaches back nearly half a century. After 170 or so years of mutual suspicion, punctuated by overt hostility and, twice, actual war, the two Atlantic democracies in the spring of 1940 found themselves suddenly drawn together by a common repugnance to Nazism. Nurtured by war and by a British prime minister who saw an Anglo–

American partnership as a means to escape the consequences of the decline in British power that two global conflicts had brought about, the British–American alliance retained much of its wartime saliency after the cessation of fighting in 1945. Over the next forty-odd years, relations between London and Washington waxed and waned, but always within the context of the "special relationship" that fact and fantasy had woven around the British–American connection.

Of course, there were always skeptics who doubted that the special relationship represented anything more than the wishful thinking of small groups of American East Coast Anglophiles and Pilgrim Society types in the United Kingdom. "Hands-across-the-sea sentimentalism," some derisively labeled the notion. But while a fair amount of sentimental nonsense has undoubtedly been written about this relationship, it is nonetheless true that an exceptionally intimate relationship has bound the two nations over the past half–century. Even their quarrels assumed a distinctive flavor, if for no other reason than because each demanded a higher standard of conduct from the other than is customarily expected in international discourse.

At bottom, a special relationship rests on a shared view of the desirable directions in which each nation should be trying to move. Agreement over the best means to achieve these objectives, over tactics, is not always necessary. Indeed, the effort to hammer out common policies might well place more strain on the relationship than it can easily handle. But nations enjoying a special relationship share, by definition, a fundamental consensus, a common vision of the basic shape of the world in which each desires to live, and of the acceptable rules of behavior each ought to follow in pursuit of that vision.

But more than this, in the special relationship that has linked the United States and the United Kingdom since the fall of France in 1940, the two nations have been drawn together by largely identical views on the nature of the external challenge confronting both—a challenge posed first by Nazi Germany, later by the Soviet Union. Over the past half-century strategic interest has furnished the underpinnings of the special relationship. "Most of all," one historian has succinctly stated, "the Anglo–American 'Special Relationship' has been about security."[2] For the United States, another has written, the British tie has furnished "a sense of company in a confusing, unfriendly world."[3] And what was true for the Americans was doubly true for the British. An "absolute lifeline," Foreign Secretary R. A. Butler termed his country's links to Washington.[4]

Of course, the special relationship has not been equally special to the two nations. At the root of the relationship—any relationship—lay the matter of comparative power. Because of the asymmetries of power between the two, the British were always more conscious of Anglo–American ties than were the Americans. Stated baldly, Great Britain needed the United States far more than the Americans needed Britain. This basic disparity shaped all aspects of the transatlantic partnership. The British feared losing American support even as they resented the very dependence they feared losing. Bereft of many of the traditional measures of power, officials in Whitehall sought instead to exert influence. As part of this strategy they endeavored to make their ties with the United States *the* special relationship, whereas the Americans always preferred *a* special relationship, less exclusive, less confining, less overt than what the British had in mind.

Exploring the special relationship between the United Kingdom and the United States presents special difficulties. As D. C. Watt has rightly pointed out, the distinguishing mark of the international historian is a bias toward the study of crises.[5] But with the obvious exceptions, the real story of the postwar Anglo–American alliance lies not in the crises but in the steady workaday routine functioning of what were indeed unusually close ties. Thus, the historian of British–American relations, instinctively drawn toward conflict, is presented with an interpretative dilemma suggested by the image of the partially filled glass. Is it half full, or half empty? Should the historian of the special relationship emphasize the exceptional intimacy of the ties between the two countries, or the repeated and sometimes heated differences that provided a more or less constant refrain to that intimacy?

Another difficulty with generalizing about the special relationship is the inescapable fact that it did not operate uniformly in all parts of the world, or with respect to all types of issues, or in all portions of the American and British governments. It was in the first place Eurocentric, functioning most easily in European soil and the surrounding waters. In Asia, the Middle East, and other areas of the world, it could frequently be marginal or even nonexistent. In addition, the special relationship operated more smoothly on defense issues than in political matters, less contentiously in political matters than in commercial questions. The total breakdown in nuclear cooperation after 1945, however, suggests that even this generalization must be qualified. Again speaking broadly, there was usually less of a commitment to British–American partnership in Westminster than Whitehall, on Capitol Hill than in the White House. So whether one finds a special relationship depends in good measure on where one seeks it.

A third difficulty, particularly for recent decades, is that the Anglo-American relationship cannot be viewed in a vacuum. It comprised one subset of a larger Atlantic community, itself only a portion of an even more extensive global community. How these various communities should mesh was a matter of continuing debate between Washington and London, and within each capital, both before and after Britain's entry into the European Economic Community. But especially in recent years American decision-makers have thought of "Europe" rather than "Britain," which complicates matters for the historian who wishes to isolate the unique aspects of British–American ties.

One cannot study postwar Anglo–American relations very long without being struck by the central role played by individual statesmen. In recent decades a focus on political leaders has not been in vogue among professional historians, who frequently view an emphasis on kings and captains as an anachronism that mistakes the ephemeral and the idiosyncratic for the underlying social and economic forces that drive men and women and determine the destinies of nations. Of course no account of British–American ties in the period after 1945 can afford to ignore the century-long decline in British power and influence relative to its friends, neighbors, and rivals. That having been said, the role individual statesmen have played in Anglo–American relations still holds an importance not found in relations between, say, Washington and Tokyo, or London and Bonn. Prime Minister Harold Macmillan, for example, by cultivating a personal relationship with first Eisenhower and then Kennedy, succeeded for a time in obscuring the extent to which the power equilibrium had shifted against Britain. More recently, the particular personalities of Ronald Reagan and Margaret Thatcher once again gave London a standing in Washington that its economic and military might alone hardly warranted.

Nonetheless, and Thatcher's influence in Reagan's Washington notwithstanding, the long-term trend in the British–American relationship clearly lay—and lies—in the direction of reduced intimacy and less exclusivity. Even in the late 1950s, Britain's utility to the United States had begun to decline, as other Western powers matched and then surpassed the United Kingdom in the various measures that denote power. And as the global power balance shifted, so too did the nature of the special relationship. This metamorphosis, moreover, was accelerated by the channeling of East–West competition into less directly menacing forms and by the emergence of nonsecurity issues—economics, the environment, energy—in international affairs. The autumn of 1963, with Kennedy's death following so closely on the heels of Macmillan's retirement, might be seen as a symbolic turning point in the bilateral relationship. Certainly the eighteen years following 1963 were not marked by the same collaborative spirit that characterized the relationship in the eighteen years preceding that symbolic divide.

But like all symbols, the year 1963 simplifies and obscures as well as elucidates. Even during the prime ministership of Edward Heath (without a doubt the postwar prime minister least enamored of close British–American ties) and the presidency of Gerald Ford (the postwar president with the fewest Anglophilic tendencies), British–American cooperation flourished in a variety of forms unmatched by two major powers anywhere else in the world. More recently, American assistance to Britain in its 1982 war against Argentina once again demonstrated the continued vitality and significance of Anglo–American ties. So too did Thatcher's support, at considerable domestic cost, for Washington's 1986 air strike against Libya.

In short, like Mark Twain's demise, reports of the death of the special relationship between Great Britain and the United States have been greatly exaggerated.

Authorship by its very nature is a solitary enterprise. Yet there can hardly be a writer laboring today behind typewriter or word processor who is not conscious of the contributions others have made to his or her work. Certainly I have not escaped this burden of obligation, even if some of those who have assisted with this study think me unusually obtuse for not having incorporated more of their suggestions. I should particularly like to thank Doug Waller and J. Kenneth McDonald for their many creative and constructive comments that forced me to tighten up phrases, rethink assumptions, and clarify otherwise mysterious passages.

I also wish to express my appreciation to Akira Iriye, who invited me to participate in Twayne's International History Series, and to G.K. Hall's Meghan Wander, who displayed infinite patience and tact when it seemed that I might never finish this manuscript.

Assistance of a different sort was provided by research grants from the Lyndon B. Johnson and Gerald R. Ford libraries. I want to thank the officers and trustees of those institutions, as well as the highly professional staffs who make working there so enjoyable. Our country's presidential libraries are truly a national treasure.

I take special pleasure in acknowledging the extraordinary debt I owe Lelia Gardner Hathaway. It was she, with her finely honed sense of the past, who first introduced me to the delights of history, and who in this fashion has so directly molded the patterns of my life.

Every author has his muse; I have four. And so this book is dedicated to Amy, Kristin, and Kelly, whose laughter and vitality provided essential respite when the task of writing seemed too oppressive; and to Susie, who more than anyone understands and sustains this compulsion I have to "do history." Without her forbearance, her encouragement, and most of all, her love, this book would not have been written. Ours is indeed a "special relationship."

Robert M. Hathaway

Washington, D.C.

chapter 1

ALLIANCE CREATED: 1776–1945

From the beginning, Anglo–American ties have exhibited a two-sided, almost schizoid character. Embittered by the personal rejection that the American rebellion signified, George III refused even to appoint a minister to the United States for a full decade after Yorktown. Yet at other times the British monarch viewed his former subjects far more benignly. In a speech to Parliament shortly after agreeing to peace terms with the Americans, George approvingly predicted eventual reconciliation: "Religion—language—interest—affections may, and I hope will, yet prove a bond of permanent union between the two countries."[1]

In his broader vision George proved prescient, but the bonds of which he spoke were not quick in forming. For the first century or more of America's national existence, Great Britain occupied the same place in American demonology that the Soviet Union has held in recent decades. The British, for their part, looked upon the upstart new nation, when they deemed to consider it at all, with a mixture of distaste and disdain. This combination led London to disregard American grievances until, in 1812, the Americans once more sought recourse in war. As an episode in British history, the second American war rates barely a footnote. Americans, on the other hand, widely viewed the War of 1812 as a second war of independence, and its passably successful termination enabled them to reorient their bearings away from the Atlantic. For the next century Britain remained a distant bogeyman, despised more than feared, but at any rate of little or no consequence in the daily lives of most Americans, intent upon the business of settling a continent.

The decades after 1815 brought periodic war scares and, on the western side of the Atlantic, considerable anti-British posturing. Conflicts or potential conflicts over Central America, the Canadian border, Oregon, California, Texas, fisheries, the slave trade, and British actions favoring the Confederacy during the American Civil War all threatened at one time or another to draw the two peoples into renewed warfare. The presence in the United States after mid-century of several million outspokenly Anglophobic Irish-Americans gave every minor dispute the potential for erupting into a major controversy. Yet in each case a way was discovered to calm inflamed passions, soothe wounded pride, and assuage points of contention peacefully. As often as not, this meant a British willingness to back down before the frequently obstreperous Americans—implicit acknowledgment by London that few fundamental British and American interests clashed, that a friendly America offered advantages over one hostilely disposed, and that Canada remained a hostage to at least tolerable Anglo-American ties.

As the nineteenth century gave way to the twentieth, the two nations, somewhat to their surprise, found themselves with complementary interests in many areas of the globe. London was content to leave unchallenged American pretensions to hegemony in the Western Hemisphere, while the United States remained uninterested in Britain's new aspirations in Africa. Whitehall pursued a friendly neutrality during the Spanish-American war, and Washington returned the favor during the Boer War. In the Far East, each recognized that the promotion of Chinese territorial integrity facilitated economic penetration of the region. In Europe a newly assertive Germany gave statesmen in Washington and London a common point of concern. Still, there were limits to this rapprochement, as evidenced by the unhappy fate of a succession of Anglo–American arbitration treaties negotiated between 1895 and 1911, each emasculated by the U.S. Senate. Not for the last time, Americans demonstrated a preference for regulating their affairs with the British more by informal understandings than by formal accords.

World War I placed tremendous strains on the recent rapprochement, even though the two nations faced a common enemy in Kaiser Wilhelm. The wartime connection between Washington and London was sufficiently close to create ill feelings, but not close enough to promote mutual understanding. America had entered the war with obvious reluctance, and only after pronounced attempts at neutrality and mediation. As late as the end of 1916, Woodrow Wilson had made few distinctions between Britain and Germany; both were hostile to American neutral rights. Wilson's grandiose rhetoric about making the world safe for democracy could not fully mask the absence of ideological affinity between America and the Allies. The president's actions revealed far more than his words, as he held the United States aloof from its wartime associates—refusing alliance, sharply circumscribing participation in the Supreme War Council, and generally adopting an air of moral superiority.

Wilson's performance at the Versailles peace conference, marked by this same smug posture of disinterestedness, rankled the British further, especially in combination with the president's tendency to magnify America's role in bringing victory. London feared that Wilsonian notions of a peace without victors rested upon a naive understanding of world realities. Worse, they failed to acknowledge, and implicitly to appreciate, the terrible suffering the war had inflicted upon the ostensible winners. John Maynard Keynes's devastating portrait of Wilson in *The Economic Consequences of the Peace* illustrated the extent to which victory had divided the former associates, simultaneously reinforcing British resentment against the Americans and infuriating Wilsonians in the United States. Senate rejection of the peace treaty seemed an altogether appropriate ending to an enterprise gone sour.

In the aftermath of the war, an embittered petulance prevailed on both sides of the Atlantic. Many Americans came to believe that the conflict had been for naught, that they had been suckered into hostilities by the crafty British simply to bail out London bankers. It was not the first time Americans would see themselves as unsuspecting victims of the duplicitous British, nor the last. On the east side of the ocean, similar disgruntlement was the order of the day. America, having foisted an imperfect treaty on Europe, had then turned its back on the League of Nations and left Britain and France to cope as best they could with Wilson's mistakes. Moreover, Washington, in demanding full repayment for the monies loaned Britain for the common war effort, was now intent upon extracting the last possible pound of flesh.

World War I proved a pivotal point in British–American relations. As II. G. Nicholas has written, the war "transposed their relative significance in the world."[2] For the United States to have sent two million men to fight in Europe represented a step whose significance cannot be overstated. Britain, indeed all of Western Europe, had irretrievably lost its independence. Hereafter, America would be the arbiter of Europe's destiny, even when Washington actively sought to escape that role. The war years also saw the pound sterling displaced by the dollar as the preeminent world currency, a development suggestive of the vast economic changes the conflict had both caused and ratified. Even the Royal Navy, for centuries unchallenged on the high seas, now faced a rival mightier than any since the Spanish Armada more than three hundred years earlier.

The two interwar decades saw each nation determined to ignore the other. Such a stance was possible in part because the Washington treaties of 1921–22 successfully defused British–American naval competition, while the creation of the Irish Free State eliminated a second major irritant in Anglo–American relations. At a more fundamental level, however, neither found in the other anything to merit a more active intercourse. To most Americans who bothered to consider Britain, the old country represented decline and a genteel seediness. Britain seemed at one and the same time a class-bound aristocracy and, with the advent of a socialist government in 1924, a seedbed of radicalism. For most Americans the Empire stood for exploitation and discredited spheres of influence. The typical Briton was thought arrogant, condescending, humorless, and untrustworthy—stereotypes gleefully perpetuated by the Hearst and McCormick presses and their lesser imitators.

But Americans were not alone in their disdain for their recent comrades in arms. Caricatures of the Roaring Twenties placing the United States in the most unfavorable light possible received widespread prominence throughout Britain. Nativism, antiradicalism, gangsterism, speakeasies, and the Scopes trial were taken in Britain as quintessentially American. Sinclair Lewis and H. L. Mencken, with their blistering portraits of a soulless society awash in hedonism, found large and approving audiences in the United Kingdom. The arrival of hard times after 1929 lent final confirmation of the bankruptcy of American life.

As the global depression intensified in the early 1930s, both countries slid into an economic and political nationalism that discouraged meaningful dialogue between the two governments. It is well-known that American diplomacy in these years displayed little imagination or daring. British statesmen, however, offered few enlightened alternatives of their own. Both nations tried to pretend that they were not affected as first Japan and then Germany and Italy proceeded to tear apart the old world order. Neither Franklin Roosevelt, who entered office in 1933, nor Neville Chamberlain, who came to power four years later, saw any value in a closer association. To the contrary, both exercised special care lest they appear to embrace joint action or adopt a common front. Even after Hitler destroyed the last illusions about the true nature of his ambitions by gobbling up truncated Czechoslovakia in early 1939, there was little in the way of Anglo–American collaboration. And the world slipped into war.

But like so much else in the British–American relationship, subterranean forces pushed in the other direction as well. In 1938, naval officers of the two nations held secret staff talks in London. While purely exploratory in nature, these conversations did prompt strategic planners to consider more seriously the advantages of joint action in case of war. In addition, a wildly successful visit to Washington and New York in mid-1939 by the British king and queen eroded Americans' Anglophobic instincts. The American public was much taken by reports of the royal couple lunching on hot dogs and baked beans at Roosevelt's Hyde Park estate and accorded the visitors an enormously enthusiastic reception. Press comment on the visit was similarly effusive, as Their Majesties charmed their critics and left all but the most hard-bitten isolationists feeling it would be tactless to object too strenuously to such gracious guests.

Even so, when war came again to Europe, Washington once more proclaimed its neutrality, as it had in 1914. Unlike Wilson in that earlier conflict, however, Roosevelt did not ask Americans to remain neutral in spirit as well as deed. From the beginning he distinguished between the combatants. At the same time, powerful domestic pressures precluded overt assistance in the anti-German alliance, so for the moment Roosevelt could do little more than sit idly on the sidelines.

The startlingly swift German victories in the spring of 1940 dramatically changed this situation. France's defeat and Britain's forced evacuation of the Continent awakened many Americans to the fact that they could no longer leave to others the responsibility for thwarting Hitler's designs. The military debacle of those months also brought a new British prime minister, a development of profound significance for the future of Anglo–American ties. Winston Churchill, by his magnificent oratory, his force of character, and his certainty of ultimate victory did more than rally his countrymen. He inspired the Yanks as well. Millions of Americans thrilled at his haughty defiance of all the Germans could throw at beleaguered Britain in the bleak year of 1940.

Haltingly, yet with a certain inevitability, America over the eighteen months after the fall of France slid into war. In the process—and in contrast to the period prior to American intervention in 1917—the United States and the United Kingdom found themselves forging an ever closer relationship. As Churchill exalted in the Commons more than a year before Washington actually entered the fray, henceforth the British Empire and the United States "will have to be somewhat mixed up together." Significantly—and this distinguished Churchill from many of his predecessors in 10 Downing Street—he quickly added: "For my own part . . . I do not view the process with any misgivings. I could not stop it if I wished; no one can stop it. Like the Mississippi, it just keeps rolling along. Let it roll. Let it roll on—full flood, inexorable, irresistible."[3]

The alliance achieved formal status only in the weeks after Pearl Harbor, although it had been a reality from at least the autumn of 1940. As alliances go, it was unprecedented—closer than any between two sovereign states in the history of war. Even so, it was not nearly as intimate as subsequent recollections—Churchill's above all—would paint it. It was, first of all, closer in Europe than in the Pacific and the Middle East. It was, as the war progressed, an alliance increasingly dominated by the stronger member, the United States. Suspicions and acrimony were pervasive, rivalry often intense. The diary of General Joseph Stilwell, the American commander in China, offers an antidote to any tendency to overromanticize the partnership: "The more I see of the Limies, the worse I hate them," he penned at one point. "[T]he bastardly hypocrites do their best to cut our throats on all occasions."[4] Stilwell's was not the dominant tone, but neither was it uncommon. Differences over military strategy, the British empire, economic and political goals and the means to achieve them, and relations with the defeated enemy states provided a continuing refrain in the alliance. Jostling for postwar advantage—financial, commercial, political, and strategic—added further disharmony.

Still, the far more significant aspect of the wartime relationship was the degree to which the two nations overlooked these differences to forge a common front against the enemy. Their bitter disagreements notwithstanding,

London and Washington followed a joint military strategy that subordinated America's intense desire for revenge against the Japanese to a Germany-first strategy. In the field, troops of each nation fought under commanders of the other. On the homefront, joint committees and combined boards regulated everything from rice to rubber, petroleum to propaganda. Lend-lease and its less well-known British counterpart, mutual aid, represented a vast improvement over the intergovernmental loans of World War I. In pursuit of the atom's secrets, British and American scientists, while not always working together easily or as equals, established within the larger anti-Axis coalition a smaller coterie that pointedly excluded the Soviets. Suggesting the extent to which national perspectives had been shunted aside by the common exigencies of war, the English even took to joining their American colleagues every Fourth of July in celebrating the successful American revolt from British rule.

The wartime partnership offered London, and above all Churchill, an opportunity to make Anglo–American collaboration a permanent fixture of the postwar world. The British prime minister was determined to transform his personal ties with Roosevelt into a broader understanding between their two nations that would ensure a continuation of the wartime collaboration. For British officials the trick, of course, was to draw the Americans close without smothering themselves at the same time.

The notion of a special relationship was accepted in Washington as well, but it was never as compelling or as highly prized. American officials rightly recognized that in the postwar world, they would need the British far less than London would rely on them. Upon this calculus of power rested much of the history of relations between the two.

The wartime alliance also bequeathed a legacy of personal ties that would shape future Anglo–American relations. The most celebrated personal relationship, that between Roosevelt and Churchill, did not survive the hostilities, as death removed one party and the voters the other. But among those second- and third-level officers and officials who would play primary roles in running their respective nations' affairs for the next several decades, recollections of the anti-Axis partnership molded their actions for years to come. The war also created personal ties of a different sort that would survive the war; after the German defeat perhaps as many as 20,000 American GIs returned to the States with new British wives.

The war fostered habits of consultation, cooperation, and compromise between the two nations that, although never as fully developed as the British would have liked, were real all the same. And they too shaped future Anglo–American dealings in military affairs, intelligence, diplomacy, and economics, as well as the way officials in each country sought to manage relations with the Soviet Union.

Even so, the end of the fighting brought an inevitable loosening of the ties that had bound the two nations since 1940. World War II turned out to be the high-water mark of British–American collaboration. It also exposed the futility of trying any longer to deny London's extensive dependence upon American power. If World War I had been the point at which the United States matched and then surpassed Great Britain in relative economic strengths, World War II marked that point in the psychological sense. No longer would Britain be anything other than the junior member in the British–American equation.

Certainly the mother–daughter analogy no longer possessed any relevance. Churchill, casting around for a new metaphor to solidify an old relationship, confided to Truman at Potsdam that he hoped the United States would be like a wife to Great Britain. The redoubtable Englishman was in effect suggesting an intimacy surpassing even that between parent and child. That Churchill found the new president decidedly uninterested in his proposal should have warned the prime minister that his ideas on the appropriate nature of future British–American ties would not go unchallenged.

But while no one knew any longer how to characterize the Anglo–American bond, their efforts to do so suggest an awareness of its unusual nature. All involved appreciated that this was not simply another bilateral relationship. As H. C. Allen, perhaps the preeminent chronicler of links between the two peoples, has observed, British–American ties through the years have displayed "some of the tension and tortuousness of family relationships."[5] Or as an official in the British Foreign Office resignedly noted during the war, in America "a higher standard is expected of us" than of other nations.[6]

The reasons for these elevated expectations lay in a combination of history, culture, and demography. The language common to the two peoples, the surface similarities in their governing processes, their shared heritage, their joint love of Shakespeare and veneration of Magna Carta, the tide of immigrants that for three hundred years had flowed from the United Kingdom to Anglicize the New World—all these factors converged to foster the impression that the interests of the two nations should and did parallel one another. Frequently, this impression was accurate enough. Just as often, however, it was inaccurate, leading to dashed expectations, then bitterness and a feeling of betrayal not customarily encountered in international discourse.

By 1945, the mother–daughter analogy had not applied for several generations, but the image continued to shape Anglo–American relations. Its influence cut both ways: it facilitated a closeness, yet led to expectations that could not be met. This perception of kinship encouraged coordinated or common efforts in a wide variety of endeavors not usually attempted by sovereign states—the joint development of the atomic bomb, for instance. But here again, collaboration failed to alter the fact that each nation had interests of its own that did not automatically coincide with those of the other. And this too begat friction.

World War II had reaffirmed, for both the United States and the United Kingdom, the utility and indeed the uniqueness of the bonds linking them.

Shared values, collective memory, and a common foe had driven the two into an intimacy not seen since Whitehall had reluctantly relinquished rule of its principal American colonies more than 150 years earlier. This time, however, it was America, not Britain, that held the predominant power. Much of the world's subsequent history would be determined by how wisely the United States exercised that power, and how gracefully the British adapted to their new position of unequal and subordinate partner.

chapter 2

ALLIANCE CEMENTED: 1945–1950

August 14, 1945: VJ-day. At 7:00 P.M. Washington time, the word goes out from the capitals of a wartorn world. One by one—in Manchuria and Indochina, aboard the U.S.S. *Missouri* and H.M.S. *King George V,* in the air over Tokyo and on isolated atolls sprinkled about the western Pacific—the guns fall silent. In Washington a beaming, bespeckled man, arguably at that moment the most powerful individual in the world, briefly speaks to the cheering crowds outside the White House and then telephones his aged mother in Missouri with the news. Across the ocean, in London, though the hour is late, a mad cacophony of auto horns, church bells, ship sirens, train whistles, fireworks, and even dust bin lids screeches out the "dot, dot, dot, dash" V for victory. A similar delirious sense of relief sweeps Moscow, while in Tokyo, half the globe away, a numbness, a sense of disbelief, of a world come crashing down, greets the emperor's order that his imperial forces lay down their arms.

Only in the days that followed did the actual import of the war's end become apparent. For Japan it meant the ignominy of foreign occupation and national debasement. For many Chinese, caught up in internal rivalries, it brought little more than a change in adversaries. In Moscow, whose victorious armies stood astride two continents, it signified redemption for the stream of snubs that had been its lot in international affairs ever since czarist Russia's defeat at the hands of the Japanese forty years earlier. For statesmen and common folk alike, in Berlin, Rome, Paris, and the lesser capitals of the world, the return of peace held its own individual significance.

So too in London and Washington. VJ-day found both the United States

9

and the United Kingdom, each amidst unprecedented circumstances, searching for their proper role in world affairs. For the United States the war had
been in many respects a liberating experience. Defense spending had finally
lifted the country out of its decade-long depression, invigorating not only the
war industries but the entire economy. Between 1939 and 1945 the nation's
gross national product soared from $91 billion to $212 billion. Manufacturing
volume nearly tripled; raw material output increased by 60 percent. "The
American people," one official exulted shortly before the Japanese surrender,
"are in the pleasant predicament of having to learn to live 50 percent better
than they have ever lived before."[1] Freed at last from economic depression,
beneficiary of the world's mightiest industrial plant, protected by an experienced army and navy numbering nearly twelve million men and women, sole
owner of a bomb widely regarded as the ultimate weapon, the United States
in August 1945 was possessed of that self-confidence born of total victory not
yet tempered by the burden of success.

For Britain, the end of hostilities promised release but not necessarily
relief. Ostensibly victorious, Great Britain in 1945 found itself nearly as
exhausted as its former enemies. German bombs and rockets had damaged or
destroyed four million houses. Enemy action, excessive wear, and inadequate
investment had ground down industrial capacity. After six years of rationing,
consumer goods were increasingly scarce. Meat consumption was down nearly
one-fourth from prewar levels; butter consumption was off two-thirds; fruit,
tea, eggs, and sugar all markedly lower. Overseas assets had been liquidated,
so that net income from foreign investment was less than 40 percent of its
prewar value. In addition, the United Kingdom had consumed most of its
gold and dollar reserves and incurred vast overseas debts approaching nearly
10 percent of the country's total prewar national wealth. Having begun the
war with a net creditor position of approximately £3.5 billion, Britain ended
it a debtor with liabilities of roughly £2 billion. The British export situation
was no brighter. Exports from the United Kingdom at the end of the war
comprised barely one-third their prewar volume. The United States, by comparison, had maintained the prewar value of its cash exports during the war
years, in addition to its enormous lend-lease shipments. While the war had
enriched America, it had impoverished the United Kingdom, although it
would take some years before most Britons fully appreciated the extent of
their insolvency.

Both the British and the Americans spent the five years separating the
Japanese surrender from the outbreak of fighting in Korea trying to digest the
implications of these dramatically differing circumstances. For one thing, the
role each was to play in world affairs needed to be defined. For the United
States the broad dimensions of this role were readily apparent even in 1945 to
those who cared to see. As the world's most powerful nation, the United
States could no longer merely offer advice from the sidelines while declining
to get its own hands sullied. No longer possible was a posture of disinterested-

ness, of standing above the fray shielded by some sort of moral superiority. Henceforth, the order of the day would be active participation—leading the newly created United Nations, shaping the international economic system, preserving world peace.

The situation facing the United Kingdom was considerably more complex, the more so insofar as British officials failed to appreciate the implications of their nation's drastically weakened condition. As one of the victorious Big Three, Britain expected a place of equality with the Soviet Union and the United States. As head of a worldwide empire, the British assumed that they would maintain their global role in the years after 1945, exercising dominion over substantial portions of Asia, Africa, and the Middle East in much the same manner they had before 1939.

And yet the paucity of their resources for such a role could scarcely be denied. No longer could Britain rely upon the weapons of the wealthy—credits, loans, and subsidies. Its financial exhaustion, its relative decline in military might and industrial power vis-à-vis its two major allies, its new strategic vulnerability now that rockets, jet engines, and guided missiles had largely negated the defensive value of the English Channel—all combined to restrict Britain's freedom of initiative and to limit the options available to its diplomats. In the future, Whitehall realized, there would have to be a greater reliance on "pure diplomacy"—friendly personal relations, efficiency and expertise, good advice. Or as one Foreign Office veteran caustically remarked in the autumn of 1944, Britain would need, for some years to come, "to make bricks without straw."[2]

London officials saw several ways to compensate for their dearth of resources. They might look to the newly created United Nations to ensure their security. They might make Britain's ties to the Commonwealth and Empire the center of British postwar policy. They could promote the formation of a Western European bloc led by Britain and a revitalized France. Or they might seek to carry the wartime partnership with the United States into the postwar period and rely upon the combined might of the two Atlantic democracies to defend Britain's essential interests.

Each of these approaches possessed liabilities, but of the four only the last, the maintenance of close ties with the United States, promised immediate help. Of course British policymakers tried to combine elements of all four approaches, but as London officials increasingly turned their thoughts from the war to the postwar world, many concluded that only by preserving the current intimacy with the United States could British interests be adequately safeguarded. Churchill was the leading but hardly the only proponent of this strategy. The sole hope for a durable peace, he argued—and not incidentally, the best guarantee of British security—lay in an agreement between Washington and London to use their combined force, should that become necessary, to maintain the peace. The Soviet Union, he added, could join this partnership if it wished, but in his mind it was an Anglo–American understanding that mattered. "Our friendship is the rock on which I build for the future of the world, so long as I am one of the builders," he wrote Roosevelt shortly before the president's death.[3] A year later, and now out of office, he repeated this refrain in his much-publicized "iron curtain speech" in Fulton, Missouri: "Neither the sure prevention of war, nor the continuous rise of world organization will be gained without . . . the fraternal association of the English-speaking peoples."[4]

Officials of Clement Attlee's Labour government, swept into power in July 1945, were not as outspoken as the old Tory about the value of Anglo–American ties. Nonetheless, they quickly came to realize that Britain's strategic and economic weaknesses left them no choice but to pursue a course that in its essentials differed little from that Churchill might have followed had he retained office. And so it would be for the next four decades: conservative or socialist, Britain's foreign policy would have as a basic premise the centrality of close Anglo–American relations.

Such ideas voiced in the months immediately after the war's end left many Washington policymakers uneasy. Few denied that the two Atlantic democracies shared many interests, and fewer still wanted a return to the strained prewar relationship. Yet American officials demonstrated remarkably little disposition in the first months of peace to translate this perception of parallel interests into any sort of concerted policy with the British. In part, this reflected the still healthy distrust of London's intentions and ambitions that the wartime partnership had failed to erase. Lingering suspicions of British imperialism played a role, as did newly awakened fears of British socialism. Opposition to specific British policies, such as those in Palestine, also contributed to this reluctance to embrace the United Kingdom too closely. "I sometimes feel that the Mother Country needs to be reminded that the umbilical cord was cut in 1776," one American diplomat wrote in a not untypical statement.[5]

But much of Washington's unwillingness to forge a common policy with the British can be attributed to hopes regarding the Soviet Union. The notion that the establishment of a lasting peace required continued collaboration with the Soviets died hard in the American capital. Few wished to take actions that hypersensitive men in the Kremlin might construe as directed toward the creation of an Anglo–American bloc aimed at Moscow. Fears of conveying the impression that London and Washington were "ganging up" on Russia led many Americans to avoid anything that could possibly be interpreted in that light. Some carried this caution a step further, concluding that the United States should serve as the mediator between its two great allies.

Attlee and his foreign secretary, the plain-spoken Ernest Bevin, appreciated the need to assuage Kremlin sensibilities, but almost from the first they were more prepared than the Americans to be firm with the Soviets. By the autumn of 1945, most of London's senior officials had abandoned their initial hopes that Labour's socialist sympathies might enable this government to work more easily with the Kremlin than the Tories had done. Indeed, Labour's triumph at the polls seemed to have produced just the opposite result, since the Soviets apparently feared that a successful Labour Party in the United Kingdom might strengthen moderate socialists on the Continent and siphon off support for the communists. By the end of the year growing numbers of British policymakers were complaining about the Truman administration's unwillingness to stand up to the Russians. "In spite of accumulating evidence of Soviet intransigence," Lord Halifax, the British ambassador in Washington, cabled in December, "there is a stubborn determination in responsible quarters to rationalise the actions of the Soviet Union wherever possible and to make conciliatory moves as and when the opportunity presents itself."[6]

American policy was bad enough, British officials grumbled, but the underlying American attitude was downright offensive. Complaints about being relegated to a position of "junior partner" were frequently voiced. Whitehall particularly came to resent Washington's reluctance to confer with London before taking action that inevitably affected Britain as well as the United States. Averell Harriman, wartime U.S. ambassador to the Soviet Union and a senior figure in American foreign policy circles for four decades, remembered that the British "were ready to support American policies provided they had a chance to thrash out questions before we took decisions." But with increasing frequency, Harriman recalled, Washington placed London authorities in the embarrassing position of having "to defend matters with which they did not agree and on which they had not had a chance to express their views."[7] Finally an exasperated Bevin told Jimmy Byrnes, Truman's secretary of state, that he simply refused to attend another conference without knowing in advance Washington's view of things, only to have the American cavalierly dismiss his concerns.

Perhaps nothing better illustrates Washington's lack of interest in coordinating policy with London than the abrupt way lend-lease was terminated shortly after VJ-day. The British had realized that the whole question of lend-lease would have to be reconsidered once the hostilities ceased, but had expected an orderly tapering off of aid over a relatively lengthy period. Instead, they were confronted with a sudden and complete cutoff of American assistance, even as many of the needs that lend-lease had funded continued. Truman's precipitant action here was not deliberately aimed at the British—nor for that matter, at the Soviets—but was judged necessary to fulfill commitments repeatedly given the Congress. Technically, the lend-lease legislation permitted the extension of goods and services beyond the period of actual hostilities, but Congress had expressly prohibited the use of lend-lease for postwar rehabilitation. Not to halt American aid, Truman's advisers cautioned, would be breaking faith with the Congress. To Truman, so recently a member of the Senate himself, terminating the program seemed nothing more than a routine decision. The anguished cries from London that followed met with little sympathy and less understanding.

As the months slipped by and it became apparent that Washington officials saw little need to keep American policy closely aligned with Britain's, the Foreign Office came more and more to miss Roosevelt's imaginative leadership and dashing flair. The abrupt termination of lend-lease, the patronizing attitude sometimes displayed by American negotiators during the talks that autumn about an American credit for the British, the unilateral actions of United States authorities in Japan, Truman's determination to cut the British out of the wartime atomic partnership, the administration's irresponsibility (as Whitehall deemed it) in matters relating to Palestine—each led London to forget a little more the frustrations and bitterness that working with FDR had also engendered. Ambassador Halifax, for instance, compared Roosevelt's "inspired leadership" and "admirable sense of timing" in guiding American opinion with the Truman administration's disposition to "chart [its] course in the manner best calculated to propitiate what [it conceives] to be the prevailing sentiments of Congress and of important pressure groups."[8]

Whatever the merits of American policy in those first months of peace, these complaints revealed as much about the British state of mind as about Washington's actions. The shrill, alarmist tone of some of its assessments underscored the inferiority Whitehall felt in the face of American might. By 1945 it was beyond denying that the ultimate guarantee of British security lay in the hands of another nation, a galling situation for a proud people who within living memory had dominated the international scene. Confronted with daily reminders of America's strength and their own dependence, many Britons found it far easier to spot defects in other nations' policies than in those of their own. Behind London's ill-tempered outbursts, the famed British economist Lord Keynes explained to a friend, lay an "inner reluctance of England to accept a situation so wholly reversed from what she is used to. . . . I am afraid it is not easy for us to accept the new situation gracefully, and that is what makes sane and acceptable counsel so difficult to give and unacceptable to receive."[9]

Would things have been markedly different had Roosevelt survived? Probably not. A certain loosening of the wartime bonds between the two nations was inevitable with the return of peace. Given Roosevelt's commitment to working with Stalin, it is likely that he would have been no more responsive to British exhortations to stand up to the Russians than Truman proved to be. Moreover, even at the height of the wartime alliance, Roosevelt had shown himself prepared to give British wishes short shrift. To be sure, the substitution of Truman for Roosevelt did shift emphases and reorder priorities in places. Roosevelt, for instance, had been a leader of American anticolonialism in a way Truman never would be. But in their fundamental assumptions about the nature of the world and America's place in it, and in their ideas on what policies the United States should pursue to ensure that a better world followed this war than had the last, the two presidents differed but little.

In some respects Truman and Attlee came to power in 1945 carrying similar burdens—overshadowed by giants, perceived as men of far lesser stature than their predecessors, greeted with open skepticism that they were large enough to handle the grave responsibilities each had inherited. This might have drawn them together, even provided the basis for a personal bond of the sort their predecessors enjoyed. But it did not. In Truman's first month in the White House, he received forty-four wires from Churchill. Truman and Attlee did not exchange that many cables during an entire year. Churchill and Roosevelt met nine times in the four years between 1941 and 1945; Truman and Attlee met three times in six years. A new reserve and formality, a distance, crept into the Anglo–American relationship at the highest levels as a result of the ascensions of Truman and Attlee, gradually replacing the warmth and camaraderie that had bound Roosevelt and Churchill.

Some Britons thought they also detected an antisocialist prejudice in the American reluctance to maintain the wartime cordiality. Indeed, Americans made no secret of their affection for Churchill or suspicions about British socialism. Many greeted the news of Churchill's rejection by the voters with incredulity. Apprehension was widespread, and at least one American congressman openly worried that Churchill's defeat indicated a communist trend in Europe.

But British concerns that America's historical bias against socialism would unduly influence Anglo–American relations proved overblown. Liberal and labor circles in the United States hailed Attlee's victory in 1945, and even the moderately conservative press, once the initial shock had passed, quickly accepted the new government. Antisocialist sentiments played almost no role in the protracted negotiations that autumn for an American credit for the British. Meanwhile, the British embassy in Washington took great pains to defuse the socialism issue. Individual rights and fundamental British liberties remained unchallenged, British spokesmen emphasized, while even under a socialist government most British industry would continue in private hands.

More to the point, however, American apprehensions about Labour's rather tame socialism paled in the face of growing fears about Soviet communism. As Americans' opinions of the Soviet Union hardened throughout 1946 and 1947, British stock rose. A welcome corollary to the new American toughness toward the Soviets, one Foreign Office diplomat observed, was that Great Britain had "graduated from a poor to a useful relation."[10] British concern in the winter of 1945–46 that the United States was too apt to play a mediating role between the United Kingdom and the Soviet Union looked naive only twelve months later. Indeed, Washington now worried whether the Labour government could be counted upon to be sufficiently firm in its dealings with Moscow.

U.S. RESERVE BEGINS TO CRUMBLE

For the first year or so after VJ-day, London had taken the lead in resisting Soviet actions thought unreasonable or provocative. But by the end of 1946, the British were increasingly content to cede this task to the United States. In part this reflected Whitehall's growing appreciation of the limited resources at its disposal. In part it represented a conscious attempt to encourage Washington to accept the great responsibilities inherent in American power. But above all else, this role reversal signified the similarity of outlooks held in the two capitals about the threat posed by the Soviet Union. Perhaps nowhere was this conjunction of views more striking than in the collaboration between George Kennan and Frank Roberts. As the father of containment, Kennan—in the early postwar period the senior career foreign service officer in the American embassy in Moscow—needs no introduction. Roberts, his counterpart in the British embassy in Moscow, has slipped into that historical obscurity that is the fate of all but a handful of professional diplomats. But a comparison of the dispatches each drafted suggests extensive intellectual cross-fertilization. Roberts may have had a far greater impact on Kennan's thinking—and hence, on the movement toward cold war—than has usually been recognized.

At any rate, London publicly applauded the Truman administration's new firmness with the Soviets beginning in mid-1946, and Whitehall worked to mesh its policies with Washington's. British officialdom lauded Truman's 12 March 1947 address setting forth the tenets of what would become known as the Truman Doctrine. Officials in the two capitals responded with identical dismay to the Czech coup a year later. And when Stalin tightened the noose around Berlin in mid-1948, Whitehall reacted with enthusiasm to Truman's decision to resupply the western sectors of the city by air. American policy had evolved so rapidly in directions the British thought wise that London was even prepared to overlook the fact that the president had not bothered to consult the British before deciding to resist Soviet efforts to force the West from Berlin.

On strategic matters, and with the important exception of atomic energy, the two countries increasingly came to coordinate their policies. What was widely perceived as Soviet intransigence led the Americans to jettison their initial hesitation, which had given British strategists some anxious months in 1945 and 1946 pondering the implications of Britain standing alone against the Soviets. British lobbying undoubtedly played a part as well in overcoming American reservations, as British military officials pushed for intelligence exchanges, information pooling on guided missiles and other new technologies, coordination of training procedures, and standardization of weaponry between the armed forces of the two nations. As a senior British officer wrote Dwight Eisenhower, now Army chief of staff, at the end of 1945: "If your armed forces and ours had more or less the same equipment, more or less the same doctrine, more or less the same organization—AND NO SECRETS of any kind between them—they would at once constitute a hard core of resistance to any breach of the peace."[11] Not that war was anticipated; early in 1946, policymakers in London officially adopted a ten year no-war planning assumption. Rather, this desire for the closest of ties with the United States arose from more general anxieties caused by Britain's weakened condition.

Military officers of the two countries held secret staff talks beginning in 1946, probably without the knowledge of the president. Personal contacts established during the war were utilized to channel the exchange of information on an unofficial basis. By the end of 1946, the wartime practice that permitted British and American warships to call at each other's bases without prior diplomatic approval had been resurrected. Naval authorities of the two nations coordinated the movements of their fleets in the Mediterranean and quietly worked together to build Cyprus into an important naval and air base. In 1947, British and American officials signed a still-secret agreement providing for the sharing of signals intelligence.

But perhaps most remarkably, the United States transferred several dozen B-29s to forward bases in East Anglia during the summer of 1948, at the height of the Berlin crisis. While none of these "atomic bombers" had been modified to carry nuclear weapons, their deployment demonstrated just how closely the defense establishments of the two nations were working. The truly novel aspect about this step, however, was that no formal agreement preceded it, only an informal understanding. "Never before in history," marveled one American Air Force commander, "has one first-class power gone into another first-class power's country without any agreement. We were just told to come over and 'we should be pleased to have you.' "[12]

Behind these collaborative measures, of course, lay a growing conviction that in matters pertaining to the basic security of the two nations, each was the other's best friend. A February 1946 article in the *Economist* precisely captured sentiment in Whitehall when it urged, "Let there be no doubt . . . of the unalterably pro-American bias of British policy. Let it be recited regularly, as a diplomatic litany, that agreement with the United States on the fundamental issues is a first commandment of British policy, with a superiority over all other objects."[13] Three months later, James Reston concluded in the *New York Times* that a consensus existed in Washington that there was "no future in trying to break up the Anglo-American bloc or denying that it exists."[14]

Reston was essentially correct in this assessment, but his stating it so plainly made many Americans uncomfortable. To an important degree the Anglo–American partnership thrived best, at least in the United States, when largely unnoticed. So much had been said about the new United Nations and the need for cooperation with all countries that the American public took some time to accept a special degree of Anglo–American collaboration. Hence the storm of public protest that greeted Churchill's Fulton speech in March 1946. This also explains the American unwillingness to formally carry the wartime Anglo–American Combined Chiefs of Staff organization into the postwar period, despite active British lobbying for such a step. Finally, this same reluctance to admit that the United Nations could not by itself eradicate all international rivalries was one of the factors behind Washington's casual disregard of its wartime pledges of cooperation in the vital field of atomic energy.

ATOMIC TROUBLES

Writing of the late 1940s, H. G. Nicholas observed that "the field of atomic weapons and atomic energy represented the most conspicuous failure of the so-called special relationship."[15] Widely viewed as possessing immense industrial and commercial potential as well as military uses, atomic energy in the early postwar period ratified a country's status as a Great Power. Although the military retained a certain skepticism, many Americans thought their monopoly of atomic weapons gave the United States unspecified but valuable advantages. The atomic bomb, the usually understated Dean Acheson wrote in 1945, was "a discovery more revolutionary in human society than the invention of the wheel, the use of metals, or the steam or internal combustion engine."[16] Not surprisingly, the British wanted an atomic bomb of their own. Moreover, they believed that they had firm promises from the Americans to assist them in developing such a weapon, and American refusal to carry out these pledges generated great bitterness in the United Kingdom for many years.

Churchill in 1944 had secured from Roosevelt a pledge of "full collaboration" after the war in developing atomic energy "for military and commercial purposes."[17] The president's actual intentions in initialing this agreement remain obscure, but Admiral William Leahy, Roosevelt's senior military aide, later assured Truman that FDR never contemplated sharing details concerning the manufacture of atomic bombs with the British. Churchill, on the other hand, apparently believed he had obtained a promise of total postwar partnership.

In the months after Hiroshima, Truman made it clear that he intended to regard possession of the bomb as a uniquely American responsibility. He distinguished between basic scientific principles, which were widely known, and the actual manufacturing processes involved in the production of an atomic bomb, which were not to be shared with Britain or any other country, "any more than we would make freely available any of our trade secrets."[18] British protests that America's bomb had been acquired only with the help of British researchers made no impression. In 1946, Congress adopted the McMahon Act, placing stringent restrictions on the dissemination of information to foreign nationals, including the British. Some years later, when informed of the 1944 Churchill–Roosevelt agreement, Senator Brien McMahon confessed that had he known in 1946 of this accord, he would never have sponsored the legislation bearing his name. That provided the British little consolation, however, for with passage of the McMahon Act, all exchange of weapons-related atomic information ceased.

How does one explain American actions? Concern lest Anglo–American cooperation undermine efforts to secure international control of atomic energy provides part of the answer. So does the uncertainty over what Roosevelt had actually intended. Fears that an atomic facility in the United Kingdom would be too vulnerable to Soviet attack, or that the British government was riddled with spies and could not be trusted with sensitive information, influenced some officials. Truman's preoccupation with securing legislation incorporating the principle of civilian control over atomic energy undoubtedly led him to disregard British protests, which in his mind only complicated an already complex political problem. But there was a specifically anti-British element in this as well. A full interchange of information on atomic energy, the American military advised, would be tantamount to an outright alliance. Very few in the American government in 1946 were prepared for such a step.

As a consequence, Britain's task of developing its own bomb was made considerably more costly and time-consuming. But build the bomb it would. To do otherwise would have been to forsake Great Power status. "It had become essential," Attlee recalled years later. "We had to hold up our position vis-à-vis the Americans. We couldn't allow ourselves to be wholly in their hands."[19] Not until 1952 would Britain explode its first atomic bomb. And when the British succeeded in producing a hydrogen bomb five years later, it too was developed without American assistance.

Undoubtedly, Washington's refusal to honor its wartime pledges left Britain to rely on its own scarce resources and hence retarded the speed with which Britain developed a nuclear capability. But it is considerably less certain that the withholding of American assistance made any real difference in a larger sense. During the Suez crisis, for instance, Britain had the bomb but found it no more useful than the Americans would in Indochina a decade later. In truth, nuclear weaponry provided few of the political or strategic advantages many had anticipated in the first months after Hiroshima. Viewed in this way, American aloofness proved far less costly than the British had feared.

CONFLICT AND COOPERATION

As for the Americans, friction with the British in other areas of the globe reinforced this disposition not to acknowledge too openly the closeness of Anglo–American ties or the similarity of the two nations' interests. China remained as much a source of disagreement after the war as it had during the fighting, as London showed itself far more willing than the Americans to accord Mao Tse-tung's communists the standing their military prowess had earned them. In Japan, General Douglas MacArthur, with strong backing from Washington, insisted upon running the occupation without interference from British, Soviet, or other allies, an attitude that irritated authorities in London even though they were perfectly willing to concede Washington the leading role in the occupation.

In the Middle East—traditionally an area of extensive British influence—the two Atlantic democracies frequently rubbed up against one another as well. Whitehall was understandably concerned with protecting its large oil concessions in the region, a task made all the more urgent by Britain's generally shaky financial situation. American policymakers, on the other hand, worried that London's inability to acknowledge the new forces of nationalism sweeping the region gave Moscow an opportunity to extend its influence. Still, while the Americans energetically worked to expand their oil holdings in the Middle East, this did not produce the wholesale rivalry with their British competitors one might have expected. Indeed, London in many instances welcomed American petroleum investments because they brought an added American political involvement that would buttress the West's position generally. Ultimately, of course, the British were following a self-defeating policy. Once the United States involved itself in the region in any substantial way, it was not likely to remain content with a secondary political role.

Palestine provided a particularly emotional irritant to the smooth functioning of Anglo–American ties. The British, holder of the League of Nations mandate in Palestine, viewed the Palestine question largely in geopolitical terms. Indeed, a British wartime study had likened the significance of the eastern Mediterranean for the Commonwealth to that of the Caribbean and the Canal Zone for the United States. Anything that destabilized the region or agitated Arab nationalism, Whitehall came to believe, worked against British interests, but also against the interests of the entire West. Truman, on the other hand, displayed little understanding of, interest in, or sympathy for the Arab inhabitants of Palestine and thought of Palestine first of all as a place of refuge for the Jewish survivors of Hitler's Holocaust. American electoral politics, of course, reinforced this view. Out of these conflicting perspectives came three years of intense Anglo–American bitterness, punctuated by extensive bickering and public accusations of betrayal. "One would have to go back a long time to find anything that has so exacerbated Anglo–American feelings," the *New York Times* reported in mid-1948 in the midst of a Palestine-related flareup.[20] Only with the British surrender of its mandate to the United Nations did Palestine cease to agitate Anglo–American ties.

London's dilemma in Palestine suggests something of the larger problems facing Whitehall in the years after 1945. The British were determined to retain their position of preeminence in the Middle East but lacked the resources to do so unassisted. Should Britain be forced from Palestine, London feared, its position in Egypt, Suez, and the entire region would be challenged. Bevin, therefore, sought a settlement in Palestine that would preserve Britain's political influence and economic interests, but that would not require British arms to enforce. This necessitated an active American presence in the region. At the same time, Washington must not become so heavily involved as to develop a set of interests at variance with Britain's. The task of squaring this circle not infrequently proved impossible.

British weakness: here was a thread that ran throughout virtually everything London sought to do in these years. "[F]or practically all of my plans Mr. Dalton [the chancellor of the exchequer] puts in a caveat as regards our resources," Bevin lamented in 1947.[21] The American credit, negotiated in the autumn of 1945, proved little more than a stopgap measure in slowing Britain's financial hemorrhage. And while quite liberal in many of its terms, it did force the British to allow full convertibility of sterling prematurely, a disastrous move that had to be rescinded within weeks of its implementation—though not soon enough to save the British economy from a debilitating run on the pound.

The entire episode of the credit illustrates a good deal about British–American ties in the early postwar period. Negotiations took place amidst intense bargaining, which often degenerated to a level more appropriate of bitter enemies than close allies. Hugh Dalton's subsequent recollections of the talks exaggerate only slightly the situation as it appeared to London. As the negotiations progressed, he wrote, "we retreated, slowly and with a bad grace and with increasing irritation, from a free gift to an interest-free loan, and from this again to a loan bearing interest; from a larger to a smaller total of aid; and from the prospect of loose strings, some of which would be only general declarations of intention, to the most unwilling acceptance of strings so tight that they might strangle our trade and, indeed, our whole economic life."[22] The atmosphere around the negotiating table, according to another London official, was one of "incomprehension and blackmail."[23]

Still, much of the British disappointment—and this is essential for understanding far more about the British–American relationship than only the credit—arose not from a comparison with the norm in international affairs, but from unrealistic hopes that the Americans would be disposed to accord Great Britain not simply special treatment, but a largesse unprecedented in relations between two sovereign states. When measured against less exalted standards, Washington's terms were remarkably generous—and the British in their less hysterical moments realized this. The Americans, Halifax wrote from Washington, "have made very genuine efforts to help and to have regard to our difficulties."[24] The chief British negotiator, Lord Keynes, echoed this assessment. "There is no question that we are working in an atmosphere of great friendliness and an intense desire on their part to work something out to our advantage," he wired London after several weeks of meetings.[25]

Here then was a pattern that would appear repeatedly in the years to come. Hard bargaining and, at times, deeply felt resentment often characterized the relationship. A sense of betrayal, a feeling that the Americans cavalierly disregarded British interests and sensibilities or—worse yet—that the United

States deliberately sought to take advantage of Britain's weakness frequently seized London officials. On the other side of the Atlantic, Washington policymakers often saw British desires for close ties as a devious trick to harness American strength for narrow British purposes. Again and again, Washington complained about British provincialism, about an apparent inability in London to see global issues except through the lens of a self-centered imperial power.

Yet, at bottom, what was more impressive—and more significant—was the degree to which the concept of partnership, of a similarity if not identity of interests prevailed. The widening split between the Soviet Union and its former allies was undoubtedly the most notable development in global affairs in those early postwar years. And in this emerging cold war confrontation, British and American officials shared to a startling degree a common conception of both the threat posed by the Soviet Union and the proper means to counter that threat. Seen in this context, the differences that divided London and Washington in dealing with Moscow were little more than matters of emphasis or tone.

Similarly, officials of the two nations found themselves drawn together on a host of major international issues. In Germany, London and Washington merged their occupation zones by the end of 1946, acknowledging their fundamental unity even as they continued to differ over specific aspects of occupation policy. In Greece and Turkey, Washington officials quite consciously saw their nation as the inheritor of Britain's imperial responsibilities. In Asia and the Middle East, the late 1940s witnessed a dramatic diminution in America's longtime hostility toward Britain's colonial policies, as Whitehall deliberately moved to give self-government to many parts of the empire.

What was perhaps most startling about the Anglo–American partnership after 1945 was not its difficulties, but the way it differed from the period following World War I. One did not have to go back a generation, however, to be struck by the transformation in British–American ties. Merely comparing the experiences of 1939–40 to the situation in, say, 1947 underscored the extent to which American thinking had shifted. By the latter date, American neutrality, should Britain ever again be involved in a world conflict, was no longer conceivable. The security of the United States had become too closely entwined with that of the United Kingdom for Washington to watch from the sidelines, as it had done before 1941, while Great Britain struggled for its life. In some ways, this represented the realization of London's hopes for at least a generation, and may well have been the most important development for British security in over a century. Placed in this context, Anglo–American differences in these years, even those that generated great bitterness, seem of secondary import.

Still, even as they quietly rejoiced in Washington's newfound commitment to British security, London policymakers could not forget that they remained more dependent upon the power of another nation than at any other time of peace in England's proud history. Nor could they forget that this dependency was not reciprocal; Great Britain needed the United States far more than the Americans relied upon Britain. Statesmen in London could never be as cavalier toward Anglo–American relations as their counterparts in Washington could be—and were. As a consequence, Whitehall devoted considerably more thought and energy than Washington to ensuring that business between the two nations went as smoothly as possible. And as a corollary to this concern, British officials actively sought to mold American opinion—and through it, American policy.

The Foreign Office postulated a direct linkage between American public opinion and the fulfillment of British interests, and the early postwar years saw unprecedented efforts devoted to influencing American opinion at both the popular and the elite levels. In spite of its financial constraints, London continued to fund its overseas publicity and information services generously—a recognition of the heightened interconnection between opinion and diplomacy in democratic America, but also implicit acknowledgment that Britain's economic and military decline left it more dependent upon less traditional forms of diplomacy.

Personal ties and the creation of contacts within the American government remained a priority for all British officials. The cultivation of friendly relations with American journalists was considered essential. Consular officials conducted extensive surveys of grassroots opinion in the various regions of the United States. Visits to the United Kingdom were promoted. BBC officials beamed broadcasts from the United Kingdom specially designed for American audiences. The New York–based British Information Services (BIS) maintained a staff of over two hundred in the late 1940s. BIS organized British speakers, exhibitions, and tours; produced and distributed magazine articles, press releases, pamphlets, and background information; supervised the distribution of British films; set up educational and cultural exchanges; and met on a daily basis with representatives of the American news media.[26]

A small number of themes appeared repeatedly in this British campaign to shape American thinking: London's indispensability in the face of Soviet hostility; the devoutly pro-Western orientation of the Labour government; the austerity and sacrifices under which Britons labored; British efforts toward recovery and self-help; and the democratic nature of British socialism. The cumulative impact of these messages is impossible to gauge, but it is worth noting that despite rather constant grumbling, Congress never failed to appropriate funds for the British—first the credit, later Marshall Plan aid, and finally MAP, the Military Assistance Program. Moreover, of the sixteen recipients of Marshall Plan assistance, the United Kingdom received more aid than any other nation—nearly a quarter of the total. Still, the effectiveness of these efforts should not be overstated. According to BIS, the extensive coverage in the American press of Princess Elizabeth's wedding to Philip in 1947 contributed more to winning American goodwill than the work of a dozen British publicists.

THE MARSHALL PLAN AND NATO

More traditional methods of diplomacy played their part as well. The speed with which Bevin picked up George Marshall's suggestion of an American aid program for Europe greatly impressed officials in Washington— and, not incidentally, had much to do with the subsequent success of the Marshall Plan. But as discussions proceeded, it became apparent that London and Washington held very different views on what Marshall's Harvard speech implied for Anglo–American relations. The Americans envisioned European leaders, including those from Britain, getting together and hammering out a single comprehensive plan for Europe's rehabilitation. Britain had a dollar shortage like the other European countries, and the solution to Britain's problems should be part of an integrated European solution. Europe's recon- struction could not be attacked on a piecemeal basis, Washington insisted.

Whitehall, on the other hand, bristled at the suggestion that the Marshall Plan should treat Great Britain as just another European country. The British would not enter the program solely as a supplicant, Bevin declared, for this would sacrifice the "little bit of dignity we have left." Before long, the United Kingdom might find itself in a relationship similar to that between the Soviet Union and its Eastern European satellites. Instead, the foreign secretary spoke of establishing a "financial partnership" with the United States, conveniently neglecting to explain just what Britain had to contribute to such a partner- ship. As envisioned by one of Bevin's aides, "American water-cans handled by British gardeners" would rebuild Europe.[27] Ultimately, of course, the American view prevailed, and as Alastair Buchan has noted, for the first time in 170 years of British–American relations, the United States treated Great Britain not as an isolated island in the Atlantic, but as an integral portion of the European continent.[28]

Even Bevin was at times tempted by the idea of closer ties to Europe. In the 1947 Treaty of Dunkirk, the United Kingdom pledged itself to a long-term commitment on the Continent. In a widely reported speech in January 1948, the foreign secretary called for a "Western union" of Europe's noncommunist states.[29] Britain by itself, Bevin admitted, could no longer stand indepen- dently. Only by taking the lead in a rejuvenated Europe was there "a possibil- ity of restoring a better equilibrium and a better balance in the world between the three powers."[30]

But while Bevin flirted for another year or so with the idea of a West European union or confederation, ultimately neither he nor his Cabinet colleagues were willing to embrace anything more than the loosest of ties. "Simplified, spectacular" steps such as a Western European constitutional assembly or a European federation were far bolder than anything the British could countenance.[31] London was not yet prepared to accept the psychological implications of such measures, for closer ties with Europe inevitably meant a diminution in the importance of Britain's relations with the Empire and Commonwealth—and with the United States.

Still, if the Americans could be induced to become more actively involved in the defense of Western Europe, Britain might yet have it both ways. Following the collapse of the London foreign ministers conference in December 1947, Bevin stepped up his campaign for a more visible American role in Western Europe. Washington's initial reaction was hesitant, but by March 1948 highly secret discussions among British, Canadian, and American defense planners were under way in the Pentagon. The joint recommendation coming out of these talks envisioned a collective defense agreement for Western Europe. Within a year, the North Atlantic Treaty Organization was a reality. If NATO has a founding father, Ernie Bevin more than any other single individual (save perhaps for Joseph Stalin) can lay claim to that title. At every point during 1948 when it seemed that Washington might back out of a formal commitment to West Europe's security, Bevin stepped in to cajole, plead, and persuade the Americans into accepting a North Atlantic pact. Since at least 1914, London had sought to involve the United States in maintaining the European balance of power. Thirty-five years later, Bevin succeeded. (Less frequently noted was the fact that a peacetime military commitment on the Continent was as alien to British traditions as to American.)

Not everyone applauded these developments. As head of the State Department's Policy Planning Staff, George Kennan argued that a military pact was an inappropriate response to a Soviet challenge that was primarily political and psychological. NATO promised only to distract Europeans from the more important task of economic recovery, which was the surest means of combating Soviet influence in Western Europe. London officials did not disagree with Kennan's description of the Soviet threat, but they more than the Americans were conscious of the need to satisfy European apprehensions that Washington was not fully committed to Europe's security. And only a formal military treaty provided the necessary assurances. Both Kennan and the British may have been correct in their reasoning, although in retrospect it seems legitimate to ask whether NATO did not unnecessarily militarize what up until then had been primarily a political competition with the Soviet Union. To the extent that this is the case, the British, as the driving force behind NATO's creation, must shoulder a larger share of the responsibility for heating up the cold war than is usually acknowledged.

THE ANGLO–AMERICAN PARTNERSHIP IN 1950

By 1950 and the eve of the Korean War, then, the Anglo–American partnership had evolved in directions few had foreseen five years earlier. Washington had completely eclipsed London as the seat of power in world affairs. In 1945, most knowledgeable observers still worried that America might draw back within its own borders, and leave to others the task of repairing a world ravaged by war. By 1950, such a possibility seemed far-fetched. In 1945, many Washington officials still viewed their role in world affairs as one largely of mediating between London and Moscow. By 1950, the United States had accepted, even embraced, leadership of the anti-Soviet forces around the globe, a role Britain had encouraged Washington to assume. In 1945, officials in both Western capitals believed Britain's weakness temporary. Only over the next five years did policymakers in either nation come to understand just how badly British resources had been overextended. In 1945, most observers still considered valid Britain's wartime role as one of the world's Big Three. By 1950, Britain had clearly been relegated to the status of junior partner to the United States. Nor were Foreign Office officials talking about an "independent" British foreign policy in 1950 with the same ease they had five years earlier. Britain's dependence upon the United States had become too obvious to ignore.

And with these dramatic shifts in global roles and power relationships came other, more subtle changes. American ethnic groups traditionally hostile to Great Britain—notably the Irish and the Germans—may have retained many of their old prejudices, but these same groups were also virulently anticommunist. As a consequence, by 1950 Anglophobia had lost much of its salience in American politics. In addition, Britain's more or less graceful retreat from colonialism defused that issue for many Americans. Indeed, as London's value as a cold war ally became more apparent, many Americans discovered a new sympathy for a British presence in what would soon become known as the Third World. One should not overstate the warmth of feelings for Great Britain in the United States; executive branch officials felt a partnership with the British that was not shared to nearly the same extent by members of Congress or the general public. Even so, comparing American sentiments toward the United Kingdom in 1950 to those of, say, 1938, the magnitude of the shift is impressive.

British opinion toward the United States was somewhat more complex, if for no other reason than because British dependency upon the Americans fostered ambivalence. Many Britons found this new dependence galling, and American aid was sometimes accepted with ill-disguised bitterness. Whereas most Americans viewed the Marshall Plan as an example of American generosity and magnanimity, the British were much more likely to see it as a belated attempt to atone for Washington's earlier indifference to British interests. Nor were matters helped when some American officials and congressmen acted as if the Marshall Plan entitled them to further concessions in Britain's financial and trade policies and even its domestic economic affairs. As Aneurin Bevan—no doubt thinking of the abrupt cancellation of lend-lease, the 1947 currency convertibility crisis, and American pressures to open the sterling area to American exports—once told the American ambassador, "the British were getting tired of American dollars being pushed into pockets from which the bottoms had been cut by American policies."[32] The British attitude toward the United States, the American ambassador reported in 1948, at times "borders on the pathological."[33]

But an equally compelling case can be made that British feelings for the Americans retained their generally positive wartime character. For the most part, reaction in Great Britain to America's Marshall Plan aid was favorable. In early 1948, left-wing M.P. Richard Crossman confessed in the Commons that his view of the United States had shifted dramatically over the preceding six months. The absence of political strings to the Marshall Plan aid impressed him greatly. In mid-1947, the British Gallup organization found that 22 percent of Britons believed that the United States sought to dominate the world. A year later, following congressional approval of the Marshall Plan, this figure had dropped to 14 percent, while in August 1950, shortly after the outbreak of fighting in Korea, only 4 percent of Britons professed to believe this anymore.[34] But even then the British were not content simply to turn over management of the world's affairs to the Americans. An article published in early 1950 says much about British ideas concerning differences between the two nations. "The Americans provide the hustle, the resilience, and [the] strength of their capitalist economy," it reported, while "we provide diplomacy, interpretation, conciliation, wisdom, and poise."[35]

At an official level, both nations predicated much of their foreign and strategic policy by the time of the Korean War on not simply close, but intimate, Anglo–American ties. In the Mideast, for example, a 1949 Foreign Office paper endorsed by the Cabinet noted that "[a]lignment of policy with the United States is . . . essential."[36] A year later, the Foreign Office's Michael Wright informed State Department representatives that British policy in the Middle East "has been premised on [the] conviction that if we work at cross purposes, things go badly."[37] Nor was the Middle East an anomaly in this regard. In discussions with Washington officials, the British continually referred to the uniqueness of Anglo–American relations. All Western policy, Wright observed at one point, depended upon those ties. In this, Attlee's Labour government acted no differently than a Tory government under Churchill would have.

Official Washington placed a somewhat different emphasis on the relationship, but in its underlying thrust of policy differed not at all from Whitehall. Two months before the North Korean attack on South Korea, the State Department completed a major study, "Essential Elements of US–UK Relations," that spelled out in detail American thinking on this topic. The dissolution of the Anglo–American relationship, the paper declared, "would be a major disaster." The United States by itself had neither the power nor the resources to turn back the Soviet challenge; allies were essential. But who? "No other country has the same qualifications for being our principal ally and partner as the UK." This was a reality of immeasurable importance, one which by itself set Britain, and British–American ties, apart. "The British and with them the rest of the Commonwealth, particularly the older dominions, are our most reliable and useful allies, with whom a special relationship should exist," this paper continued. A "serious impairment" of relations between London and Washington "would require a whole reorientation of US foreign policy, since the achievement of many of our objectives . . . depends on the British agreeing with those objectives and taking the necessary action to accomplish them." "We cannot afford to permit a deterioration in our relationship," based as it was on a "fundamental identity of our interests."[38]

Not that officials of the two countries agreed on all matters, of course. The British, this study continued, "are inclined to wish to make this relationship more overt than we feel desirable." They "react strongly against being treated as 'just another European power.' "[39] This question of how to balance Anglo–American ties with Britain's links to the rest of Europe was not resolved by this State Department analysis and continued to trouble diplomats in the two countries for many years. London sought to maintain political power and prestige on the Continent but worried that close European ties would undermine Britain's position as a world power. Whitehall went to elaborate lengths to distinguish between "unity" and "union." Efforts leading to European unity were acceptable, but not those pointing toward union.

The Americans replied that this was a false dichotomy. Washington, they emphasized, was not asking for European union or for a surrender of British sovereignty. Even so, there were many steps London could take to strengthen European unity. An active British presence on the Continent was needed to counterbalance the revival of German strength and to integrate West Germany into the Western bloc. The United Kingdom, Washington officials believed, was the "key" to European integration. Closer economic ties between London and the other European countries were also desirable, since Europe could regain its economic health only with British collaboration. "It should be our line with the British to assure them that we recognize the special relationship between our two countries and that we recognize their special position with regard to the Commonwealth," the 1950 State Department paper prescribed. "We should insist, however, that these relationships are not incompatible with close association in a European framework."[40]

And what exactly would this mean? "We should insist . . . that the British recognize that it is necessary for us, when we are dealing with a generalized European problem, not to make overt distinctions between them and other European countries." The "special close relation" between the two nations, "is one of the premises of our foreign policy. It is not, however, a substitute for but a foundation under closer British (and perhaps U.S.) relations with the Continent. In dealing with other Europeans, however, we cannot overtly treat the British differently." This point was repeated. "The British will have to recognize that in the European context, we must deal with them as a

European country and they must not try to demonstrate overtly a special relation to us." Any mark of favoritism "could only have the effect of seriously upsetting the Continental countries, particularly France, adding to the everpresent fear that both we and the British will abandon them in case of an emergency."[41]

These differences over what Britain's ties with the Continent should mean for Anglo–American relations were not insignificant, but neither were they fundamental. In fact, the far more impressive aspect of British–American ties on the eve of the Korean War was the widespread agreement and the concerted effort to harmonize policy that they displayed. Dean Acheson, Truman's secretary of state for four years, largely captured the essence of those ties when he remarked after leaving office that during the Truman period, "British–American relations were regarded as domestic relations in both countries." Only in later years, Acheson would recall, did American policymakers come to regard Great Britain as a foreign country, and Anglo–American links a matter of foreign policy.[42]

Acheson overstates the case. Even so, his remarks are telling. Acheson himself enjoyed exceptional rapport with Sir Oliver Franks, the capable British ambassador. His relationship with Bevin, according to Bevin biographer Alan Bullock, was closer than that between any other British foreign secretary and American secretary of state.[43] Building upon these personal ties, and drawn together by a similarity of views on most major issues of the day (China, atomic energy, and for a time Palestine being the prominent exceptions), Washington and London succeeded in the years after 1945 in carrying their wartime partnership over to the postwar period. Their relationship was characterized by a mutual confidence, by a belief in the basic goodwill and integrity of the other side—a belief essentially at odds with the notion of foreign relations. And in this respect, Acheson's observation is entirely accurate.

chapter 3

ALLIANCE THREATENED: 1950–1956

North Korea's invasion of its sister state to the south on 25 June 1950 threw the world once more into war. But the political repercussions of Pyongyang's surprise strike would be felt long after the fighting on the Korean peninsula had ceased. The outbreak of hostilities and China's subsequent entry into the war led to the freezing of Sino–American relations, which took nearly three decades to thaw. In addition, the unexpected attack triggered a series of decisions in Washington that institutionalized a cold war mentality that would dominate American foreign policy until the 1970s.

Pyongyang's invasion of the south also introduced a new set of strains into the Anglo–American equation. In the United States, the war in Korea reinforced existing doubts about Britain's constancy and dependability, its willingness to subordinate narrow British interests to the more important objective of blocking the spread of communism. In the United Kingdom, the Korean hostilities encouraged renewed questioning about American judgment and the wisdom of tying Great Britain too closely to the United States. For a period officials in the two countries managed to contain these reinvigorated doubts. But while kept in check, the doubts were not erased, and in 1956 they resurfaced, this time far more virulently.

Indeed, the six and a half years after June 1950 were not easy ones in Anglo–American relations. In both London and Washington, European concerns increasingly took second place to issues involving Asia and the Middle East, regions of the world where British–American cooperation had always been more problematic. Not only in Korea, but in China and Japan, Indochina and

30

Iran, Egypt and Buraimi, officials of the two Atlantic democracies found the close collaboration they enjoyed in Europe impossible to replicate.

From the moment of Tokyo's surrender in 1945, the two allies quarreled over the occupation of Japan. American authorities both in Washington and at MacArthur's headquarters in Japan were determined to run the occupation without interference from others—and this included the British. Whitehall was less than happy with this American attitude and protested such high-handedness. But seeing that their complaints got them nowhere, the British with more or less grace accepted their subordinate position in Japan.

China was another story. The British were no more enthusiastic than the Americans about the prospects of a communist victory in China. But as such a possibility grew more and more likely, the British far more than the Americans were prepared to accept the inevitable. British diplomats were instructed to work for a modus vivendi with Mao Tse-tung and the new Chinese leadership in order to retain a modicum of influence for the West in China. In the United States, on the other hand, whose citizens for several generations had prided themselves on holding a special place in Chinese hearts, domestic pressures and indecision within the administration made such a practical approach more difficult.

The issue of whether to accord formal diplomatic recognition to the new regime in Peking finally brought matters to a head and found London and Washington moving in opposite directions. For a variety of reasons Britain chose to recognize the new Chinese government. Financial interests in Hong Kong seemed to dictate this course, and the Asian members of the Commonwealth weighed in heavily on behalf of recognition as well. But beyond these specifically British concerns, London was reluctant to abandon the hope of retaining Western influence in China and keeping the Chinese from a total dependence on Moscow. Viewed from the perspective of several decades, it is difficult to see that America's nonrecognition policy achieved anything of value. But while Britain's course may have been the more logical one, it is also true that recognition produced no more tangible advantages than Washington's nonrecognition.

Whatever possibility existed that the United States would formally recognize the new Chinese regime disappeared on 25 June 1950. Early that morning, crack units of the North Korean army streamed across the border and drove toward Seoul. Caught by surprise, the South Koreans gave ground. Withdrawal turned into rout, and before the South Koreans could stabilize their defensive lines, they had been pushed almost off the peninsula.

For both the United States and the United Kingdom, the Korean peninsula had been little more than a geographical backwater prior to 25 June. The North Korean invasion, however, evoking as it did memories of Axis aggression prior to September 1939, radically altered the situation. Truman decided almost instantly that the nations of the noncommunist world could not let

Pyongyang's action go unchallenged. Two days later, the president ordered American planes to cover the South Korean retreat and resolved to seek the commitment of United Nations forces to assist South Korea in defending itself.

The decision to oppose North Korea by force of arms was made exclusively in Washington. Britain harbored no enthusiasm for sending troops to Korea, but the memory of the 1930s remained strong. More to the point perhaps, London understood that a half-heartedness in supporting collective security in Asia would encourage a similar hesitancy in the United States on behalf of European collective security. With their proverbial stiff upper lip, therefore, the British resignedly determined to pull their full load. Washington, of course, ran the show in Korea, even though it was ostensibly a United Nations action. The United States also supplied by far the largest contingent of troops—and suffered casualties accordingly. Turkey's contribution was the next largest, then Britain's. But prior to the Chinese intervention that autumn, London was content to give Washington pretty much a free hand. The British Cabinet worried about Truman's sending the Seventh Fleet into the Taiwan straits but said nothing. The decision to cross the 38th parallel and unify the entire peninsula troubled the British chiefs of staff as well, but Bevin refused to introduce a discordant note into Anglo–American relations by raising the issue. Like Washington, London took little notice of Chinese warnings that Peking might be forced to intervene, and in the United Nations, the British, at American behest, sponsored a resolution calling for all-Korea elections, which, of course, could take place only if the North were liberated along with the South.

China's entry into the war, and the initial successes Chinese troops enjoyed, completely transformed the situation. Suddenly the prospects for another global war appeared very real. At the least, the military emergency in Asia threatened to curtail America's allocation of resources to Europe, which remained in British eyes the key strategic prize. (The Truman administration, though not its Republican critics, agreed with this assessment of Europe's importance.) The American tendency to describe the Chinese offensive as part of a global strategy of aggression orchestrated by Moscow also alarmed the Attlee government. Whitehall largely abandoned its earlier reticence and now kept a close watch to ensure that Washington did not take any rash actions.

A HURRIED TRIP TO WASHINGTON

At the end of November a remarkably inept reply by Truman to a press query further raised the level of concern in London. Asked if the United States would consider using the atomic bomb in Korea, the president responded, with greater accuracy than discretion, that no option had been foreclosed; there "always" had been "active consideration" of its use.[1] The

British responded with outrage. Already in the midst of a general foreign policy debate, the Commons reverberated with condemnations of American adventurism and irresponsibility. The Labour party threatened to split, endangering Attlee's hold on 10 Downing Street and, if the situation were not managed carefully, even Britain's continued participation in the Korean police action. The worried prime minister, buffeted at home by friend and foe alike and unsure of Truman's intentions, hurriedly secured an invitation to visit Washington. It would be his first conference with Truman in five years.

In the United Kingdom, the week preceding the Attlee–Truman meeting saw anxious and frequently heated debate over the alarming course international developments had taken in recent weeks. Korean strategy and, lurking in the background, the ever-present bomb dominated the discussion, but relations with the United States, and the degree to which Britain could or should rely on Washington, figured prominently in the debate as well. No one of any standing suggested that the United Kingdom reconsider its decision to support the U.N. police action in Korea. There were, however, numerous calls for a more limited and well-defined statement of military objectives, and for negotiations looking toward a political settlement of the conflict. Great Britain, went a frequent refrain, must ensure that the United States not use the atomic bomb except with London's concurrence. Nor should Washington undertake other steps of escalation, such as bombing Manchuria, without bringing the British into the decision.

Discussion of these matters inevitably exposed British uneasiness over American policy beyond the Korean peninsula. Washington's insistence upon viewing a Taiwan-bound Chiang Kai-shek as the legitimate ruler of China was deemed equally unrealistic and unprofitable. Many worried that the United States would so heavily commit itself in Asia as to leave Europe defenseless. And this naturally led to an exploration of Anglo–American differences over the rearming of Germany. Not the least of the ramifications of North Korea's 25 June attack had been the American decision three months later to raise in allied councils the topic of German rearmament. Washington's logic in pointing out the need for a German contribution to Western Europe's defense was unassailable, but the administration had clearly discounted the emotions such a prospect would evoke. London officials fumed at Washington's failure to warn them of this demarche, let alone to consult with Britain before laying so sensitive a matter before the public.

How best to order relations with the Soviet Union figured prominently in the British debate as well. In this regard, conservatives no less than Labourites insisted that the Western powers formulate a genuine if cautious response to recent Soviet calls for a meeting of the foreign secretaries. Churchill, as he had done previously, urged an East–West summit before the Soviets accumulated a large stockpile of atomic bombs. Careful observers noted, however, that virtually no one advocated "appeasement."

Implicit in all this talk was widespread skepticism about the steadiness and predictability of American policy. Considerable apprehension was voiced that the world was drifting toward full-scale war, and that belligerent or thoughtless American actions were exacerbating the situation needlessly. Doubts about the administration's capability to restrain the ever-belligerent MacArthur lent these anxieties a special edge. So did the apparent clout demonstrated in the November elections just past by Senator Joe McCarthy, already as despised in Britain as he was in more thoughtful American circles.

Underlying the entire debate lay a resentment, but also an embarrassment, at Britain's continuing status as junior partner in the Anglo–American alliance. Washington, ran a frequent refrain, did not accord the views of His Majesty's government proper weight in its decisions and failed to appreciate the very real sacrifices for the common cause the United Kingdom was making. But here London's financial woes, which its Korea-induced rearmament had badly accentuated, and its continuing dependence upon American financial aid underscored Britain's secondary position in the partnership, and undermined its desire to end dependence upon the Americans.

In the United States as well, informed opinion was examining many of these issues, but with a difference—one suggesting the asymmetry of the Anglo–American partnership. In Washington, discussion rarely focused on British–American ties per se. Word of Attlee's planned visit was generally received with approval except by congressional Republicans, who believed that the administration was already too susceptible to European views. This unwarranted influence, they complained, had caused Washington to neglect Asia and had led the North Koreans to believe they could attack the South with impunity. The British were "appeasers" in dealing with Peking, several legislators warned. Special diligence must be exercised to ensure that the British prime minister did not persuade Truman to gut American policy.

After such a buildup, the five-day Washington summit proved oddly anticlimatic. As for Truman's implied threat to use the bomb—the precipitant for the conference—Attlee professed satisfaction with American assurances that the United States would consult with Great Britain before its employment, although both parties understood that an American promise to consult left Washington with virtually a free hand. In addition, the two leaders easily agreed on the need to continue resisting Chinese aggression in Korea. Attlee was reassured that the president was not bent on a showdown with Peking regardless of the costs, although Truman refused to offer China diplomatic inducements for a cease-fire. London officials were similarly pleased by Truman's statement that Europe remained the decisive theater in the cold war conflict.

On the narrower issue of military strategy, Attlee's trip may have borne some fruit. While the Americans had already decided against full-scale hostilities with China, more limited action—perhaps bombing Manchuria, blockading the Chinese coast, or assisting Nationalist attacks against the mainland—still had many proponents in Washington. Attlee's pointed warnings that such steps held little promise of military effectiveness but could escalate a limited war into a full-fledged conflict irritated many Americans, who attributed the prime minister's caution to unseemly concern for British interests in Hong Kong. It cannot really be said that Attlee convinced the Americans not to undertake limited war against China. Rather, he reinforced existing doubts by making it clear that such action would not be supported by either the United Nations or Washington's NATO partners. Indeed, by requesting the summit in the first place, Attlee had caused Washington to delay its decision-making and had given those fearful of escalating the conflict time to overcome the first panicky reactions prompted by the military reversals in Korea.[2]

In retrospect, the entire affair has something of a tempest-in-a-teapot character to it. No one in Washington had seriously contemplated using the bomb against the Chinese, so British concerns on this score had been largely unfounded. The formulation about consultation merely reaffirmed Britain's exclusion from any real say in the American atomic decision-making process. Moreover, a unified Western approach to China was no nearer after the conference than before, and this issue would continue to poison international affairs for several decades.

Viewed at another level, the Washington meetings had something of a soothing effect on Anglo–American relations. His talks with the president, Attlee informed Bevin with obvious satisfaction, had reaffirmed Britain's special standing with the United States. Great Britain had been "lifted out of 'the European queue,' " Attlee crowed. "[W]e were treated as partners, unequal no doubt in power but still equal in counsel."[3] Indeed, the Americans did seem to have a new consciousness of Britain's importance to the United States. Prior to the conference, the British search for a diplomatic resolution to the crisis in Korea had led an exasperated Truman to complain, "The position of the British on Asia is, to say the least, fantastic. We cannot agree to their suggestions."[4] By the summit's conclusion, however, Washington opinion was more faithfully reflected in Acheson's observation that the United Kingdom was "the only real ally on whom [the Americans] could rely."[5] And despite the many irritants in the partnership, this assessment continued to serve as the controlling factor in the bilateral relationship.

For the next two and a half years, until a cease-fire took hold in Korea in mid-1953, British and American policies with respect to the war coexisted uneasily. Up until the very moment the guns stopped firing, London displayed a vastly greater interest than Washington in finding a diplomatic solution to the fighting, and was far more concerned about provoking a wider war, although MacArthur's recall did ease British fears somewhat on this score. Calls for a policy more independent of the Americans were frequently voiced, at both the official and the unofficial level, and not just by the opposition. Washington, for its part, remained greatly irritated by London's refusal to sever diplomatic relations or commercial ties with Peking, even at the height of the crisis in Korea.

This absence of any real consensus on Korea spilled over into other Asian issues. Washington, not wishing to take on an obligation to defend British colonies, pointedly excluded the United Kingdom from the discussions leading to the 1951 ANZUS treaty tying Australia and New Zealand into the American defense network. ANZUS stood as stark testimony to the extent to which London had lost its prewar primacy in the Western Pacific. It also illustrated the American tendency to think more and more of Britain as primarily a European rather than a global power.

The manner in which John Foster Dulles, negotiating for the Truman administration, handled the peace treaty with Japan revealed this same disposition. By insisting that Tokyo regard Taipei as the only legitimate Chinese government, Dulles did more than simply run roughshod over British fears about pushing Peking ever more tightly into the Soviet embrace. He also set Japan on a course that skewed Far East politics for a quarter century. Like his Democratic colleagues, Dulles believed that British reservations about the wisdom of this policy merely reflected British self-interest. London wanted a Japan oriented toward Peking, the American believed, in order to foster Sino–Japanese trade ties. Only in this fashion would Japan be prevented from branching out and challenging traditional British markets elsewhere in the region. This suspicious incomprehension of British concerns did not augur well for Anglo–American relations, for Dulles's appointment to a high position in a future Republican administration was certainly not unlikely.

NEW FACES BUT OLD PROBLEMS

Churchill's return to power in the autumn of 1951, while generally viewed with pleasure in the United States, did not markedly alter the substance of British foreign policy or of Anglo–American relations. The tone of the exchanges between the White House and 10 Downing Street, on the other hand, almost immediately took on something of the wartime cordiality that had been noticeably lacking during the Attlee years. The old Tory, Eisenhower observed a year or two later, retained "an almost childlike faith that all of the answers are to be found in British–American partnership."[6] Almost instinctively, Churchill reached out to Washington, arranging a journey to the States as one of his first actions after taking office. His trip thus reestablished the wartime pattern of summitry, which had largely been abandoned in the years since 1945.

Eisenhower's election as president a year later brought to the scene another veteran of the wartime alliance. Unlike Truman, Eisenhower knew the British well and regarded his wartime collaboration with them as one of the high points of his career. Moreover, he was personally inclined to the type of summitry Churchill relished, but for which Truman had little patience. Periodic, then regular, meetings between the American president and the British prime minister hereafter became a feature of the Anglo–American connection.

Eisenhower's elevation to the White House also brought to center stage the individual who every bit as much as Churchill or the president himself established both the tone and the substance of British–American ties through much of the 1950s: John Foster Dulles. After years as the heir presumptive, Dulles finally realized his life's ambition in the winter of 1952–53 by being named American secretary of state. A man of immense capabilities, but with equally great idiosyncrasies, Dulles brought to American foreign policy renewed dosages of the self-righteous moralism and the inflexible legalism that had frequently been among its distinguishing characteristics. He was convinced, as he informed the Senate at one point, "that in all the history of the world, no nation has been as free from the temptation to use its power for its selfish purposes" as the United States.[7] From there he inexorably moved to the conclusion that all other nations should subordinate their interests to those of the United States, in light of the moral superiority with which the latter was imbued. Needless to say, such sentiments did not endear Dulles to a people as proud as the British, nor one with as long a tradition of dealing on equal, if not superior, terms with the rest of the world. It is reported that Anthony Eden, Churchill's foreign secretary and eventual successor in 10 Downing Street, tried to dissuade Eisenhower from naming Dulles secretary of state.

Dulles, for his part, found this "nation of shopkeepers" equally difficult. As one of his biographers has noted, the secretary "was not exactly anti-British. But he was always particularly suspicious of them, often profoundly irritated by them, and sometimes despairingly contemptuous of them. The British were apt to be the last people whose views he wished to hear."[8] Almost invariably, Dulles came to believe, London defined issues in terms of narrow, often commercial, self-interest. British claims to a special relationship with the United States particularly provoked his disdain.

Yet, for all the importance of individuals, Anglo–American ties remained very much a function of larger impersonal forces over which mere mortals exercised only limited influence. Chief among these forces, as it had been since 1940, was Britain's financial debilitation—a decrepitude made all the more noticeable not only by the extraordinary economic boom the United States experienced in the first two postwar decades, but also by the equally remarkable recovery made by Britain's former foes, the Germans, the Italians, and, a bit later, the Japanese. In the United Kingdom, by contrast, financial crises followed one another like seasons of the year, with each further depleting Britain's limited resources, each further sapping British initiative, and each more severely than the last constraining British diplomats.

This insidious financial cancer shaped the Anglo–American partnership in almost its every respect. It lay behind London's fears that the United States was demanding too speedy and too large a rearmament program for the Atlantic community. It played a role in Britain's more conciliatory approach toward the Chinese communists. For a long time it hampered efforts to reach a common policy with the Americans for Germany. It helped explain the divergent perspectives the two countries brought to the consideration of Middle East questions—Suez above all, but also Iran and the Saudi Arabian inroads into Buraimi. It encouraged the belief among American congressmen that Britain was not doing all it could to better its own economic situation—a conviction most prominent when Labour held power, but also present after Churchill and the Conservatives regained office. And it became a factor each time Congress was called upon to appropriate new funds for the Marshall Plan and subsequent American assistance programs.

The British, of course, bravely maintained otherwise. When Churchill's plans to visit Washington shortly after he assumed office were made public, the British press pointedly reminded Americans that the prime minister was coming with his hat on his head, not in his hand. But no amount of bravado could alter the reality of Britain's dependence upon the United States. In the ten years after 1945, Washington provided $7.67 billion in economic assistance and nearly $1 billion in military aid to the United Kingdom. Of all the nations in the world, only France received more during this period. This dependence gnawed at Churchill. "They have become so great and we are now so small. Poor England!" he lamented at one point. Churchill's physician wrote in his diary of "that sense of inequality that devours him like a cancer."[9]

CONFRONTING THE SOVIET THREAT

Yet, despite Britain's economic anemia, the United Kingdom remained a valued military partner to America throughout the 1950s. Indeed, collaboration in defense, security, and intelligence matters played a central role in cementing the Anglo–American partnership. Measured in terms of men actually under arms, the differences between the two nations were not as great as one might have expected. Moreover, American strategists continued to value British bases, especially in the Middle East, for the projection of United States air power. But undoubtedly the most obvious manifestation of this partnership lay in the dramatic rise in the number of American bases in the United Kingdom. By one reckoning, Britain housed forty-three major American airfields in 1953 (although this figure declined as strategic doctrine and operational requirements evolved during the decade).

Washington continued to oppose occasional British suggestions for a re-creation of the wartime Combined Chiefs of Staff, on the grounds that this was likely to disquiet the other European allies. In many other respects, however, there thrived a quiet collaboration, frequently involving the Canadians as well. The movement toward the standardization of weaponry and other defense articles continued unabated. Air force officers of the two nations worked closely together at the technical and operational levels on the development of high-performance aircraft, helicopters, missiles, and such specialized procedures as in-flight refueling. And in a pattern that speaks eloquently about the closeness of the bilateral relationship (as well as the intensity of the interservice rivalries within each nation), the navies of the two countries often conspired together against the two air forces, and vice versa, adding an odd international dimension to the traditional competition between sister services.

Above all, military officers of both countries predicated all their planning on the assumption that the two would stand side-by-side in any future war. Contrary to hopes held by American officials early in the Eisenhower years, the United States maintained its guarantee of European security through the tangible step of keeping its troops in Europe. This was key. It overrode specific disagreements between Washington and its allies. And it furnished one of the touchstones of the British–American partnership.

Intelligence furnished another. "No feature of the special relationship, other than the trade in nuclear weapons know-how, has been of comparable importance in binding together British and American political and military establishments," one authority has concluded. "Secret pacts, whether established by treaty or merely by custom and practice, have virtually created integrated multinational intelligence agencies."[10] Officials of the two countries collaborated extensively in cryptanalysis and in the collection and exploitation of electronic intelligence. Their partnership was somewhat less productive in espionage and covert action, where a spectacularly botched joint operation against Albania in 1949 (possibly betrayed by British intelligence officer and Soviet double agent Kim Philby) illustrated the difficulties of cooperation in such enterprises. But another combined operation met with greater success a few years later, as British intelligence worked closely with the CIA in overthrowing Iranian Prime Minister Mohammed Mossadegh and returning the shah to his throne. Once the United States began to employ sophisticated overhead surveillance techniques—first the U-2 and its successors, later satellites—Washington frequently shared the take from these systems as well. Indeed, RAF pilots may actually have manned some of the U-2 missions. Finally, analytical intelligence reports were routinely exchanged, including at least some that London did not permit even the Canadians to see. These intelligence links, historian David Reynolds has judged, lay "at the heart of what [made] the Anglo–American tie so different from other alliances."[11]

Collaboration in nuclear matters remained a touchy issue, although Eisenhower proved more sympathetic to British wishes than Truman had been. From London's perspective, Britain was being asked to serve as a base for American atomic weapons, thereby making itself a potential target, but was denied either a voice in the use of these weapons or American help in acquiring its own nuclear arsenal. Churchill in particular, remembering the expectations of far more generous treatment he had once held, was wont to brood at what he considered Washington's bad faith in this area. But while Eisenhower directed his subordinates to be as forthcoming as possible, the restrictions imposed by the 1946 McMahon Act limited what they could do.

Only after the administration sought legislative relief in 1958 did anything approaching true collaboration in the nuclear field resume.

In the interim, the United Kingdom strode determinedly ahead on its own. The successful test of an atomic bomb in the autumn of 1952 brought London officials temporary cheer. This, however, largely dissipated when only a month later the American detonation of the world's first hydrogen bomb once again reminded Whitehall of the wide gap between the nuclear programs of the two nations. Britain's decision to develop its own thermonuclear weapon predictably followed. Only in this manner, Churchill informed the Cabinet, could the United Kingdom expect to maintain its influence as a world power.

Sometime later, during a debate in the Commons on the country's defense policies, Churchill amplified this reasoning. Britain required its own hydrogen bomb, he explained, because the United Kingdom's targeting priorities were entirely different from those of the United States. In a future war, London needed to ensure that targets of life-and-death importance to the United Kingdom would in fact be selected. Churchill went on to add that as long as Britain remained largely dependent on American protection, London would not enjoy much influence over American policy. But a British H-bomb would augment Britain's voice in Washington. Harold Macmillan, then minister of defence, echoed this combination of strategic and political considerations. The proposition that the United Kingdom needed no deterrent force of its own was "a very dangerous doctrine," he told the Commons. "Politically, it surrenders our power to influence American policy and then, strategically and tactically, it equally deprives us of any influence over the selection of targets and use of our vital striking forces. The one, therefore, weakens our prestige and our influence in the world and the other might imperil our safety."[12] Labourites as well as Conservatives generally accepted this argument for an independent British nuclear deterrent, although an influential minority repeatedly challenged the party's official line. "[W]e did not think it right that this country should be so dependent" on the United States, Labour leader Hugh Gaitskell observed in explaining his party's endorsement of the government's decision to develop a hydrogen bomb.[13]

Much of London's distress over Washington's unwillingness to accept Great Britain as a nuclear equal arose from a genuine concern that American policies might lead to a third, and this time catastrophic, global war. The Eisenhower administration's apparent disposition to regard atomic weaponry as simply another element in the Western arsenal—a disposition that increased the longer NATO forces remained manpower poor—produced considerable anxiety in London. Backed by the French, Whitehall vigorously resisted the idea that Western military planners should view nuclear arms as more or less routine weapons to be automatically used in case of war.

"Appeasement," of course, continued to be a nasty word in the British vocabulary. London no less than Washington remained convinced of the necessity of containment, supported the concept of Western rearmament, backed NATO, and believed that the maintenance of peace rested on America's continued commitment to the defense of Western Europe.

That having been said, London—and the old anti-Bolshevik Churchill above all—was far more willing than Washington to seek out areas of agreement with Moscow and to see the potential for fruitful negotiations. The American ambassador in Britain cabled his superiors back home that the prime minister, "firm in [the] belief in his own genius," viewed negotiations with the Soviets as a way of achieving "one last crowning act on [the] world stage."[14] More generally, Washington attributed London's greater willingness to sit down with the Soviets to Britain's more exposed geographical position. Whitehall, for its part, explained Washington's reluctance to talk by pointing to an unfortunate inflexibility in American policy, an intransigence encouraged by both McCarthyism and the unbending moralism of Secretary of State Dulles. None of these explanations was completely off the mark.

Recent research tends to support the claim that Stalin's death in 1953 may have offered the West an opportunity to ease world tensions and establish some more acceptable modus vivendi with the Soviet Union. Churchill lobbied energetically to persuade Eisenhower to agree to a summit meeting with the new Soviet leadership. But the Republican administration in Washington preferred trying to capitalize on Eastern European discontent with Soviet rule to working for a general settlement that would implicitly accept Moscow's dominance over half the continent. Neither Eisenhower nor Dulles was prepared to allow a fragile detente to jeopardize their hopes for the European Defense Community or West Germany's integration into the Western bloc. In light of our knowledge of what has transpired in the years since 1953, one cannot help but wish that the possibilities of that day had been pursued more vigorously, that London had been more willing or able to challenge the Americans on these fundamental matters of policy.

Things look far clearer in hindsight, however, than they did to policymakers at the time. Moreover, British wisdom was so obviously in short supply on other important questions of the day—various Middle East issues spring most readily to mind—that there is little reason to believe that British eloquence or logic, if only presented more forcefully, would have won over the Americans. In addition, the British Cabinet was itself split on the value of dealing with the Soviets. Foreign Secretary Eden, for instance, rather consistently opposed his prime minister on this issue, on the grounds that Moscow was not prepared to make any substantial concessions in either policies or tactics. But beyond these internal disagreements there was the matter of power, of the one unalterable reality that British security lay in the closest of partnerships with the United States. Constrained by their dependence, London officials concluded that they could resist the Americans only so far.

THE DIFFICULTIES OF COLLABORATION

On other issues the two allies frequently differed—but always within this larger context of a sense of shared interests against the Soviet threat. Washington's insistence upon naming an American rather than a British admiral as the first commander of NATO's Atlantic forces triggered an anguished and angry outcry in Great Britain. Even on the oceans that the British navy had ruled for hundreds of years, it seemed, the United States was now intent on elbowing the United Kingdom into a secondary position. As for matters on the Continent, Washington was forever pushing London to work more vigorously for European integration, economically and militarily if not politically. Churchill was never able to summon up any great enthusiasm for the European Defense Community, although he did grudgingly go along with it as the most acceptable means of achieving West German rearmament. Far more aware than Whitehall that Britain's future lay within Europe, Washington found this half-heartedness exasperating—and said so. At last, Oliver Franks, one of Britain's most pro-American U.S. ambassadors, could stand no more. The Americans, he complained, were "trying all the time to impose their own way of doing things on the Europeans. If it isn't German rearmament it is European unity, if it isn't their view of the Middle East it is their view of China." Washington, he protested, had "acquired a habit of putting on all the pressures whenever the Europeans do not follow. . . . Americans behave in Europe as if it belonged to them."[15] The unhappy Franks was undeniably accurate in describing this American confidence that Washington more than London had all the answers. But at the same time, this tirade from the normally unflappable diplomat suggests just how difficult many British found the fact that their global role had passed to another.

More than anything else, an unwillingness, or perhaps an inability, to accept their new role prevented the British from joining France, Germany, Italy, and the Benelux nations in creating the European Economic Community. Many analysts have deemed this failure the major blunder in British postwar foreign policy. And a good many of those have blamed the Anglo–American relationship for deceiving Whitehall into believing that Britain was different from the other Western European states, that its power allowed it to remain aloof from the movement toward European unity.

While not entirely gratuitous, this argument ignores several salient points. The Anglo–American partnership, after all, was responsible for neither the Commonwealth nor those portions of the Empire that still existed in the 1950s, vestiges of a past that led many Britons to place themselves in a different category from that of Italians or Germans. Nor could the United States be held accountable for the fact that Britain alone among Western European countries possessed nuclear weapons. Indeed, Washington had placed major obstacles in the way of Britain's acquiring such an arsenal. Moreover, the Americans from the start had encouraged London to join its

European neighbors in the discussions leading to the creation of the EEC. But as David Owen, British foreign and commonwealth secretary in the 1970s, later explained, the national mood in Great Britain precluded its becoming a founding member of the EEC. "Britain still *felt* a major power" in the 1950s, he recalls.[16] And while the close ties with the United States may have contributed to this feeling, there is little reason to think that without those ties, Britain would have been any more prepared to turn its back on a four-centuries-old national tradition of avoiding European entanglements.

As Ambassador Franks's lament suggests, Anglo–American difficulties were not confined to Europe. Indeed, European-generated squabbles were restrained in comparison to disputes arising elsewhere. The American role in overthrowing the Arbenz government in Guatemala in 1954, for example, produced friction that, as Dulles informed Eisenhower, became "almost unbearable." The president angrily replied that the United States had been "too damned nice" to the British and that perhaps Washington should "give them a lesson" about interfering in matters involving the Western hemisphere.[17] Called on the carpet, Whitehall backed away from its plans to raise the issue in the United Nations.

In the Far East, the cessation of fighting in Korea did little to bring British and American policies into harmony. The two continued to differ over the most appropriate approach to the People's Republic of China, with London consistently pushing for greater flexibility in dealing with the world's most populous nation. Increased trade, Churchill assured Dulles, could serve as a weapon for penetrating the iron curtain. Nor would it hurt British commercial interests, the American secretary of state acidly responded.

Heightened tensions in 1955 over the Chinese offshore islands of Quemoy and Matsu served to underscore Anglo–American differences. The Nationalist outposts on the two islands could not be abandoned without producing shocks far beyond the Formosa straits, Washington maintained in an argument that would be repeatedly applied elsewhere in Asia during the 1960s. American resolve and reliability around the globe would come into question. But Quemoy and Matsu were not worth a global war, London rejoined, and the stated American policy of massive retaliation threatened to transform a localized Asian conflict into a worldwide holocaust. Few in London wished to hand Taiwan over to the mainland Communists, although Chiang was frequently viewed as little more than an American creation. But Whitehall did wonder about the military feasibility of holding coastal islands within artillery range of the mainland and argued that their orderly abandonment could lead to conditions making possible a general settlement in the area, with Taiwan remaining free of Peking's control.

British anxiety during the Quemoy-Matsu crisis was undoubtedly heightened by recollections of the crisis in Indochina a year earlier. Besieged at Dien Bien Phu by the communist forces of Ho Chi Minh, the French had desperately turned to the Americans to rescue them from a disaster that was almost certain to terminate the French presence in Indochina. French pleas fell on receptive ears in Washington, and for several weeks in March and April of 1954, the American capital was ripe with rumors of air strikes and expeditionary forces. It is not at all certain that Eisenhower seriously considered an American intervention, but Dulles, Vice President Richard M. Nixon, and Joint Chiefs of Staff chairman Arthur Radford all vigorously lobbied for some sort of military action.

Ultimately, of course, cooler heads prevailed, in part because the British made it clear that they wanted nothing to do with such adventures. It was hardly likely, Churchill pointedly told Radford, that British soldiers would be prepared to fight and die so that France could retain Indochina when they had not fought to hold India for Great Britain. More generally, Whitehall doubted that a French defeat in Indochina would have the devastating strategic consequences the State Department feared. Rather, London worried that a Western intervention could set off a wider war with China. For the moment, America had been saved from itself. British–American ties, on the other hand, had suffered a setback, as Dulles bitterly denounced London for refusing to support his plans for intervention. Never one to forget a slight, the American secretary two years later would easily recall how London let him down in Indochina in 1954.

But it was in the Middle East that Whitehall and Washington found themselves most at cross purposes. The 1950s saw the British position in the region increasingly under siege. Iran in 1951 nationalized the Anglo–Iranian Oil Company and its lucrative oil fields. Demands for a British withdrawal from Egypt came with mounting frequency. Iraq pressed for a revision of the one-sided alliance that had accorded the United Kingdom pre-eminence in that country. And Saudi Arabia's occupation of the Buraimi oasis on the southeastern tip of the Arabian peninsula threatened to undermine Britain's presence in the Persian Gulf.

Official Washington felt, with some reason, that London's refusal to recognize awakening Arab nationalism had encouraged anti-Western sentiment in the Middle East. Blessed with enormous petroleum reserves and situated at the crossroads of three continents, the region, Americans believed, must be kept free of Soviet influence. As the decade progressed, more and more Washington decisionmakers concluded that the only way to maintain Western predominance and keep the Soviets out of the region was to supplant the British presence with America's. And this meant accommodating the rising tide of Arab nationalism, even when, as in Iran and Buraimi, this placed Washington and London at odds.

Matters could hardly have looked differently to the British. London viewed the Middle East not in terms of Soviet expansionism, but as an arena of competition with the United States for both oil supplies and political influence. To the British, the enormous petroleum reserves of the region offered a potential solution for Britain's ailing economy, and Whitehall decisionmakers resented being muscled out of this market by American oil companies. Undoubtedly, a determination to hold on to the remainder of their empire also motivated London officials. Strategic considerations—most notably a desire to protect the Suez Canal and the shipping lanes to India and the Far East—counted heavily as well. Lumped together, this combination of strategy, economics, and bruised national pride formed a combustible mix. And in the second half of 1956, this mix burst into open flame at Suez, bringing on the worst crisis in Anglo–American relations of the postwar period.

THE SUEZ IMBROGLIO

As Lord Harlech, Britain's U.S. ambassador during the 1960s, has observed, the Suez-induced breach in British–American comity was a product of the divergent histories, interests, and psychological forces operating on London and Washington.[18] Compounding these differences was a fundamental inability on the part of these closest of allies to communicate with each other. Of such are diplomatic debacles made.

The essentials of the story can be quickly summarized. In July 1956, the United States, angered by Cairo's increasingly cordial ties with the Soviet Union and its allies, and put off by Egyptian President Gamal Nasser's anti-Western rhetoric, withdrew its earlier offer to assist Egypt in financing the huge Aswan Dam project on which Nasser had staked a good deal of prestige. A week later, Nasser retaliated by nationalizing the British-owned Suez Canal. There then followed three months of tortured diplomatic maneuvering, which repeatedly ran afoul of the fundamental fact that neither Cairo nor London felt able to back down on a matter that had become a point of national honor. Finally, on 29 October, as the opening move in a carefully orchestrated operation with Britain and France, Israeli troops invaded Egypt. Without giving prior notice to the Americans, who were a week away from their presidential election, the British then bombed Egyptian airfields and, joined by the French, parachuted soldiers into the Canal Zone. British forces sought only to protect the canal, London explained, though by the time the troops arrived, fighting around the canal had virtually ceased. In the United Nations, Washington joined Moscow in condemning the Anglo–French–Israeli invasion. When this brought no result, the Kremlin proposed a joint intervention to Eisenhower. The American president emphatically replied that he would not tolerate the introduction of Soviet forces into the region, but at the same time used Washington's financial strength to pressure London into halting its advance. Around noon on 6 November, Eden, who had succeeded Churchill in 1955, gave in, announcing British acceptance of a cease-fire.

Three-plus decades later, the Suez misadventure stands as a monument of misjudgment and mismanagement. The British, and Eden above all, acted as if London were leading from strength, when in fact Britain's position, in terms of power if not legality, was a very exposed one. This represented a fundamental British miscalculation, that with sufficient will Britain could intimidate Nasser in 1956 as it had his predecessors. Diplomatic means proved inadequate to the task, but Eden came to understand this only at a point where he felt compelled to turn to a military option. Here too he failed—first because he was unable to prevent Nasser from closing the canal, then because he found it impossible to retake the canal in the face of intense American opposition.

Nor was Eden at all imaginative in assessing the likely consequences of an Anglo–French intervention. Little thought seems to have been given to what Britain might actually do if it succeeded. Was London prepared, in the face of certain Egyptian sullenness if not outright hostility, to occupy the Canal Zone indefinitely? Did Whitehall actually think that a successor government to Nasser could both cooperate with Britain and remain in power? Did the British really believe that the United Nations would meekly condone the intervention, and was London prepared to abandon the high moral ground that a negative General Assembly response would entail? Finally, might not the Soviet Union, even if Washington were to support the Anglo–French–Israeli action, inconvenience Britain elsewhere?

In predicting the likely American reaction, Eden labored under three misconceptions. First, he allowed himself to believe that Eisenhower would not move at the climatic moment of the American election. This error arose from his second and more fundamental misconception—that Washington's very tepid support of London in the weeks leading up to the intervention was a function of the election and of Dulles's personal opposition, but that at the moment of reckoning, neither the president nor the American people would turn on their good friends the British. And this misjudgment was in turn a function of a third and still more basic misconception—that a greater identity of interests bound the United States and the United Kingdom than actually existed. Even in later years, Eden failed to understand that for the United States, Britain's fight at Suez was not America's. If only the United States "had approached this issue in the spirit of an ally," he lamented some years after his retirement. Instead, nothing about American policy "was geared to the long-term purpose of serving a joint cause."[19] That, however, was precisely the point: it was not a joint cause. That London could seriously have believed that the Americans would have judged it in their interest to side with the colonial powers in the dispute with Nasser represents the triumph of hope over reality.

Of course, American policy left something to be desired as well. "While it is quite legitimate for any person or government to have their own views about what we should have done and the way we should have done it," an embittered official in the Foreign Office wrote shortly after the crisis subsided, "it is not legitimate for the United States to pour out a series of emotional criticisms when one of the causes of the difficulties in the Middle East has been the failure of the United States to arrive at a definite, clear and active policy."[20] Indeed, confusion and inconsistency had characterized Washington's course in the months preceding the attack. Dulles at times led Eden to believe—or perhaps Eden only hoped this was so—that the United States did not exclude the use of force against Nasser if all other methods failed. In the absence of firm guidance, Eden was allowed to persuade himself that Washington could be counted upon for, at a minimum, benign neutrality. Eisenhower, on the other hand, publicly stated in a press conference at the end of August that the United States would "exhaust every possible, every feasible method of peaceful settlement," which may have encouraged Nasser to resist a negotiated compromise.[21] And although Washington had helped to precipitate the crisis by retracting its offer to assist with the Aswan Dam project (without, incidentally, consulting the British, although London was also a partner in the deal), the Americans failed to suggest an acceptable alternative to the armed force ultimately chosen. Perhaps there was no alternative, but neither did Washington seriously address that possibility. The abrupt withdrawal of the Aswan offer itself appears impulsive and vindictive, and all the more so since London was left hanging. At a minimum, Dulles seems not to have asked what might be the likely consequences of his action.

Underlying these individual failures, however, lay a more fundamental inability in Washington and London even to agree on the meaning of Nasser's actions. For Dulles the Suez crisis represented an unnecessary and unfortunate diversion from what should have been the West's principal focus—the struggle against communist expansion. Eden, on the other hand, saw Nasser's provocations not only as a challenge to British influence throughout the non-European world, but as precisely the sort of lawlessness that had been allowed to go unchecked in the 1930s. For the Americans, the use of European military force against a Third World country was an inflammatory act that practically invited the Arab states to turn to Moscow. Whitehall, however, viewed the dispatch of British and French troops as the type of restrained response that, had it been used against Hitler and Mussolini in the years before 1939, might have prevented a world war.[22] Neither country, it should be added, displayed any real comprehension of the Egyptian and pan-Arab nationalism that perhaps best explained the crisis.

The whole sorry episode, of course, diverted attention, in a way not even the boldest Soviet scriptwriter might have dared portray, from Moscow's brutal suppression of the revolt in Hungary. Indeed, the Soviet Union, rather than receiving the universal condemnation its actions in Budapest deserved, emerged from the events that fall with an enhanced reputation in the Third World as the protector of less developed peoples from imperial designs. Seldom, if ever, in the long record of alliances have nations as closely linked as Britain and the United States worked at such cross purposes, or with greater ill effect.

As for ties between Washington and London, the Suez debacle led policymakers in both nations to reassess the fundamental meaning and usefulness of a relationship in which two partners could come to such public odds. That his friends would have taken actions expected only of the Soviets seemed to Eisenhower a betrayal of the values for which the Western alliance stood. "Of course, there's just nobody, in a war, I'd rather have fighting alongside me than the British . . . ," the president complained. "But—*this* thing! My God!"[23] What the British and the French had done, Dulles informed the National Security Council at the height of the crisis, "was nothing but the straight old-fashioned variety of colonialism of the most obvious sort." The invasion of Egypt threatened the West by suggesting that there really was little to distinguish it from the East. Unless the United States acted to oppose the intervention, Dulles argued, "all of these newly independent countries will turn from us to the USSR. We will be looked upon as forever tied to British and French colonialist policies."[24] Reportedly, the president wanted to seek a United Nations resolution branding his allies "aggressors," as had been done with China in Korea, in order to make the point that such actions were no more acceptable to the United States when carried out by friends than when undertaken by adversaries.

At a more personal level, Eisenhower felt betrayed by the stealth with which the British acted on their plans, as did officials in the American foreign policy, defense, and intelligence bureaucracies. London's timing—not only on the eve of the American election, but also just as Soviet brutality in Eastern Europe was at its most apparent—angered the American president as well. Finally, many Americans were simply disgusted at the sheer incompetence displayed by the British military once the operation was under way. Had the Western allies executed their plans swiftly and presented the world with a fait accompli, American ire might soon have been tempered by the realization that little could be achieved by outrage. Instead, British and French troops arrived at the canal—supposedly to separate the combatants—only after London and Paris had tipped their hands by vetoing the Security Council resolution calling for a cease-fire.

The British, for their part, were stung not only by the virulence of American opposition, but by the pressure the American Treasury placed upon them, which seemed far more severe than anything required by electoral considerations or geopolitical necessities. In effect, Washington presented Whitehall with an ultimatum: either call off its war against Egypt or lose access to American dollars, which would soon ruin the pound. But more was to come. The United States was not content merely to save Nasser. It also required the evacuation of all British and French troops, forcing London to hand back its military gains and unilaterally abandon the diplomatic leverage these offered. Again, the British felt unable to do anything other than give way. And so they did, but not without undisguised rancor and resentment at their supposed friend. As Eden would later say, "I did not foresee then that the United

States Government would harden against us on almost every point and become harsher after the cease-fire than before."[25]

The Suez crisis did have its ironic aspects, even if these gave the participants little solace. In Britain, where the Conservatives had always been the most ardent proponents of the American connection, it was now the Labour party that suddenly discovered great wisdom in the admonitions of a conservative American administration. Moreover, the Americans, who had sponsored the creation of the Israeli state, now opposed Tel Aviv, while the British, who had been so roundly castigated in America for their allegedly pro-Arab bias, found themselves in league with Israel. Finally, the debacle had led the United States to make common cause in the U.N. with the Soviet Union against Washington's closest friends.

Viewed in its broader dimensions, the Suez crisis was simply one more in a series of extra-European crises where one of the Atlantic democracies sought the support, or at least the acquiescence, of the other. In Indochina in the spring of 1954, as in the Middle East two years later, outright opposition by one partner brought the efforts of the other to nought. And then in the 1960s, the positions would once more reverse, as the United States for a second time solicited London's assistance in dealing with Indochinese troubles. Again, the British turned the Americans down. All these episodes suggested a larger truth about the Anglo–American partnership—that in spite of the repeated disagreements over Britain's proper role in Europe, the special relationship functioned best in its European context.

At the same time, Eisenhower's public reaffirmation that Britain and France were still friends, even if misguided in this instance, was also revealing. Issued in the face of Soviet threats to intervene militarily, it served to remind observers on both sides of the ocean that the deplorable business at Suez had not altered the many interests that had furnished the reason for the closeness of the relationship in the first place. Indeed, in America, once the heat of indignation had passed, the primary sense was more of sorrow than of anger, and even of understanding how the British might have taken such wrongheaded action. "I shall never be happy until our old-time closeness has been restored," Eisenhower wrote Churchill at the end of November.[26] Thus, even as tempers still flared, the ingredients for a return to the pre-Suez ties remained in place.

chapter 4

ALLIANCE SUSTAINED: 1957–1963

Worn down by ill health and diplomatic debacle, Anthony Eden informed the queen early in the new year that he could no longer continue as her first minister. As his successor she appointed Harold Macmillan, who as chancellor of the Exchequer the previous autumn had insisted that Britain's depleted treasury left London no choice but to abandon the Suez enterprise. A figure of patrician elegance, Macmillan had about him the reassuring appearance of times and glories past. Yet the air of Victorian languor he sometimes assumed masked instincts that had gained him a reputation for political adroitness of the first order. "This is no mean man," American ambassador David Bruce cabled Washington a few years later. "He represents Edwardian and eighteenth century England in the grand tradition of the establishment," yet at the same time "has an extensive appreciation of contemporary public opinion." The prime minister, Bruce judged, was "a political animal, shrewd, subtle in maneuver, undisputed master in his Cabinet house."[1]

Few individuals were better suited than Macmillan to restoring some semblance of order and comity to Britain's ties with its most important ally. And in this task he must be counted a notable success. Indeed, one of the most remarkable aspects of the entire Suez affair is the speed with which feelings of great bitterness gave way to a renewed sense of the intimacy that had characterized Anglo–American relations in the decade prior to 1956. Only a few months after the Suez debacle, to cite one example, the State Department sent out instructions to American diplomats around the world that its general proscription against disclosing classified information to foreigners was not meant to apply to British colleagues. And barely a year and a half after the crisis, the two Atlantic democracies, doubtless to their own surprise, found themselves conducting loosely coordinated military operations in—of all places—the Middle East, the area of the world where one would have least expected Anglo–American collaboration of this nature. The precipitant for so extraordinary a development was the toppling, in July 1958, of a pro-Western Iraqi government. Convinced that Nasser was behind the coup, Washington landed marines in Lebanon while Britain dispatched airborne troops to Jordan. That the United States was prepared to join the British to block Egyptian ambitions is a testament to the salvage job on Anglo–American relations Macmillan had performed.

Like Churchill, whom he revered, Macmillan had an American mother. Like Churchill, Macmillan had enjoyed, during his wartime service as British Resident Minister in North Africa, a working relationship with Eisenhower that had blossomed into full-fledged friendship. Like Churchill, Macmillan had come to believe that only the closest of ties with the Americans would safeguard British interests adequately. In working toward re-establishing those ties, he found a willing collaborator in Eisenhower, who had himself been shaken by the rift in Anglo–American relations that the Suez embarrassment had engendered.

And still again like Churchill, one of Macmillan's first actions after moving into Number 10 was to arrange a private tête-à-tête with the American president. Their March 1957 meeting in Bermuda had as its principal purpose the restoration of the spirit of partnership that the events of recent months had so badly eroded. The extent to which they succeeded can be gauged by Eisenhower's later recollection that the Bermuda meeting was "by far" the most successful international conference he had attended since the close of the war.[2]

Here again, however, personal ties and feelings of friendship were supplemented by less transitory forces. In Washington these included continued recognition of the important role even a weakened Britain could play in the ongoing competition with the Soviet Union. The United Kingdom still retained a consequential presence in the Indian Ocean, the Middle East, the southwest Pacific, and the Caribbean. Naval and air bases in places such as Gibraltar, Aden, Hong Kong, and Singapore enabled the British to project their power around the globe. Except for the two superpowers, the United Kingdom was the world's only nuclear weapons state. Even Britain's traditional domestic political stability took on a new importance in light of the manifest instability that wracked France, Italy, and some of Washington's other allies. Anglo–American ties, a senior American diplomat reaffirmed a year after the Suez crisis, remained "at the core" of the NATO alliance.[3]

A similar appreciation of the transatlantic relationship reasserted itself in London. "Suez proved that without American support we could not sustain the most tin-pot of campaigns for more than three days," a Conservative M.P.

declared in some bitterness.[4] A year or so later, a former British minister warned that "with the enemy at the gate this is no time for bickering." Speaking only slightly hyperbolically, he added: "On a close relationship between the two countries rests the best hope for the future of the world."[5] Somewhat less excitedly, but equally reflective of British assumptions was the 1961 observation by a longtime commentator on British–American ties that "however much of a cliché it has now become that the future of the Western world depends primarily on understanding between the American and British peoples, it is—like so many clichés—still fundamentally true."[6]

Clichés aside, London in the months and then the years after the Suez disaster went through a thorough if not always systematic reassessment of the British position worldwide. Macmillan's widely noted "wind of change" speech in South Africa in 1960 reflected this rethinking of Britain's position. So did London's more or less graceful acceptance of independence for many of its former possessions in the decade or so after 1956. So did Macmillan's historic announcement in 1961 that the United Kingdom planned to seek membership in the Common Market. Stunned by the wholesale nature of the failure Suez represented, British policymakers decidedly, if not always consciously, lowered their expectations about the role Britain should henceforth play in world affairs. As the American ambassador in London reported in the autumn of 1957, the British were increasingly "disposed to be more realistic than before about their weakened world position and to cut their coat to fit a relatively smaller piece of cloth."[7]

The Macmillan government's 1957 White Paper on Defense, which marks a turning point in British postwar defense policy, gave official expression to these reduced expectations. The product of the Suez imbroglio (although its outlines had been foreshadowed earlier), it was also the nearly inevitable result of spiraling defense costs since 1950, of the less threatening nature of the cold war since Stalin's death, and of Britain's chronic inability to right its economy. The White Paper set forth sweeping cuts in the defense program. The armed forces would be slashed from 690,000 to 375,000 men and women over the next five years. The strength of the British Army on the Rhine would be reduced. Conscription would end. These reductions were to be partly offset by a greater reliance on Britain's nuclear deterrent. Thus, the Macmillan government found itself adopting the "new look" of the Eisenhower administration, a defense posture made possible by changes in the McMahon Act and Washington's new willingness to share its nuclear expertise.

Nowhere was the post-Suez rapprochement between Washington and London more manifest than in the nuclear sphere. At Bermuda in March 1957, Eisenhower agreed to provide Britain with sixty intermediate-range Thor missiles capable of carrying atomic warheads. This represented the first time Washington had ever shared missiles with another country. The "two-key" system that ensured American approval before their use further demonstrated the unique defense ties linking the two nations. The provision of the Thors meant that, unlike Britain's development of its nuclear weapons, London would receive extensive American cooperation in obtaining the means to deliver its warheads. Britain's successful test two months later of its first thermonuclear weapon made possession of an advanced delivery system all the more significant.

The following year Eisenhower succeeded in having the McMahon Act amended to permit far more extensive collaboration with the British on weapons design and production. With this step, the British at last secured the wholesale nuclear cooperation they had desired–and expected–since 1943. London wasted no time; the day after Eisenhower signed the measure, the two governments initialed an accord providing for the pooling of much of their knowledge. Nor was this the end of matters. In 1959, agreement was reached for London to buy nuclear weapons components from the United States. Finally, at Camp David in 1960, the British offered to base American Polaris submarines at Scotland's Holy Loch, thus giving the United States its first Polaris base in European waters. In return—although it was not presented as a quid pro quo—Eisenhower pledged to sell Britain, at bargain-basement prices, the air-to-surface Skybolt missile then under development, thereby completing the job of linking both Britain's warheads and its delivery systems to the United States. Even before these agreements, Britain's nuclear relations with the Americans had rested on a unique footing. With the completion of these arrangements, however, London had acquired unprecedented access to American weapons and technology.

Britain derived substantial advantages from these various agreements. For one thing, they made it possible for London to proceed in its nuclear development without duplicating much of the costly work already completed in the United States. For another, they prolonged the usefulness of Britain's bomber force and allowed London to postpone development of a prohibitively expensive new generation of strategic bombers. But there were costs as well. The advent of the missile age, dramatized by the Soviet satellite *Sputnik* in 1957, and the gradual downgrading of the manned bomber served to de-emphasize areas of British strength. *Sputnik* and Thor, each in its own way, pushed the United Kingdom into an ever greater reliance upon the United States. This, however, made more problematic Britain's entry into Europe, once London decided to seek admission. As events soon enough demonstrated, not all of Britain's Western allies, and certainly not the French, viewed London's special nuclear partnership with Washington with unreserved favor.

The French—"if we could only sit down and talk to them man to man like we can with the British when things get tough," Eisenhower lamented at one point.[8] The distinction the American president drew between his two European allies repeatedly worked to Britain's advantage. So, for that matter, did Charles de Gaulle's moves beginning in 1959 to distance France somewhat from NATO, which made British constancy all the more admirable in American eyes. Eisenhower's assessment of the importance of links with the British, offered two years before the Suez business but equally pertinent post-Suez, is revealing. Pointing out his window to the bridges spanning the Potomac and filtering traffic into Washington, Eisenhower remarked that thousands of people used them daily without ever thinking about it. But if one of the bridges collapsed, then immediately everybody would take notice and a ruckus would ensue. And that, the president observed, was "exactly the way it is between the British and ourselves," accurately predicting the impact of the Suez debacle two years later.[9]

Suez had been such a disaster in part because it had enabled the Soviets to wriggle off the hook on which their brutal actions in Hungary had impaled them. Eden's being replaced by Macmillan had served to realign Anglo–American policy with respect to Moscow as well, and Washington officials noted with satisfaction that the Macmillan government brought a new firmness in dealing with the Soviet bloc. Moscow's efforts to extend its influence into Africa, Asia, and the Middle East brought it into sharp conflict with the United Kingdom and essentially negated its earlier policy of courting London in an effort to separate Whitehall from Washington. The Berlin crisis that erupted in late 1958, and that episodically over the next several years threatened the world with a full-fledged nuclear war, saw the two Atlantic democracies coordinating their policy as closely as they had at any time since 1945. Similarly, the crisis precipitated by the Soviet downing of an American U-2 reconnaissance plane in May 1960, and the subsequent scuttling of the Big Four summit, found Whitehall loyally lining up with its American partner.

As had frequently been the case, there were differences in tone and nuance in managing relations with the Russians, but these seem far less significant today than they did at the time. In a pattern going back a decade or more, London was apt to see greater possibilities for fruitful negotiation with the Kremlin than did Washington. Notwithstanding the extensive coordination of Anglo–American policy, Pentagon officials grumbled during the Berlin crisis that London's caution bordered on the defeatist. Macmillan's 1959 trip to Moscow occasioned anguished worries in some American quarters about a new mood of appeasement in the United Kingdom. Not to be outdone, British newspapers frequently complained about trigger-happy American generals eager for a showdown with the Soviet Union and barely controlled by a president too tired to restrain them. Dulles's saber-rattling rhetoric and apparent lack of interest in easing tensions with Moscow continued to alarm Britain, a country far more exposed to Soviet power than was the United States.

POPULAR ATTITUDES

As these examples suggest, an intimacy now approaching two decades in duration had not fully erased the easily evoked stereotypes each held of the other, even though close association had succeeded in toning down many of the more starkly unfavorable aspects of those images. The British Left less frequently viewed the United States as the archetypical capitalist exploiter and enemy of the workingman. Indeed, leftist politicians and commentators were increasingly apt to cite America as a model of a classless egalitarianism that Great Britain should strive to emulate. At the same time, America's power and its frequent diplomatic heavy-handedness—personified in British minds by Dulles's unique combination of apocalyptic rhetoric and ponderous moralism—continued to alienate large segments of the British public. Portions of the Labour Left also outspokenly opposed nuclear weapons—particularly American weapons in Britain—and called for a unilateral disarmament laden with anti-American implications.

The British Right regarded the United States with something of this same ambivalence, admiring American anticommunism, but nurturing a suspicion about the social and cultural influence on Britain of the vaunted American way of life. British industrialists frequently complained about unfair American competition. In the area of international arms sales, for instance, British manufacturers and exporters widely believed that undue pressure by the United States government on behalf of American suppliers explained why British firms seemed to lose so many major orders. Right-wing anti-Americanism never achieved the prominence of its left-wing counterpart in Britain, but the nationalistic "Suez group" of Tory M.P.s found it very hard to forgive Washington's "betrayal" in 1956. Openly resentful of what they viewed as America's usurpation of Britain's power, these M.P.s considerably complicated Macmillan's years as prime minister by vocally condemning any sign of weakness in dealing with the United States.

And yet, despite all this, observers on the scene reported a basic trust of and liking for Americans, and British anti-Americanism should not be overstated. Opinion polls suggested that most Britons believed that the United States could be trusted as an ally, even though many remained convinced that Washington did not treat the United Kingdom as an equal partner. In mid-1961, a few months after the Bay of Pigs debacle and just as the Berlin crisis once again heated up, a Gallup poll asked Britons whether they would select the United States or the Continent if Britain were forced to join with other powers. Fifty-five percent wished to join with the United States, while only 22 percent preferred Europe. Perhaps it was not surprising that Conservatives chose the United States by a 62–18 margin. What was noteworthy, however, was that Labourites also opted for ties with the Americans, by a substantial 47–28 margin.[10] So much for the ever-ready complaints that Americans ruined the domestic labor market with their high wages and outbid everyone else for the best flats.

In the United States, one heard the more virulent strains of Anglophobia with less frequency, although they were not totally absent. For the first time in nearly two hundred years British-baiting was neither good politics nor good patriotism. On the whole, Americans were less and less inclined than in earlier years to view Great Britain as an arrogant, hypocritical power living off its ill-gotten colonies. Americans of all political stripes hailed Macmillan's 1960 "wind of change" speech, in which he frankly said that the evolving directions of modern life required a new and less one-sided relationship between Britain and its former dependencies. Indeed, London's relatively graceful retreat from empire had the quite remarkable effect in the fifteen or so years after 1945 of defusing an American anticolonialism that for the better part of two centuries had furnished a major irritant to Anglo–American ties. How greatly matters had changed can be gauged by the testimony offered by Dulles's successor, Christian Herter, who told the Senate Foreign Relations Committee in the waning days of the Eisenhower administration that the United Kingdom was doing "a superb job" with its colonies.[11] Scarcely a decade earlier it would have been inconceivable to have heard an American secretary of state make such an admission.

On balance, Americans were probably less likely than Britons to think of their transatlantic partners in one-dimensional stereotypes. This, of course, did not mean that Americans were a more rational people. At bottom, this difference arose from the more fundamental fact of the unequal distribution of power between the two nations, and even more from the fact that its distribution was becoming more rather than less unequal. Americans could be charitable toward their British allies for the simple reason that they could afford to ignore the British for long periods of time. The typical Briton did not have this luxury. Britain's position, its ability to function as a world actor, even its continued independence, depended too heavily upon the United States. The English found it easy to blame the United States for Britain's reduced position in the world, and envy of American power and wealth combined with suspicion of American motives to fan the flames of anti-Americanism in the United Kingdom. Washington's frequently casual attitude toward British sensibilities did not help matters either.

At another level, many Britons remained unconvinced that Washington possessed either the experience or the sophistication to employ its great power wisely. Eisenhower's succession of public statements at the time of the U-2 crisis, each in turn retracted or amended, did much to reinforce British inclinations to see the American president as a bumbler. A year later, the fiasco of the Bay of Pigs invasion early in the Kennedy administration led many to fear that a younger president was not necessarily going to bring a higher level of competence to the design and execution of American policy.

Underlying these British fears—some reasonable, some baseless or irrational—lay a deeper concern about the transformation in British life that increasing contact with America was effecting. As consumers, music listeners, book and magazine readers, moviegoers, and, as the 1950s ended, television viewers, the British generation born after, say, 1940 found itself profoundly influenced by American trends, fashions, and fads. Nowhere else did American predominance in the postwar world assert itself more conspicuously, or in more ways. Even before the stepped-up transoceanic exchanges of the 1960s, a British observer judged the young people of his country "to an astonishing degree Americanized."[12] Indeed, American products and American tastes may have bound the two nations together far more effectively than the efforts of all the diplomats. As anthropologist Geoffrey Gorer noted more than a quarter century ago, this overseas transmission of American jeans, jukeboxes, and junk food had created "one of the first great international communities since the breakup of the medieval Church."[13]

Nor was this cultural and material migration in an exclusively easternly direction, even before the so-called English invasion of America in the 1960s. In perhaps less obvious ways the British shaped American attitudes just as surely as the Americans altered those of the British. American political scientists in the 1950s, for instance, widely admired the British party system, and in their American government courses they regularly contrasted the strong cabinet leadership and disciplined parties of the United Kingdom with the dispersion of power and tendency toward immobilism they found characteristic of American government. For many of these same reasons, American reformers, frustrated by the American system's capacity for obstruction, extolled the more structured British political system.

Economic and financial ties continued to draw the two nations together as well. Beginning in the 1950s, following a dip in the first years of peace, trade and investment links rose steadily. In 1949, for instance, the United Kingdom supplied only 3.4 percent of American imports. A decade later this figure had more than doubled to 7.5 percent. By value, the increase was even more dramatic, from $228 million to $1.1 billion. A similar if less spectacular rise in American exports to Great Britain occurred during the 1950s as well. By the end of the decade the British market took more than a billion dollars of American products annually, making the United Kingdom the second largest foreign market for U.S. exporters, trailing only Canada. Stated somewhat differently, the United States in 1959 supplied Great Britain with 9.3 percent of its imports, while the American market took 10.4 percent of British exports. In 1949, the United States was Britain's fifth largest overseas customer; Australia bought more than three times as much from the United Kingdom as Americans purchased. But by 1959, the United States was easily Britain's largest foreign buyer.

Investment links were even more pronounced. By 1960, British direct investment in the United States stood at $2.25 billion. This constituted nearly one-third of all foreign investment in the country and made the United Kingdom America's largest foreign investor. America's position in the British economy was, if anything, more dominant. In 1960, American investments in the United Kingdom totaled nearly three and a quarter billion dollars, and within a few years the British government would be publicly raising alarm about the penetration of Great Britain by American capital. By 1967, American-owned firms employed one out of every 17 British workers, prompting Prime Minister Harold Wilson to warn that the British, along with the rest of Europe, risked becoming "economic helots" of the United States.[14]

A NEW AMERICAN ADMINISTRATION

These financial and commercial links were both the progenitor and the product of the political ties binding the two nations. But in an equally important sense, they operated independently of the political relationship that prevailed at any given time. Even so, ties between the United States and the United Kingdom had shown themselves unusually sensitive to and dependent on whatever personal relationship then existed between the American president and the British prime minister. And since the winter of 1960–61 brought a changing of the guard in Washington, Macmillan's carefully nurtured relationship with Eisenhower assumed, at best, an instantaneous irrelevance. Indeed, it could have been a positive liability, had John Kennedy chosen to freeze out those who enjoyed close ties with his predecessor. There was, in fact, some speculation in the early months of the new administration that Macmillan and Kennedy would find it difficult to work together, if for no other reason than because of their nearly quarter-century age difference. And in the absence of a close relationship between the heads of government, the pessimists predicted, the intimacy of Anglo–American ties would inevitably decline.

Macmillan, of course, had other plans. Indeed, he did not even await Kennedy's inauguration before proposing they get together, a suggestion that led to the first of four meetings in 1961 alone. To the surprise of some, the two soon discovered a temperamental affinity. They shared an abiding interest in and sense of history. They displayed the same ironic wit. Kennedy enjoyed the prime minister's patrician bearing, his urbanity and unflappability, his lack of pomposity, and his sense of humor, and came to admire the detachment long experience had given Macmillan. According to a close Kennedy associate, the president found Macmillan's "breadth of vision" stimulating, and was captivated by the prime minister's propensity to relate events of the present to those of a bygone era.[15] As the months passed, Kennedy came to think of Macmillan not merely as the leader of a reliable ally, but as a valued friend. It was a perception the prime minister carefully cultivated and, moreover, one that the difficulties of working with de Gaulle and German Chancellor Konrad Adenauer did nothing to diminish.

For his part, Macmillan found the idealism and the youthful dynamism of the younger man refreshing. The American president turned out to be a more serious person than he had been led to expect. Kennedy's forthright acceptance of responsibility for the Bay of Pigs fiasco profoundly impressed the prime minister, who could not have avoided comparing Kennedy's behavior with Eisenhower's embarrassing attempts a year earlier to portray the loss of the U-2 as something other than the disaster it actually was. Unknowingly echoing the description provided some years earlier by Dean Acheson, the *Economist* observed in mid-1962 that the relationship between the two leaders "can only be described as domestic."[16]

Augmenting and enhancing this personal bond was the quite extraordinary friendship—no other word conveys the warmth of the relationship—between Kennedy and the British ambassador in Washington, David Ormsby-Gore (later Lord Harlech). Indeed, Kennedy reportedly took the unusual step of requesting that Ormsby-Gore, a personal friend of long standing, be sent to Washington. Ormsby-Gore was distantly related to Macmillan and, through the marriage of one of Kennedy's sisters, to the president as well. But remote family ties do not begin to explain the closeness of the relationship or the remarkable access Ormsby-Gore enjoyed in the Washington of John F. Kennedy. A frequent visitor not only at the White House but at the Kennedy compounds in Florida and Massachusetts, Ormsby-Gore was the only diplomat in Washington regularly to address Kennedy as "Jack." At the peak of the Cuban missile crisis, the White House quietly issued instructions that the British envoy and his family be brought to the presidential nuclear retreat in the mountains west of Washington should the capital have to be evacuated. Recalling this web of personal ties between the president, the prime minister, and himself, Ormsby-Gore would later say "it was almost like a family discussion when we all met."[17]

Of course, access is not identical with influence, which is far more difficult to establish. The minister of state for disarmament prior to his appointment as ambassador, Ormsby-Gore brought to Washington a passion for and expertise in nuclear disarmament and test ban negotiations. It is not unreasonable, though ultimately unprovable, to surmise that his views influenced Kennedy in moving toward the 1963 test ban treaty, the first important agreement with Moscow since the 1955 accord ending the postwar occupation of Austria.

Ironically, given the close ties that developed between Kennedy and Macmillan, many senior officials in the new American administration openly disparaged the significance of bilateral relations with the United Kingdom. Many of Kennedy's appointees, too young to have participated in the grand Anglo–American collaboration of World War II, frequently tended to lump Britain with France, West Germany, and perhaps Italy. The creation in 1957 of the European Economic Community, the Common Market, and the accomplishments of its early years convinced many that the era of fully autonomous European states had passed, and that the future favored those nations that pooled their resources to act in concert. This was not, of course, a novel proposition, but the inauguration of a new administration in 1961 gave these ideas a renewed force, as well as articulate spokesmen strategically placed throughout the government. Thus, Macmillan's decision in mid-1961 to seek British membership in the EEC received widespread endorsement in Washington.

Indeed, American enthusiasm for British entry into the Common Market was far more pronounced than London's own eagerness, a situation attributable to the very different significance each country assigned to British participation. For Macmillan, the decision to seek entry was something of an admission of failure, an acknowledgement that he had succeeded neither in revitalizing Britain's economy nor in restoring his nation to its prewar preeminence in world affairs. This public confession of Britain's decline, even if implicit rather than explicit, required a difficult adjustment for many Britons. The drawn-out negotiations that followed London's application for membership fully reflected the ambivalence with which many in Britain viewed the prospects of EEC participation. London's newly discovered desire for Common Market membership, Macmillan instructed the British negotiating team, must be balanced with older loyalties and obligations toward the Commonwealth and the European Free Trade Association.

Whitehall's reserve irritated not only its potential European partners, but many Americans as well, for Washington viewed the prospects of an expanded Common Market through very different lenses. In retrospect, it seems apparent that American officials rather badly overestimated the benefits of British membership in the EEC. But at the time an enlarged Common Market seemed to promise a solution to a whole range of political, economic, and strategic problems, including the always difficult question of how to reintegrate Germany into the Western security structure. Indeed, for Washington the political potential of the EEC far outweighed its economic benefits—or, for that matter, its economic disadvantages to American commercial interests. "We must never lose sight of the primary consideration," Under Secretary of State George Ball reminded Kennedy a week after Macmillan announced Britain's application, "that for political reasons the forthcoming negotiations between the UK and the Common Market must succeed."[18] Sixteen months later Ball was still arguing this case. Failure of the negotiations, he cautioned, would represent "a major blow to free world strength."[19]

Nor was Ball alone in these expectations. A few days after Macmillan's announcement that the United Kingdom would apply for EEC membership, David Bruce, the American ambassador in London, recorded in his diary that the decision was "the most thrilling and momentous made by a British Government in peacetime for generations." It constituted "one of the historical events of our century," which in time could lead to "lasting Western unity, with all that would connote for the preservation of Western civilization against aggression from elsewhere."[20]

Having endowed British membership with such significance, American officials found exasperating London's hesitation during the course of the complex negotiations with the EEC commissioners. The future of Commonwealth trade preferences proved a particularly perplexing problem. The Macmillan government was convinced that a failure to obtain an agreement perceived as fair to the Commonwealth would make parliamentary approval far more problematic. While sympathizing with London's concerns on this score, Washington tended to downplay their importance. The British had an unfortunate tendency, Ball informed the president in December 1962, "to treat the negotiations as a commercial haggle rather than a major political undertaking."[21]

To their credit, Ball and his colleagues realized that too visible a stand by the United States on these issues would only further complicate an already complex situation. Thus, while remaining convinced that London and the continental countries needed to find a way to surmount their individual nationalist perspectives, American officials consciously tried to remain in the background throughout the negotiations. Even so, Washington's preferences were widely enough known that at one point the chief British negotiator felt compelled to deny on television that the United States had pushed the United Kingdom into the negotiations.

Washington's caution was well-advised. The continental powers, and France above all, worried that British membership in the EEC could provide the opportunity for the proverbial camel's nose—in this instance, an American camel—to slip under the European tent. Was Britain, the Europeans asked, prepared to renounce its old relationship with the United States in order to enter into a new relationship with Europe? Macmillan tried to straddle the issue, denying that the one necessarily precluded the other. Ironically, a major crisis with Washington at the end of 1962, which for a period threatened to wreck London's old special relationship, ultimately gave the skeptics in Europe an excuse to scuttle British hopes for a new special relationship.

SKYBOLT

The nuclear partnership that the post-Suez rapprochement between London and Washington had established had not, at least for many Americans, settled the question of the proper role for Britain's nuclear deterrent, or of the part the United States should play in helping Britain maintain that deterrent. John Kennedy's election in 1960 gave those who had doubts about an independent British deterrent an opportunity to reopen the issue. National nuclear forces, contended a number of senior Kennedy appointees in the State Department and elsewhere, would only encourage nuclear proliferation. A British nuclear force would inevitably push France in the same direction, and with Paris busily acquiring a *force de frappe*, Bonn would demand the same right—at a time when many were not yet prepared to trust the Germans to act as responsible members of the world community. Moreover, a special nuclear partnership between Britain and America could be an obstacle to Britain's incorporation into the EEC. Far better, they concluded, to deemphasize the special Anglo–American relationship—both in its nuclear aspect and more generally—and to place American policy toward the United Kingdom on an equal footing with policy toward France and West Germany.

Other American officials argued on entirely different grounds against Britain's possession of nuclear weapons. The British arsenal, they pointed out, was neither large nor secure enough to deter a Soviet first strike or to provide a convincing second-strike capability. Indeed, Britain's nuclear weapons were militarily useless, and therefore economically wasteful. They represented little more than a frivolous diversion of scarce resources at a time when those could more profitably be used to augment NATO's conventional strength. In a widely publicized speech in mid-1962, Robert McNamara, Kennedy's high-powered secretary of defense, pointedly remarked that "limited nuclear capabilities, operating independently, are dangerous, expensive, prone to obsolescence and lacking in credibility as a deterrent."[22] Although he subsequently denied that he had been referring specifically to Britain's nuclear force, his words caused more than passing concern among a London officialdom well aware of the doubts existing in some American quarters.

Many Washington officials came to view the establishment of a multilateral force (MLF) under NATO auspices as a preferable alternative to an independent British deterrent. The MLF would be comprised of a fleet armed with Polaris missiles and manned by multinational crews that would, in the words of one senior Kennedy official, be "so integrated—through multilateral manning, control, and ownership—that no country could withdraw its contribution and reconstitute it as a national force."[23] Regardless of the merits of such a scheme—McNamara for one thought it totally lacking in military value—it did seem to provide the means for incorporating Germany into the Western security structure. Moreover, it meshed nicely with Kennedy's vision of a grand design for Europe in which the nations of the Continent would gradually subordinate their individual identities in favor of some larger collective identity.

Needless to say, London regarded any suggestion that it give up its independent deterrent for some vague multilateral grouping with the utmost suspicion. "Our acceptance as a great power now rests to a large extent on our having a military nuclear programme," Britain's U.S. ambassador had written as far back as 1957. "It would be difficult to over-estimate at this juncture the importance of our having megaton as well as kiloton weapons."[24] As British strength continued to ebb relative not only to the superpowers, but to France, Germany, Japan, and other second-tier states, its status as the only non-superpower with nuclear weaponry assumed an ever greater importance. This consensus behind Britain's independent deterrent crossed party lines, notwithstanding the antinuclear rhetoric frequently employed by Labour spokesmen. The mere fact that Britain possessed an independent deterrent, Macmillan had once explained, "makes the United States pay a greater regard to our point of view."[25] He believed that American talk about multilateral rather than national nuclear programs had to be resisted, for at bottom such talk masked a desire to force Britain from its preferential standing into a position of equality with the rest of Europe.

This, then, was the background to what became, after the Suez affair, the most serious crisis in Anglo–American relations of the postwar era. That it should have come only six years after the 1956 debacle indicates the volatility of even this closest of alliance partnerships. That is, like Suez, was smoothed over with surprising speed, given its seriousness, demonstrates the commitment to their partnership both nations retained. Finally, that it has not been followed for more than a quarter century by a comparable crisis suggests the transformation in the nature of the bilateral relationship that took place within a very few years of this crisis.

Meeting with Macmillan at Camp David in 1960, Eisenhower had promised to sell Great Britain the air-launched Skybolt missile, then in the early stages of development. Acquisition of the Skybolt meant that British bombers would no longer have to penetrate Soviet air defenses. Instead, they could stand 800 miles off their target and release their weapons. Thus the Camp David agreement extended the life of the Royal Air Force's V-bombers, the mainstay of the British deterrent. At a time when long-range, ground-based missiles were still at a rudimentary stage, it ensured that Britain retained its independent nuclear strike force.

Over the next two years, however, the Skybolt program ran into one snag after another, as testing indicated the missile could not match the performance of either the Polaris or the Minuteman. By early 1962, rumors abounded that McNamara and the "whiz kids" he had brought into the Pentagon were seriously disenchanted with the missile. But the British complacently chose to ignore the warning signs that Washington might be having doubts about Skybolt. After all, they had a "deal" with the Americans, didn't they? American officials might have been more forthcoming with the British in their concerns about the program. McNamara, for instance, failed to reveal the full extent of his doubts, which by this time were considerable, when he met with Defense Minister Peter Thorneycroft in September 1962. But even so, American reticence does not adequately explain why Whitehall was so slow in realizing the serious trouble Skybolt faced.

Part of the problem arose from the fact that while the Americans viewed Skybolt in terms of technology and cost-effectiveness, the missile had taken on far more sweeping implications for the British. First of all, it had become a domestic issue in British politics. For Macmillan to lose Skybolt now, at a time when he was already very much on the defensive at home, would raise profound questions about the effectiveness of his leadership. Weakened as his government had become during the course of the year, it was not at all inconceivable that cancellation of Skybolt could topple the government. At a minimum, losing the missile would jeopardize the existence of Britain's independent deterrent. Thus, for Macmillan, far more was at stake than merely the future of a particular weapons program: the matter raised profound questions about the survivability of his government, his personal political fortunes, his policy of close Anglo–American ties, and the future of the British nuclear deterrent.

The Americans were remarkably slow to realize the political embarrassment Skybolt's abandonment held for Macmillan. For Washington, fresh from the triumph of the Cuban missile crisis, Skybolt was, until very late, a nuisance more than a crisis. McNamara, for instance, viewed the missile's cancellation not in terms of its impact on Anglo–American relations, but as a managerial problem of overriding the desires of the Strategic Air Command and placating the Air Force's allies in Congress. Symptomatic of Washington's failure to appreciate the difficulties cancellation would cause Britain was the inconspicuous—actually, nonexistent—role Secretary of State Dean Rusk played throughout the crisis.

Thus, when McNamara arrived in London for defense talks the second week of December 1962, all the ingredients for a monumental blowup were in place. McNamara found the British still smarting from comments Dean Acheson had made the week before that London had lost its way in the world without having any real idea of what its new role should be. McNamara immediately made things far worse with a public statement, even before sitting down with Thorneycroft, revealing the full extent of American concerns about the Skybolt program. The British reacted with indignation and a sense of betrayal. Those who had warned that Britain could not rely on the United States, Thorneycroft informed McNamara, would now "throw this into the face of those who had always stood up for close Anglo–American relations."[26] A decision to cancel Skybolt, Macmillan remarked to Ormsby-Gore, deliberately employing one of Dulles's apocalyptic phrases, could force Britain into an "agonising reappraisal" of all its foreign and defense policies."[27]

As fate would have it, Kennedy and Macmillan were scheduled to confer for several days in Nassau beginning 18 December 1962. The British contingent arrived, according to one eyewitness, the angriest of any British delegation at any Anglo–American summit since the war, harboring a "resentment and suspicion of American intentions such as I have never experienced in . . . twenty years."[28] Macmillan had spent a good portion of the flight to the Bahamas reading about the decline of the Roman empire, a choice that undoubtedly did nothing to lighten his mood.

It took the Americans little time to discover just how seriously the British viewed the situation. In one of the opening sessions with the Americans, Macmillan put on what Kennedy aide Arthur Schlesinger, Jr., would later term a "bravura performance."[29] The prime minister recalled Britain's sacrifices for the common good in two world wars and his own commitment to the closest of ties with the United States. He then grandly detailed the unfortunate consequences for Anglo–American relations and for Western security should the British public come to believe that the president sought to strip

Britain of its independent deterrent. It was, one historian has noted, "one of Macmillan's finest hours."[30]

No more willing than Macmillan to allow the issue to jeopardize the bilateral relationship between their countries, Kennedy made a remarkable offer that he and Ormsby-Gore had worked out as they had flown together to Nassua aboard Air Force One. The United States would continue with Skybolt's development, Kennedy proposed, and split the costs evenly with Britain, even though the British alone would actually deploy the missile. But by this time too many questions about the weapon's capabilities had been raised, and Macmillan was determined to settle for nothing less than the American-built Polaris. His response to Kennedy's generous offer, therefore, was bound to be negative, but his reply was couched in the grace and witticism that led the president to value his friendship so highly. "Although the proposed British marriage with Skybolt was not exactly a shotgun wedding," the prime minister told Kennedy, "the virginity of the lady must now be regarded as doubtful."[31] Britain, therefore, could not accept the president's proposal.

Ultimately, Kennedy offered Britain the submarine-launched Polaris Macmillan coveted. In doing so, the president overruled key subordinates, such as George Ball and Walt Rostow, who wished to use Skybolt's cancellation as a way to kill off Britain's independent deterrent and integrate London's nuclear forces into the MLF. As something of a sop to the multilateralists, Macmillan pledged to make Britain's Polaris-armed submarines available to NATO. But he also insisted upon an escape clause that allowed London, in a national emergency, to use the weapons unilaterally. Well could he afford such a gesture, for his principal goal had been achieved. The British nuclear deterrent—increasingly irrelevant in a strategic sense but politically indispensable—had been preserved for another generation.

Once more a full-scale break in Anglo–American ties had been averted. While considerably less attractive for the British than the Camp David agreement, the Polaris offer still represented a significant concession by the Americans. The terms of the sale, for instance, were extraordinarily generous: Britain was asked to pay almost none of the substantial research and development costs of the missile. But the political import of the agreement, by rescuing Britain's deterrent, constituted an even greater concession by the Americans. It was, moreover, a concession obtained in large measure because of Kennedy's personal commitment to British–American ties and his fondness for Macmillan. In short, the acquisition of Polaris represented a triumph for the prime minister's strategy, doggedly pursued since his first days in office in 1957, of cultivating relations with his chief ally. Or viewed in less charitable terms, it was, as a disgruntled George Ball wrote some years later, another case "where the emotional baggage of the 'special relationship' got in the way of cooler judgment."[32]

And yet there remains a rather basic question. In an alliance as close as this one, at a time when the two countries were led by men with a genuine mutual admiration and respect, and when the ambassadors of each were universally credited with uncommon skill and access, how could each nation have misread the other so badly? Why, with so much working on its behalf, did the Anglo–American partnership come so close to an open breach?

McNamara's indecision played a role, of course. Until very late in the game, the defense secretary remained uncertain whether he would be able to triumph over the Air Force and its congressional allies and actually secure cancellation of the program. Whitehall, for its part, chose not to believe that a civilian secretary of defense might succeed in making the Air Force swallow Skybolt's cancellation. Nor did it help that neither McNamara nor Thorneycroft possessed much confidence in the other—a situation that discouraged frank conversation.

But something more fundamental was at work here as well. As Richard Neustadt has shown, London's strategic planners had based so much of Britain's defense posture on Skybolt that they believed they had no alternative but to assume that the program would continue. Any other outcome would have presented Britain with monumental problems that Whitehall shied away from facing. Given the absence of options, why raise doubts about American intentions by asking questions that would only serve to legitimize the concerns about Skybolt's future already being voiced?[33]

Skybolt thus followed the pattern of the Suez affair. Lack of communication was not the problem, for there was constant back-and-forth discourse between the two capitals. Rather, those communicating displayed no ability, notwithstanding their common heritage and shared objectives, to talk meaningfully about issues that had potentially explosive domestic implications. McNamara, preoccupied with a rebellious Air Force and expecting the British to ask for Polaris to replace Skybolt, waited for London to act. But the Macmillan government, believing it had a deal with the Americans, expected McNamara to make the first move. As a consequence, neither raised the issue until it was nearly too late. Each misread the intentions and interests of the other; each followed a course that made good sense in terms of his own bureaucratic difficulties. But two prudent courses combined nearly bred a fiasco.

"Whitehall has been inexcusably naive," Michael Howard wrote in London's *Sunday Times* a few days after the summit, "if it really expected the United States to develop, at vast expense, a weapon which they no longer need, so that we could pursue a policy of which they openly disapprove. Loyalty to allies has its limits."[34] Howard's judgment remains a valid one. As long as important circles in official Washington nursed doubts about the wisdom of Britain's independent deterrent, it was inevitable that the financial and technological arguments against Skybolt would find receptive ears in the American capital. As it turned out, the British expected more of their special relationship with the Americans than it was capable of bearing.

Whether it was ultimately in Britain's long-term interest to continue its facade as a major nuclear power is another matter. The Cuban missile crisis had already demonstrated that London, its independent deterrent notwithstanding, had little more say than Lima or Liechtenstein in determining the outcome of a confrontation that jeopardized Britain's very survival. Moreover, because its Polaris-armed submarines were to be assigned under most circumstances to NATO forces, the Nassau agreement added little to Britain's capacity to act independently in areas outside of Europe.

More fundamentally, it was difficult to envision a situation where Britain's nuclear weapons would have more than marginal utility. If the United States were also threatened, the added firepower offered by Britain's arsenal would be minimal. And if the United States did not feel itself endangered, Washington was hardly likely to permit London to threaten an independent nuclear strike. Indeed, as Britain's ability to use its nuclear warheads became ever more dependent upon American delivery systems, the prospects for unilateral British moves in the nuclear sphere progressively diminished. Over time successive British governments implicitly acknowledged this situation by making less and less of the argument that Britain's deterrent gave the United Kingdom wider scope for independent action. Instead, they increasingly defended Britain's nuclear arsenal as a contribution to the Western (meaning the American) deterrent.[35]

Britain's experiences between 1946 and 1962 underscore the difficulties of any nonsuperpower competing against a superpower in the nuclear arena. The relentless rush of technology that rendered military equipment obsolete even before it came off the production line, the spiralling costs of military hardware, the mounting requirements for penetrating Soviet air defenses, and the ever-greater difficulties of guaranteeing a secure retaliatory force in the face of burgeoning Soviet power all suggested that Britain's quest for nuclear respectability alongside Moscow and Washington would ultimately fail. But London's special nuclear partnership with the United States may have blinded Whitehall to this fact. Believing themselves possessed of an independent deterrent, the British failed to appreciate just how dependent upon the Americans that deterrent actually was.

Others did not. Three weeks after the Nassau communique, de Gaulle announced that France would veto Britain's bid for EEC membership. His formal explanation pointedly avoided linking his decision to the Nassau agreement. In informal remarks, however, the proud Frenchman left little doubt but that the Anglo–American nuclear partnership renewed at Nassau struck him as inappropriate for a nation seeking entry into the European community. In all likelihood, Nassau provided de Gaulle not so much with a reason for turning the British down, but with a handy excuse. Still, by giving him a plausible pretext, the Polaris deal probably contributed to keeping Britain out of the EEC for another decade. And this may have ultimately worked to Britain's disadvantage in a way that more than offset whatever benefits retention of its independent deterrent brought.

CONFRONTATION IN CUBA

Had Lyndon Johnson rather than John Kennedy been president—that is, has the crisis occurred a year later—Skybolt in the wake of the Suez debacle could have destroyed the special Anglo–American partnership. But it never threatened the global peace, and in this sense the episode stands apart from the other great international crises of the early 1960s—of which there were many. With the important exception of Berlin, where the Soviets walled off their sector of the city and prompted a helpless and therefore embarrassed Kennedy to call up the American reserves, and where London and Washington worked more or less in tandem, most of these cold war confrontations took place outside of Europe. And as had been the case in the 1940s and 1950s, the two Atlantic allies frequently found themselves at cross purposes in dealing with extra-European crises.

In Laos, where rival factions jockeyed for domestic power and international backing, the Macmillan government vigorously opposed Washington's predisposition to become more militarily entangled. Eventually the prime minister persuaded Kennedy that support for the neutralist Souvanna Phouma represented the only real noncommunist alternative, thereby postponing by a few years America's misadventure in Indochina. In the Congo, American backing for an active United Nations role openly clashed with London's reluctance to support any attempt to impose a political solution on that tortured African nation. As in earlier years, China provided its own store of Anglo–American tensions. Especially galling to Washington was Britain's sale of six military aircraft to Peking in 1961. And then there was Cuba, where Soviet and American forces came closer to outright confrontation—"eyeball-to-eyeball," Rusk said—than at any other point in the forty-plus years since the end of World War II.

Fidel Castro's seizure of power in 1959 had set relations between Cuba and the United States on a steadily downward course. By the time Kennedy entered office, matters had deteriorated to the extent that as foolish an undertaking as the Bay of Pigs invasion could elicit extensive support in official Washington. In the United Kingdom, both the press and the general public had been unanimously critical of the bungled American effort to overthrow Castro, although the Macmillan government had, to a large extent, tempered its public comments. In the succeeding year and a half, London and Washington had found it difficult to coordinate policy on Cuban matters, although officially Whitehall sympathized with American fears about a Soviet beachhead in the Caribbean. Even so, the British were reluctant to invoke the economic sanctions against Cuba that Washington sought, and eventually they led the opposition in NATO to American proposals along these lines. In part, London took this stance because it valued Cuban trade. But Whitehall also believed—rightly, as it turned out—that such measures only bolstered Castro's domestic position by giving him a ready-made excuse for the failures of his regime. Still, British imports from Cuba dropped nearly 50 percent between 1959 and 1961, while British exports declined by two-thirds during the same period.

The discovery of Soviet intermediate-range missiles in Cuba in mid-October 1962 instantaneously elevated Cuba into a crisis of first-class proportions. In the week or so after American intelligence confirmed the presence of the missiles, a group of senior Washington officials, working in great secrecy, debated their options. Ormsby-Gore was invited to sit in on several of their sessions—the only foreigner so honored. But he was also strictly enjoined from reporting their deliberations to his own government, or even the existence of a crisis.

Kennedy informed the world of the Soviet missiles in a televised speech on the evening of Monday, 22 October, at which time he also outlined American plans to impose a naval blockade around Cuba. The quarantine was to go into effect on Wednesday morning. On Tuesday night, Ormsby-Gore dined with Kennedy at the White House. Acting solely on his own authority, the British ambassador suggested that the American blockade line be moved three hundred miles closer to Cuba, in order to give Moscow more time to appreciate the full folly of forcing the issue with the United States. Recognizing the wisdom of this advice, the president overruled his naval advisers and ordered the blockade line moved. Had this been Britain's only contribution during the crisis, it was not an inconsequential one. The extra hours this delayed the first confrontation between American and Soviet vessels may have been critical in the Kremlin's eventual decision to accept a humiliating retreat rather than challenge the United States.

In the anxious days following Kennedy's speech, Macmillan loyally supported the president, both publicly and behind the scenes. While probably tempted to seek a negotiated compromise, he resisted Soviet invitations to mediate, recognizing these as desperate efforts by Moscow to crack Western solidarity. Still, not even Macmillan could resist a gentle dig. In promising Britain's support of the United States at the U.N., the prime minister said, "I hope that whatever you do we will be able to carry through as we weren't able to do at Suez."[36]

In a fundamental sense, however, the Cuban crisis demonstrated just how little influence the British had on the policies of their great ally, even when American actions threatened to involve Britain in thermonuclear war. Only after Kennedy had made the key decision to impose a naval blockade was Macmillan apprised even of the existence of a crisis. Officially, Washington's reticence was explained by the compelling need to keep the Soviets from learning that the United States had discovered their missiles in Cuba. Others, though, suspected that Kennedy simply did not believe that the advice the British might offer would compensate for the complications expanding the circle of the knowledgeable would inevitably entail. "We are told," Labour's Richard Crossman wrote bitterly a few days after Kennedy's address,

1.   Roosevelt and Churchill with the Combined Chiefs of Staff, Quebec, September 1944. *Courtesy Franklin D. Roosevelt Library*

2.   Churchill, Truman, and Stalin at Potsdam, July 1945, in one of the conference's few light-hearted moments. Within days Churchill would be voted out of
office, and the wartime alliance would be little more than a memory. *Courtesy U.S.
Army and Harry S. Truman Library*

3.   Foreign Secretary Ernest Bevin (*left*) and Prime Minister Clement Attlee. Despite their dissimilar backgrounds, they were almost always in step in their conduct of British foreign policy. *Courtesy of the National Archives*

4.   Eisenhower points Churchill, carrying his perennial cigar, into a chair on the White House lawn, June 1954. Foreign Secretary Anthony Eden (*hands in pocket*), Secretary of State John Foster Dulles, and presidential press secretary James C. Hagerty (*behind Eisenhower*) all appear fascinated by the proceedings. *Courtesy Abbie Rowe and the National Park Service*

5.   Prime Minister Harold Macmillan, urbane, elegant, and unabashedly pro-American. *Courtesy of the United Nations*

6.　　　President John F. Kennedy, whose death in 1963 brought to a close an eighteen-year period of extremely cordial Anglo-American relations and ushered in a far more difficult eighteen years. *Courtesy of the United Nations*

7.   President Lyndon B. Johnson. During his five years in the White House,
British–American relations took a back seat to an unwanted war in Southeast Asia.
Courtesy of the United Nations

8.   Prime Minister Harold Wilson, with his trademark pipe. According to one contemporary, Wilson appeared "a plump, affable halibut" with "the eyes of a shark." *Courtesy of the United Nations*

9.   President Richard M. Nixon, who sought close ties with the British, only to be rebuffed by Edward Heath. *Courtesy of the United Nations*

10.   Prime Minister Edward Heath. Of all Britain's postwar prime ministers, he alone rejected the idea of a special relationship with the United States. *Courtesy of the United Nations*

11.   President Gerald R. Ford, whose decency and lack of pretension helped the United States get through the difficult post-Watergate, post-Vietnam period. *Courtesy of the United Nations/S. Lwin*

12.   President Jimmy Carter. Eventually his countrymen concluded that idealism and honorable intentions were insufficient in dealing with the Soviets and Iran's Ayatollah Khomeini. *Courtesy of the United Nations/T. Chen*

13.   Prime Minister Thatcher at No. 10 Downing Street with her favorite guests, President Ronald Reagan and his wife, Nancy. Under Thatcher and Reagan's tutelage, the British–American special relationship blossomed once more. *Courtesy Central Office of Information, United Kingdom*

that Britain's nuclear deterrent would "give us a place in the councils of the nations. And in particular make sure that the Americans will listen to us. . . . Well, after last Monday night, that little myth is exploded!"[37]

In the days after his 22 October address, Kennedy telephoned the prime minister frequently, but these calls were more informational than consultative. As one British official privy to these conversations later recalled, "We were kept fully informed—more fully informed than anybody else. But we were not really consulted about the actual decisions."[38] Indeed, the predominant feeling in the United Kingdom was one of helplessness, of watching from the sidelines while others decided Britain's fate. In the mocking catchword of the day, Britain faced annihilation without representation. It was a far cry from the glory days of 1940, when the British nation almost single-handedly had defied Hitler's mighty *Wehrmacht*.

Beyond the corridors of Whitehall, widespread skepticism about the necessity for the American blockade was coupled with an oft-expressed fear that a reckless American administration was about to push the world into nuclear war. Hugh Gaitskell, the respected Labour leader, drew a parallel between Kennedy's 22 October speech and Truman's careless press conference remark in 1950 about using nuclear weapons in Korea. Recollections of the Bay of Pigs invariably colored the British assessment of the October crisis, and many assumed that Kennedy, reflecting what was considered America's peculiar hypersensitivity about Cuba, had overreacted. American bases in Turkey were frequently equated with Soviet bases in Cuba, and more than one British writer professed to see little difference between the United States and the Soviet Union. On the evening after Kennedy's televised address, nearly three hundred policemen were required to keep an angry crowd from breaking into the American embassy in London. Only after the release of photographs documenting Soviet activity in Cuba did the tone of British comment noticeably soften.

Still, much of this criticism had an air of irrelevance, even of carping, for little agreement existed among the critics as to how Washington ought to have responded to the missiles. Indeed, once the Soviets had retreated and the crisis eased, acclaim for Kennedy's skill and especially his restraint became the predominant theme of British comment, a transformation suggesting that the earlier condemnations had been as much a function of a general anxiety as anything else. Moreover, although some Whitehall officials grumbled about the lack of consultation, the administration, even holding information as tightly as it had prior to 22 October, was far less guilty of deception than Britain had been at the time of the Suez incident six years earlier.

THE END OF AN ERA

Cuba, in a way that was not immediately appreciated, marked the end of the most intimate phase in the Anglo–American alliance. The fears of those October days led the two superpowers to seek less risky methods of carrying out their competition, and Cuba proved to be the last great crisis of the cold war. Within a year, the two great powers, along with Britain, had signed a limited test ban treaty. The test ban by itself did little to diminish the chances of global war, but it did represent public acknowledgment by the leaders of the world's two power blocs that even deep ideological rivalry had limitations. As such, it was one of the first important steps in a gradual lessening of cold war tensions that the Nixon administration would popularize as detente. And as, over the years, relations between Washington and Moscow became less immediately threatening, the raison d'être for the Anglo–American partnership lost much of its urgency.

Initially begun in 1958, test ban discussions between the United States, the Soviet Union, and the United Kingdom (at this point the world's only nuclear states) at first went nowhere. Not only were the Soviets less than committed to achieving an accord, but the Eisenhower administration, and Dulles above all, was quite skeptical about the value of a test ban. For the balance of Eisenhower's term Macmillan took the lead in prodding both superpowers toward some form of agreement, stubbornly refusing to allow American doubts or Soviet obstinacy to kill off the idea.

Eisenhower's being replaced by Kennedy in 1961 at first seemed to reinvigorate the talks, but Moscow's resumption of testing that autumn after a three-year moratorium represented a substantial setback to prospects for an accord, and was a particularly bitter blow to Macmillan. Even after the missile crisis, agreement on a comprehensive treaty proved elusive. Eventually the parties settled on a partial test ban prohibiting all nuclear tests except those conducted underground as the only accord possible, finally initialling the treaty in July 1963.

The test ban was a personal triumph for Macmillan. More than any other statesman, he had refused to let the talks die. He had taken the lead in looking for compromises that would satisfy Soviet objections without endangering Western security. He had repeatedly tabled new proposals and sought ways around old obstacles. He had bargained and pleaded and persistently pushed his two negotiating partners. And ultimately he had succeeded. Perhaps more than at any other time in the postwar period, Britain had acted as the broker between two larger and very wary parties.

This is not to say that as broker he occupied a place midway between Washington and Moscow, for the test ban treaty was also a testament to Anglo–American collaboration. The president's confidence in Macmillan led Kennedy to overrule his own military advisers on several sticky points. Anglo–American differences over technical matters or political assessments were overcome by the confidence each leader held in the other, by the understanding each had of the other's special problems and perspectives, and most of all by an awareness of shared interests. Macmillan's acceptance of Kennedy's request to stage American nuclear tests on Britain's Christmas

Island illustrates the workings of this collaboration. Such a request was immensely distasteful to the prime minister. He realized, however, that in the face of renewed Soviet testing, a British refusal to accede to the president's wishes would place unacceptable strains on British–American ties and would, in all likelihood, scuttle hopes for a test ban.

Still, essential as Macmillan's role was, the treaty ultimately came about when, and only when, Washington and Moscow were ready to deal. Here as elsewhere, the ultimate power of decision lay in hands other than Britain's. This does not detract from Macmillan's indispensable role in fathering the accord, but it does suggest the limits even to his indispensability.

The test ban treaty was ratified on 8 October 1963, the same day Macmillan entered the hospital for prostate surgery. Ten days later the prime minister forwarded his resignation to the queen. In truth, however, ill health was only one of Macmillan's burdens by the second half of 1963. After a period of promise, Britain's economy was once more lagging. Unemployment levels were rising, Britain's international balance of payments deficits persisted, and British exports remained as uncompetitive as ever. A series of espionage and security cases, culminating in the notorious Profumo affair (in which the British war minister was found to be sharing a mistress with a Soviet naval attaché), had provoked questions about Macmillan's ability to provide the decisive leadership Britain needed. New doubts had been raised about the prime minister's reliance upon the United States—reservations that the Cuban crisis, Skybolt, and de Gaulle's humiliating veto did nothing to resolve. More and more, the government had taken on the appearance of being run by tired old men; the Conservatives, after all, had been in power by this time for twelve years.

Barely a month after Macmillan's resignation, an assassin removed the other half of the Macmillan-Kennedy equation. British grief was palpable, recalling the shocked disbelief that had coursed through Britain following Roosevelt's death eighteen years earlier. Buckingham Palace decreed seven days of court mourning. Memorial services throughout the country taxed the embassy's capability to provide representation. Streams of people, many in working clothes on their way home in the evening, crowded the embassy to sign the condolence books. The British, C. L. Sulzberger wrote in the *New York Times,* had "a deep and wholly genuine sense of participation in the American tragedy."[39]

Why this outpouring of emotion for a foreign statesman? One could not account for it in solely logical terms, Ambassador Bruce explained: "These people, dimly fearing the future, regretting the already distant past, embodied in the President their desires and hopes for a better-ordered future."[40] Or, as London's *Sunday Times* observed, "Great statesmen are rare at any time; great statesmen with the gift of hope are even rarer."[41] This intangible "gift of hope," far more than any particular policy or program of the martyred president, explained Kennedy's hold on the British public. As one British commentator wrote, the American president "was the living embodiment of what we have all been longing for and have desperately missed[:] . . . Youth, Energy, Courage and—above all—Hope."[42] When Harold Wilson had assumed leadership of the Labour Party in early 1963, he had used his first public appearance as party leader to speak of the need to get Britain "moving ahead again," the need to restore a "spirit of hope and adventure," the need for a "new sense of purpose."[43] It had all been very Kennedyesque, and it suggested something of the way in which John Kennedy had fired British imaginations. Dallas, in other words, had robbed the British not simply of an ally, but a close friend and even a member of the family.

As for his successor, the British were uneasy. "The task of succeeding an obviously great President is an extremely difficult one," the *Sunday Times* tactfully put it.[44] But more than that, Lyndon Johnson was an unknown quantity, a man without demonstrable ties to or feelings for the United Kingdom. As a consequence, the British derived considerable comfort from assurances that relations with the United States would be maintained on the same basis as in the past. Everywhere one heard the hope expressed that while presidents might have changed, the partnership had not.

Except that the partnership had changed. Not themselves the cause of this transformation, Macmillan's retirement and Kennedy's death provide a convenient marker for it. By the early 1960s, it was no longer possible to ignore the reality that Great Britain was about to be surpassed by other Western European states, notably Germany. Macmillan's special genius had been in obscuring, or at least making less important, the extent to which the power equilibrium, and hence the basis of the special relationship, had shifted.

But with the nearly simultaneous departure of Macmillan and Kennedy, that reality could no longer be hidden, and the special relationship binding their two nations ceased to exist in the form that had shaped international relations for almost a quarter century. As the decade progressed, Britain turned increasingly toward Europe, even as de Gaulle continued to rebuff its advances. The United States, in the meanwhile, found itself more and more preoccupied with Southeast Asia. Neither Harold Wilson nor Lyndon Johnson placed the premium on close Anglo–American ties that many of their predecessors had. But most important, the lessening of tensions with the Soviet Union that haltingly occurred after 1962 reduced the most compelling compulsion for unity. And so, in November 1963, as Britons mourned the fallen president, they grieved, in a way they did not consciously comprehend, for themselves as well.

chapter 5

ALLIANCE DEPRECIATED: 1964–1972

On a raw December day nearly a year before John Kennedy's murder, Dean Acheson, long since retired and enjoying the status of elder statesman, made his way to the Military Academy at West Point, where he had been invited to speak. In the course of "a look at the general condition of NATO," Acheson referred to London's "attempt to play a separate power role," by which he meant "a role apart from Europe," one based on a "special relationship" with the United States and with a commonwealth that "has no political structure, or unity, or strength." This role, he declared, "is about played out." The former secretary of state derided Britain's efforts to act as a broker between the Soviet Union and the United States and argued that Britain's rightful place now lay as part of the European community. Finally, in a formulation reprinted throughout the United Kingdom, Acheson observed that "Great Britain has lost an empire and has not yet found a role."[1]

The British, accustomed to regarding Acheson as a friend, were stung. The *Yorkshire Post* noted that those passages of the speech "which mock Britain will no doubt make blood boil."[2] The London *Times*'s diplomatic correspondent reported that Acheson's words had produced "sharp anguish" in Whitehall.[3] Prime Minister Macmillan personally issued a response, tartly declaring that "insofar as he appeared to denigrate the resolution and will of Britain and the British people, Mr. Acheson has fallen into an error which has been made by quite a lot of people in the course of the last four hundred years, including Philip of Spain, Louis the Fourteenth, Napoleon, the Kaiser and Hitler."[4] (The Anglophilic Acheson must have marveled at the company into which he had been cast.) The British press, openly pleased with Macmillan's rejoinder, carried prominent stories on the prime minister's rebuke of Acheson.

Given the timing of the speech—amidst increasingly credible rumors that the United States was about to back out on its promise of Skybolt—Whitehall wondered if Acheson's words were not officially inspired. The State Department and the White House hurriedly denied that either had cleared the address. Kennedy directed that the press be "backgrounded strongly" (to use National Security Adviser McGeorge Bundy's words) that the administration most emphatically did not share Acheson's view of Anglo–American relations. The president believed that ties between Washington and London "are not based only on a power calculus, but also on [a] deep community of purpose and long practice of close cooperation." The phrase "special relationship" "may not be a perfect phrase," the press was informed, but "sneers at Anglo–American reality would be equally foolish."[5]

In truth, the bitter British reaction to Acheson's remarks was far out of proportion to the actual injury inflicted. British indignation reflected wounded pride, envy of American might, and an at least partial realization that Acheson's analysis was not all that far from the mark. Indeed, the *Guardian* conceded as much when it noted that Kennedy might well repeat Acheson's words, if more diplomatically, when the president met Macmillan at the forthcoming Bermuda conference.[6] Behind the scenes, Ambassador Bruce made much the same point by observing that Acheson had not said anything that had not been previously acknowledged by British officials. American diplomats argued that once Acheson's speech was absorbed in its entirety, the British would recognize it as a strong plea for strengthening the alliance by British membership in the EEC, closer economic ties between Europe and the United States, and greater European participation in nuclear decision-making.

Obviously, Acheson had jarred an exposed nerve—one that would become increasingly exposed as the 1960s wore on. For the better part of two decades Britain had avoided basic decisions on the part it was to play in world affairs. Ever since 1945, Whitehall had deferred choosing between a global role akin to that which it had pursued for four centuries, and something less magnificent but more in tune with what Kennedy had called the "power calculus." For nearly twenty years, London had sought to reconcile its imperial and commonwealth aspirations with its European obligations, and both within a framework of an Atlantic partnership with the United States. How these responsibilities and roles were to mesh had been a matter of ongoing debate between Washington and London for much of the postwar period.

This debate reached its climax in the mid-1960s. In 1967, London abandoned its last pretensions as a global power by announcing plans to withdraw from east of Suez. Almost simultaneously, its concomitant desire to participate more fully in the affairs of Europe suffered a sharp rebuff from a de Gaulle still suspicious of Britain's ties to the United States. Paradoxically, although they had consistently endorsed British efforts to join the Common Market,

American officials openly deplored London's decision to pull back from Asia. Obviously, it was not Britons alone who were confused about Britain's proper role in the world.

For its part, the United States during these years struggled to come to terms with its own place in international affairs, as a controversial war in Asia raised new questions about America's self-appointed role as guardian of the free world. The 1960s saw the highwater mark of imperial America, as well as the first politically important calls for a reduction in American commitments around the globe. As the decade progressed, there surfaced new demands, as was the case in Britain, to bring America's international posture more into line with its national means. Much to their discomfort, Americans came to discover that military might and economic efficiency did not supply all the answers.

As fate would have it, guiding their respective countries through this difficult period were men who placed less of a premium on close Anglo–American ties than had most of their recent predecessors. For more than a decade, Eisenhower and Kennedy for the Americans and Churchill, Macmillan, and, in his own way, Eden for the British had valued Anglo–American cordiality and consciously cultivated their opposite numbers across the Atlantic. After Macmillan's resignation and Kennedy's murder, however, there followed nearly two decades during which no such personal ties of admiration or affection bound the elected leaders of the two nations. Although Jimmy Carter and James Callaghan enjoyed one another's company, not until Ronald Reagan assumed the presidency in 1981 and found in Margaret Thatcher a kindred soul were ties of genuine warmth reestablished. And in the intervening seventeen years, much had changed in the relative positions of both countries to diminish the significance of this renewed cordiality.

In Lyndon Johnson the United States had a president far less interested in foreign affairs than his predecessors had been. Like Harry Truman eighteen years earlier, Johnson had quite unexpectedly been catapulted into the White House after a career centered largely on domestic issues. Indeed, his inexperience momentarily revived talk in Britain of London taking the lead in the Western alliance, although those in positions of authority were quick to point out that the death of an American president did not alter the fundamental power equation between the two nations.

Macmillan's successor, Sir Alec Douglas-Home, did not remain in office long enough to set his own stamp on Anglo–American relations. In October 1964, the British electorate turned out the Conservatives and made Harold Wilson prime minister. Together, Wilson and Johnson redirected British–American ties into the less personal, more distant character that would mark the relationship for much of the following two decades. Neither Wilson nor Johnson deliberately set out to loosen the cords that linked their nations. But neither man expended the energy or the political capital necessary to counteract the forces that worked to undo those bonds.

At forty-eight the youngest British prime minister of the twentieth century when he assumed office in 1964, Wilson was routinely credited with a shrewd mind, first-rate debating skills, a caustic wit, and perhaps a shade too much ambition. Initially skeptical about him because of his allegedly "neutralist" tendencies, Americans upon meeting the new prime minister found him reassuring. The chairman of Johnson's Council of Economic Advisers informed the president that Wilson was "an impressive, *take-charge, no-nonsense, non-stuffy Prime Minister.*"[7] The *New York Times*'s C. L. Sulzberger was especially struck by the contrast between Wilson's unassuming outward appearance and his inner strength. Watching Wilson closely, he wrote, "is like studying a plump, affable halibut and suddenly seeing the eyes of a shark."[8]

In the years preceding his appointment as prime minister, Wilson had spoken of the need to modernize the Anglo–American relationship by basing it on something more substantial than "old boy" ties. He had been particularly outspoken about abandoning the special nuclear relationship with Washington and substituting a "natural" relationship that rested on common interests rather than atomic secrets. His antinuclear stance represented neither pacifism nor unilateralism. He had no desire to remove Britain from America's atomic umbrella, but he did believe it a costly illusion for the United Kingdom to continue a nuclear posturing that added little to Western defenses. Britain, he argued, should use its limited defense resources to beef up its conventional forces instead.

Though both were consummate politicians, Johnson and Wilson never hit it off. The ever-diplomatic David Bruce recalls that their meetings were invariably characterized by "the utmost courtesy"—damning praise in light of the conviviality and even affection that had bound their predecessors.[9] Others have been less circumspect in their recollections. Johnson, one of the president's senior aides remembered, regarded Wilson as "too clever by half."[10] LBJ made no secret of his conviction that British prime ministers used their periodic visits to Washington primarily to bolster their domestic standing, although why he of all people would find this distasteful is not altogether clear. Although Wilson journeyed to Washington six times in the five years Johnson was president, LBJ never set foot in the United Kingdom. Indeed, his memoirs make no mention of any meeting with Wilson. For their part, the British frequently found the Texan patronizing and parochial. As Truman had inevitably suffered in comparison with Roosevelt, so too did Johnson appear in British eyes as something of a shabby impostor in the rosy afterglow of Camelot.

NEW FINANCIAL PRESSURES

When Labour returned to office in 1964, after an absence of thirteen years, its first and most pressing concern lay in addressing Britain's sorry economic and financial plight. Economic growth since the end of the war had been spotty, particularly when measured against the remarkable record achieved by the EEC countries. Industrial modernization had lagged as British businessmen (at least according to the CIA) had persisted in maintaining "a 19th century approach to 20th century business problems."[11] Wage hikes had run ahead of increases in productivity, making British exports less competitive and reducing the United Kingdom's share of total world commerce. Sluggish exports, combined with too many imports, had produced a persistent trade deficit, which had been a major factor in the payments imbalance, which in turn drained British gold and foreign exchange reserves and brought severe pressure on the pound.

In the autumn of 1964, Britain's most immediate economic problem was its enormous balance-of-payments deficit—the largest since the war years. Informed opinion held that devaluation was imminent. Determined to avoid this step, the Wilson government over the next several years adopted a series of increasingly stringent measures designed to promote exports, curtail consumer demand for imports, and reduce the outflow of capital. Some of these steps dampened down the economy, a risky move under any circumstances but especially in light of the government's precarious majority during its first seventeen months in office. But in spite of this daring, Britain's payments position did not noticeably improve, for the government sought to apply short-term economic solutions to what was in fact a long-term social, political, and even psychological problem: how to persuade Britain's conservative economic managers and union leadership to invest heavily in advanced technology and labor-saving capital equipment.

Failing to achieve notable success with its economic measures, the Wilson government gave increasing attention to military expenditures, particularly those that drained foreign exchange. While no one believed that defense retrenchment by itself would solve the payments imbalance, the government came under growing pressure to trim military spending substantially. Inevitably this led to talk about cutting back British commitments around the world. Just as inevitably, Washington deplored all discussion about reducing defense commitments "east of Suez" or withdrawing British troops from Germany. As a consequence, Johnson administration officials, including the president himself, spent an inordinate amount of time in the mid-1960s analyzing the British economic doldrums. Unless Britain solved its financial problems, Treasury Secretary Henry Fowler warned the president, "the United Kingdom's position, present and potential, as a world power has no meaning." Even "its opportunity to play a constructive role in Western European political, diplomatic and military affairs will be greatly minimized."[12] Other American officials concurred with Fowler's assessment. "Walking their economic tightrope," wrote one, "soaks up energy, saps initiative, and colors their approach to every policy, emphatically including their political commitments overseas."[13]

Devaluation offered another possible way out of this economic morass, but carried considerable liabilities as well as advantages. As Wilson later explained, he struggled for years to avoid this step for fear of setting off "an orgy of competitive beggar-my-neighbour currency devaluations—similar to those of the 1930s—which would have plunged the world into monetary anarchy, and left us no better off."[14] In addition, devaluation would inevitably entail domestic economic and political costs for any British government, but especially for a Labour government already regarded with suspicion in Britain's leading financial circles. Devaluing "the second most important reserve currency in the world . . . ," Wilson's chancellor of the Exchequer subsequently recalled, "was almost a moral issue."[15]

In Washington, officials feared that devaluation would bring heavy speculative pressures on the dollar, which would have serious consequences for the American balance-of-payments position and American gold reserves. Devaluation would also probably mean an end to efforts to liberalize trade. If large enough, it could trigger a chain reaction of competitive devaluations by other major trading nations. A British devaluation would, in the worried words of one senior American diplomat, "create chaos in the financial world and could very well set in train an era of economic warfare among free world countries."[16] Finally, devaluation would probably encourage a turning inward in the United Kingdom, a retreat from Britain's international responsibilities. For the past three years, a White House aide reminded the president in 1967, the United States had repeatedly warned Wilson that "we regard devaluation as mortal sin."[17]

At the same time, American officials were tired of the British repeatedly returning to Washington for emergency rescue packages. London's expectation of help from the United States even as Whitehall talked about cutting back on Britain's wider political and military responsibilities compounded this irritation. The British, McGeorge Bundy told the president, must "get it into their heads that it makes no sense for us to rescue the Pound [sic] in a situation in which there is no British flag in Vietnam, and a threatened British thinout in both east of Suez and in Germany."[18] Treasury Secretary Fowler and Defense Secretary McNamara were inclined to argue that a British military contribution in Vietnam, while not strictly a condition for American help on sterling, would nonetheless greatly improve the odds of a sympathetic attitude in Washington toward Britain's difficulties.

Still, letting the British stand alone or, worse yet, go under was even less palatable. If the United States refused to assist the British, Under Secretary of State George Ball warned in 1965, or if Washington imposed conditions London could not accept, the British would see no alternative to slashing their defense commitments around the globe even more drastically. This, Ball argued, "would be disastrous politically since it would leave us more than ever the policeman of the world."[19]

Such reasoning proved persuasive to American decisionmakers. As a consequence, the United States met British requests for help in these years with a large measure of understanding. In late 1964, the Johnson administration took the lead in arranging a multilateral $3 billion package of credits, of which the American share was $1 billion. The following year, Washington helped London obtain an additional $925 million in credits from American and European central banks. Administration officials also displayed a tolerance toward British policies, such as import surcharges, that had an adverse impact on American exports or the American balance-of-payments position.

Part of Britain's financial problem in these years arose from the heavy drain of foreign exchange—$200–$250 million annually—caused by the 51,000-man British Army on the Rhine (BAOR). This foreign exchange loss placed continual pressure on the pound, and many Britons came to resent the fact that West Germany appeared to be benefitting financially as well as militarily from the BAOR. Denis Healey, Wilson's defense minister, argued that since Europe was the place least likely to see the outbreak of war, British retrenchment should most logically begin there. When, in July 1966, the Wilson government adopted a new package of severe deflationary measures, it also threatened to reduce substantially its military forces in West Germany unless Bonn fully recompensed Britain for the foreign exchange costs of the BAOR. But the Federal Republic was in the midst of a recession, and with a budgetary deficit of its own was unlikely to be of much help to the British.

The Johnson administration also faced balance of payments pressures, which the $800 million annual foreign exchange cost of stationing American forces in West Germany only aggravated. On Capitol Hill, restive legislators, led by Senate majority leader Mike Mansfield, sought to trim back the number of American troops in Europe as one means of dealing with the payments deficit. In August 1966, Mansfield obtained forty-three co-sponsors for a resolution calling for a substantial reduction of American forces in Europe. Mansfield's move raised a fundamental political question concerning the future of the Atlantic alliance and the U.S. role in Europe. The presence of American forces in Germany was the most concrete and visible manifestation of Washington's commitment to European collective security. Europeans would inevitably regard the withdrawal of a sizable number of troops, no matter the reason, as evidence of a slackening of that commitment.

Administration officials worried that British cuts in the BAOR would fuel support in the United States for Mansfield's proposal. Even if they succeeded in blocking the Mansfield resolution, a substantial reduction in the BAOR could set off a chain reaction of undesirable developments. It would undoubtedly strain Britain's relations with Germany and the rest of Europe, thereby impeding British entry into the EEC. It might encourage Moscow to heat up tensions in central Europe, especially Berlin. It would tempt other NATO allies to pull out of the integrated NATO command, as France had recently done. Worst of all, it could ultimately lead to an unraveling of NATO defenses and sabotage the movement for greater European political and economic unity.

With concerns of this nature as the backdrop, negotiations among the British, Germans, and Americans to resolve these force-level and burden-sharing problems commenced in the autumn of 1966. Before the talks could proceed very far, however, the Christian Democratic government of Germany's Ludwig Erhard fell from power, bringing on a prolonged hiatus in the discussions while the new government in Bonn determined its position on these issues. Wilson in the meantime came under increased domestic pressure, and for a time it looked as if he would be unable to wait for the negotiations to resume. To head off hasty British action, Washington offered to purchase $35 million in military equipment from the United Kingdom in order to ease London's immediate foreign exchange burden. Wilson, in return, agreed not to withdraw British troops from Germany before July 1967.

Eventually, the negotiations produced a troop rotational scheme that, in combination with new financial arrangements, covered most of the foreign exchange costs of maintaining American and British forces in West Germany. At the last moment, however, after most of the details had been hammered out, the talks threatened to stalemate over a final $40 million gap between British costs and German offsets. Not prepared to see their efforts fail over such a relatively trifling sum, Johnson offered to cover half the difference with additional military purchases in Britain, if the Wilson government would swallow the remaining $20 million. With this final American gesture of support for a hard-pressed friend, the last-minute details of the agreement quickly fell into place, and the threat of a substantial British cutback in its BAOR commitment receded.

EAST OF SUEZ

But still the inexorable pressures on Great Britain mounted. Desperately searching for relief, Treasury analysts returned again and again to the country's high defense expenditures. Economy-minded advocates of reductions in this area correctly pointed out that Britain routinely allotted a larger share of its GNP to defense than any of its European allies. Moreover, whereas most of the European nations spent their military budgets within their own country, Britain's defense expenditures were in large measure overseas. This, of course, only aggravated the balance-of-payments problem.

British deployments east of Suez received special scrutiny from Treasury accountants. By the mid-1960s, these deployments consumed a quarter of the defense budget, more than $900 million, and cost $250 million annually in foreign exchange. At a time of serious labor shortages at home, the United Kingdom had 100,000 men east of Suez. Fifty-five thousand British troops were stationed in Malaysia alone, where they were engaged in a nasty war with communist insurgents backed by Indonesia. Like its Tory predecessor, the Wilson government felt obligated to honor Britain's commitment to defend Malaysia. Nonetheless, the idea of a substantial pullback from the Far

East after the resolution of the Malaysian crisis drew more and more proponents as the government's other measures to strengthen Britain's financial position proved wanting.

Even so, for Whitehall officials, any decision to withdraw from areas of traditional British influence would be difficult. "We are a world Power and a world influence or we are nothing," Wilson publicly stated shortly after taking office in 1964.[20] London had longstanding ties to places like Hong Kong and Singapore, and specific commitments to countries as far afield as Malaysia and the oil-rich Arabian sheikdoms. Moreover, Britain possessed far-flung financial and commercial interests, even if it was not always readily apparent how a military presence enhanced or protected them. For some members of the Wilson government, such as Navy Minister Christopher Mayhew, resignation eventually seemed preferable to sanctioning large defense cutbacks. With the contemplated reductions in the Far East, Mayhew complained, the United Kingdom would no longer be a power in its own right, but only an extension of American power.

The prospect of Britain reducing its Far Eastern commitments genuinely horrified many Americans. Washington defense planners valued the British bases at Aden and Singapore. Most felt it useful to have the British flag rather than the American "out front" in the Persian Gulf and the Indian Ocean. A British withdrawal from the region between Suez and Singapore would remove the last British troops from the area covered under SEATO, and could prove the deathblow of that alliance. Washington would feel compelled to fill the vacuum, and few American officials had any desire to take on this responsibility, especially as it was obvious that the war in Indochina was going badly and would require further commitments. Administration officials also feared that a British pullback from Asia would encourage Mansfield and other members of Congress who believed that the United States was overcommitted and ought to reduce its own role in the world.

American policymakers were not oblivious to the burden their expectations placed on the British. "Would it not be better on both sides," the American embassy in London asked rhetorically at one point, "if we allowed the British to adjust themselves 'naturally' to a lower and more manageable national power level instead of encouraging them to persevere with commitments beyond their real resources, then periodically having to bail them out?"[21] Some officials, such as George Ball, argued that a world role for Britain was more nostalgic than real, and that as long as London continued to see itself as a global power, it would not willingly pick up the mantle of European leadership. As Ball explained in a lengthy memorandum to Johnson in mid-1966, British troops in Germany had "an immediate relevance to Britain's participation in Europe," while British troops in the Far East "are a distraction from the role that Britain should play over the next few years. . . . By permitting Britain to phase out her Asian deployments we can help her make the hard decision to give up the pretensions to a world role that are today diverting her from a more constructive purpose."[22]

But Ball's views remained the minority position within the administration. Even as they realized the grave nature of Britain's financial plight, Washington officials resisted the conclusion that drastic steps were no longer avoidable. As late as June 1967, Johnson vigorously took the British to task for thinking about Far Eastern withdrawals. For what in retrospect appears an unreasonably long time, the United States continued to act as if Britain could simultaneously maintain a healthy economy, a substantial presence in the Far East, and a major role in Europe.

Moreover, although they attached great importance to a continuing British military presence east of Suez, American officials made it clear that the United States was unable to take on additional security commitments of its own in the area. Administration representatives endorsed British efforts to defend the Malaysians from Indonesia, but for Americans the fighting in Malaysia clearly took a backseat to that in Indochina. No one in the American capital suggested that the Pentagon pick up some of the British burden in Malaysia. Indeed, Washington vainly attempted to get the British to take on new responsibilities, perhaps by dispatching troops to Vietnam or playing a more active part in Thailand's defense.

But while shunning new commitments for themselves, many American officials were willing to offer the British additional financial support if London would maintain its presence east of Suez. The Pentagon, for instance, seriously floated the suggestion that Washington pick up the foreign exchange costs associated with Britain's east-of-Suez military expenditures. The State Department and the Treasury succeeded in sidetracking this proposal, but did agree to offset the cost of British defense purchases in the United States by additional American purchases of British military equipment and material. Some senior Washington decisionmakers were even prepared to lend aircraft carriers to the British to enable London to maintain a sea presence in the Indian Ocean.

In the end, of course, reality could not be eluded. The formal announcement of a reorientation in Britain's global role occurred in separate stages, although at the time of the first, it was not fully apparent what was in the offing. In May 1967, Parliament overwhelmingly approved the government's plans to reapply for EEC membership. While the debate was not cast in terms of a European versus a global role, this was implicit for those who chose to see it. Two months later, in July, Her Majesty's government announced its intention to withdraw from Singapore and Malaysia by the middle of the next decade. In November came the long-postponed, much-resisted decision to devalue the British pound. Last in this chain of concessions to reality was the announcement, in January 1968, that Britain would accelerate its military withdrawal from all points east of Suez, including South Arabia, the Persian

Gulf, and Southeast Asia. By the end of 1971 nothing would be left of the once extensive British military presence east of Suez except for small troop contingents in Hong Kong and on a pair of insignificant islands in the Arabian Sea and the Indian Ocean. Finally, albeit with mixed feelings, the British had relinquished their centuries-old global role.

Americans were saddened and sobered by the speed and extent of the decline that these decisions ratified. The announcement to devalue the pound, Johnson would later recall, was "like hearing that an old friend who has been ill has to undergo a serious operation. However much you expect it, the news is still a heavy blow."[23] Some Washington officials could not hide their disappointment and even bitterness at what seemed akin to a full-fledged rout. Their ill-humored expressions in turn irritated an obviously touchy Whitehall, where British officials believed their plans sufficiently flexible to take American needs and obligations in the Far East into account. Moreover, they pointedly reminded the Americans, Britain's overseas military spending constituted a far larger percentage of the country's national product than did comparable American expenditures. Finally, they not unreasonably added, the United States itself would largely withdraw from the Asian mainland once its Vietnam adventure had been terminated.

The New York Times was far more realistic in assessing London's decision to cut back its global commitments. The British announcement to withdraw from the Far East represented "a long-delayed but unavoidable choice between uniting with Europe and persisting in the old role of a world power." Noting that the decision would undoubtedly place new burdens on the Johnson administration, the paper went on to observe that America's true interest lay in seeing Britain live within its means and demonstrate its European orientation. In the long run, the Times concluded, a strong united Western Europe, with Britain an integral member, was surely in the American interest.[24]

BRITAIN-IN-EUROPE

Indeed, London's decision to liquidate most of its overseas commitments signified that the United Kingdom had chosen to become a full-fledged member of Europe, with a defense posture centered on NATO. But what in concrete terms this meant was not always clear. The dispute with Bonn over the foreign exchange costs of the BAOR had reflected some of the prevailing uncertainty about NATO's role as the Western alliance approached its twentieth anniversary. So, too, had the French decision in 1966 to withdraw from the military side of the alliance, a step that had momentarily seemed to threaten the vitality, even the viability, of the pact. On the whole, however, the transition to a NATO without France was accomplished smoothly, facilitated immensely by the fact that no other member challenged the premise that the Atlantic alliance remained the essential element in each's national security.

But the longer term threat to NATO's continued significance centered on the German question. Increasingly, Bonn demanded the status of full partnership, which for the other members raised the specter of German possession, or at least partial control, of nuclear weaponry. The multilateral force had been conceived in large measure to finesse this problem, but for a variety of reasons it had proved unworkable.

Labour had entered office in 1964 promising, for a combination of political, economic, and ethical reasons, to reexamine the usefulness of Britain's independent nuclear deterrent. Once saddled with the burdens of responsibility, however, the government rather quickly concluded that Britain had traveled too far down the nuclear road to opt out at this point. Nonetheless, commentators in both London and Washington continued to debate the appropriateness of a British independent deterrent. Many Americans viewed Britain's nuclear arsenal more as an impediment to closer British ties to the Continent than as a guarantor of Western security. George Ball, for instance, wrote Johnson in mid-1966 that "Britain must recognize that she is no longer the center of a world system but that she can nevertheless play a critical role by applying her talents and resources to the leadership of Western Europe. . . . Britain must adjust her national aspirations to the limitations of her resources. . . . It gains little in world prestige by being a nuclear power but it could gain great respect from the world by taking the statesman-like step of getting out of the business. . . . By giving up her national nuclear deterrent Britain could strike a dramatically effective blow against the spread of nuclear weapons."[25]

Abandoning its nuclear forces would complement Whitehall's efforts to negotiate a nonproliferation treaty with the Soviet Union, Ball, McGeorge Bundy, and other administration figures maintained. A British renunciation of its nuclear arsenal would make it easier for countries such as India and Japan to remain nonnuclear. It would simplify the German problem. And it would ease the financial pressures on London by reducing Britain's defense expenditures (although as an economic proposition this was a dubious argument). If necessary, Ball and some of his colleagues added, the United States should be prepared to curtail the technological sharing in the nuclear field that had resumed in 1958.

Wilson, his nuclear ambivalence notwithstanding, was noticeably cool to this line of argument. Nor was he attracted to any of the various proposals for a multilateral nuclear force. The idea of some sort of European nuclear sharing, he believed, had been unnecessarily generated by "enthusiasts" in the State Department, who had stimulated German interest in the concept. A European deterrent force would play a divisive role in NATO, needlessly provoke the Soviets, and jeopardize prospects for a nonproliferation treaty.[26] Somewhat half-heartedly, the Wilson government proposed an Atlantic Nuclear Force (ANF) as an alternative to the MLF. But from a strategic point of view, an ANF made even less sense than an MLF, and both schemes were quietly shelved.

If questions about NATO's nuclear force structure defined one part of the debate over Britain-in-Europe, London's relationship with the EEC formed another. Following de Gaulle's 1963 veto of British entry into the Common Market, Whitehall officials toyed with various alternatives, such as a British "associate membership" in the EEC or enhanced trade ties between the EEC and the European Free Trade Association (the alternative commercial bloc Britain and six of the smaller European nations had created as a counter-weight to the Common Market). Some Labourites spoke optimistically about a free trade zone incorporating not only the countries of the EEC and EFTA, but Eastern Europe as well. Washington opposed such proposals on the grounds that they would discriminate against American exports without offer-ing the compensatory political benefits routinely expected of Western Euro-pean unity. The United States was prepared to tolerate discriminatory Euro-pean trade arrangements, but only if accompanied by offsetting political advantages.

At the same time, it remained an article of faith among Washington officials that Britain should renew its efforts to seek admission to the Com-mon Market. Indeed, many were prepared to give the British a forceful shove in that direction. If this resulted in a diminution of the Anglo–American relationship, so be it. Europeanists in the State Department were inclined to argue anyway that the United States had received very little in return for the privileged treatment it had accorded Great Britain. "We must dispel the British tendency to feel that she must choose between entering Europe and maintaining the 'special relationship' with the United States," Under Secre-tary Ball wrote in 1966. "We should make it clear to Prime Minister Wilson in unambiguous terms that we would find it easier to work with a Britain that was leading the drive toward a unified Europe than with a Britain that continues to be isolated from the Continent."[27] Ambassador Bruce, always an outspoken enthusiast of British membership in the EEC, argued that Britain's entry "should strengthen, not impair, our easy intercourse with [the United Kingdom] and its new associates." As if to underscore this point, he added that the "so-called Anglo–American special relationship is now little more than sentimental terminology" anyway, although he did concede that its "underground waters" continued to "flow with a deep current."[28]

But as always, there existed another side to the story. Writing to a British friend in 1965, McGeorge Bundy observed: "In the very nature of things, British interest[s] and ours intersect in every continent, and usually in rather complicated ways. . . . My own thinking is governed by a conviction that, if we can understand them correctly, our real interests will nearly always turn out to be very close to each other indeed."[29] Officials in the American embassy in London echoed this assessment. Why, they rhetorically asked, does the United States continue to regard close relations with the British as an important policy objective?

The simple, hardly debatable, answer . . . is that we need the support and sympathy of the British. If they are unable to go it alone, in their relative weakness, neither can we everywhere. We touch one another at too many points and are still affected by what the other does in too many situations to be able to dispense with mutual support of some kind. We consult together more frequently and extensively than with any third countries. On many matters and in widely different circumstances our policies are made to fit agreed lines of action. They tend more to interlock than to conflict on major international issues, regardless of the character or propensities of the British or the American governments of the day. They do not perfectly match one another, but, again, the main contemporary answer to the question of whether US–UK policies broadly harmonize is that they do. In this sense, a special kind of Anglo–American relationship does exist.[30]

The embassy went on to admit that the "rhetoric of a special Anglo–American relationship and the talk of interdependence can become very empty." Alluding to American desires for closer British ties with Europe, this assessment noted that "it is not in our interest to encourage the view that Anglo–American relations shut others out while drawing the British into a preferential American circle." Indeed, the "use of 'special' to define what now exists between us is psychologically unfortunate, however descriptive it may be as a partial statement of fact." Even so, the embassy concluded, it would not be in American interests "lightly to assume that the running down of the 'special' relationship would be advantageous to us or that it would be easy to replace with some other. The alternatives are not all that available or attractive or reliable."[31]

Still, London's reorientation away from a global role to a more European-centered one inevitably had repercussions for Anglo–American ties. Lord Chalfont, Britain's chief negotiator with the EEC, publicly announced in 1967 that the United Kingdom would henceforth make no further claims on the special relationship. Similarly, Wilson promised the Commons that this time Britain would not allow "a new Nassau" to disrupt negotiations over its entry into the Common Market.[32] What the prime minister meant by this was revealed a month later when he announced that Britain would not buy the American-built Poseidon missile as the successor to the Polaris. This was widely interpreted as a demonstration of British independence from the United States and a bow to Gaullist sensitivities. True, the decision made sense economically, for the cost of the Poseidons would be immense. But it also seemed a final concession that Britain could not compete with the two superpowers in the nuclear arms race, and would no longer try to do so. It did not mean, as some said, that Britain had opted out of the arms race altogether. It did, however, constitute an admission that despite its lead in nuclear weaponry over all countries except the two superpowers, Britain in the future would rank itself with the medium-range states. Indeed, Wilson's announcement was hailed in some quarters as opening the way to a possible joint effort to develop an Anglo–French missile. Thus, de Gaulle's second veto of Britain's bid to enter the Common Market represented a severe setback for those in both Britain and America who had seen European membership as a way for the United Kingdom to retain a voice in global affairs.

EAST–WEST ISSUES

As had been the case since the end of the war, the Anglo–American partnership during the 1960s drew much of its vitality from the cold war conflict with the communist world. Of vast, even overriding, importance to the bilateral relationship was the fact that each partner continued to believe in and adhere to the goals and purposes of NATO. And whenever it appeared that reduced tensions between the communist and the noncommunist world might lead to a slackening of that commitment, Soviet heavy-handedness would prompt officials in the two capitals to recall the reasons for their partnership. Such had been the case, for instance, in August 1968, when Warsaw Pact forces invaded Czechoslovakia to crush the liberalizing sympathies of the Dubcek government.

At the same time—and this too fit into a pattern reaching back to the 1940s—some of the most visible disputes between the two allies arose from efforts by one or the other to apply cold war policies in the Third World. London, for example, took great offense when Washington refused to terminate its foreign aid to President Sukarno while the Indonesian leader was engaged in trying to subvert the British-supported federation of Malaysia. Attorney General Robert Kennedy's interest in mediating the Indonesian–Malaysian dispute turned London policymakers positively apoplectic. (Whitehall, however, was soon enough to forget the resentment engendered by allies intent on mediating Southeast Asian conflicts.)

Britain's refusal to halt trade with Castro's Cuba provided another irritant to the smooth functioning of the partnership. Indeed, for the British this issue took on something of the air of a declaration of independence from American dominance. Early in 1964, a British manufacturer agreed to sell Cuba 450 buses, with an option for a thousand more. Washington, with sensitivities still raw barely a year after the missile crisis, believed that an economic boycott would keep the Cuban economy disorganized and stagnant, and therefore represented the best way of combating communism in the Western hemisphere. In Britain, there was general agreement that Castro was a nuisance and a thorn in the side of the Americans, but most Britons also believed that the United States got far too excited about Cuba. Besides, London had serious doubts that an economic quarantine would succeed in ridding Cuba of Castro, and was certainly not inclined to sacrifice concrete British exports for a probably unworkable policy. One poll indicated that nearly 70 percent of the British public found trade with Cuba acceptable, while only 16 percent opposed the bus sale. Following a Douglas-Home visit to Washington in February 1964, British papers of every political stripe warmly applauded the prime minister's staunch insistence in the American capital that Britain intended to carry through with the sale. What made this dispute between allies more than a little silly was the fact that British exports to Cuba declined steadily after Castro's seizure of power.

As the 1960s progressed, however, cold war issues had far less salience for British–American ties than in earlier years. The British were generally ahead of the United States in pushing for what during the following decade would become known as detente. In 1967, for instance, the Wilson government actively pursued negotiations for a treaty of friendship with Moscow. Washington was generally skeptical that any good could come from such a pact and worried that it could have a divisive impact on the Western alliance. Even so, the Americans did not make a major issue of their reservations. They were, after all, negotiating with the Soviets as well.

The successful conclusion of these negotiations in 1968, resulting in the nuclear nonproliferation treaty, did more than simply set superpower relations on a course that not even Moscow's cruel crushing of the Prague Spring later that year could reverse. The nonproliferation treaty marks a milestone in Anglo–American relations as well, for it was the last major set of successful arms control negotiations in which Britain participated on more or less equal footing with the Americans. The strategic arms talks that would dominate the following decade were very much a bilateral affair between Moscow and Washington, even though the British and the world's other peoples had every bit as much at stake in the success of these talks as did the two participants.

VIETNAM TESTS THE PARTNERSHIP

For the United States, of course, the principal cold war theater during the 1960s lay in Southeast Asia. Almost from the beginning, British opinion on American policy in Vietnam was mixed. At the time of the Tonkin Gulf incident, for instance, the respected Manchester *Guardian* challenged Johnson's account of events and suggested that the White House might have manufactured the entire crisis to justify air strikes planned months earlier.[33] The *Times*, on the other hand, asserted that American destroyers in the Gulf had every right to be where they were, doing what they were. Douglas-Home's foreign secretary declared that the retaliatory American air attacks against North Vietnam were an entirely natural response to gratuitous aggression and directed British diplomats in the United Nations to support the American position in the Security Council.[34]

Many Britons vaguely sympathized with American objectives in Indochina, particularly as long as British troops fought communist insurgents in Malaysia. As late as mid-1967, polls suggested that the British people retained a favorable image of Johnson by a margin of five or six to one. Large portions of the British press tended to be supportive as well. The *Telegraph*, the country's leading Conservative paper, was outspoken in its backing for Johnson's Vietnam policies, while its deputy editor and chief diplomatic correspondent, Peregrine Worsthorne, actively organized support for American policy within the British intellectual community. The *Economist* was so friendly that one White House aide playfully proposed that Johnson "trade *Time, Newsweek* and two outfielders to the British" for the prestigious weekly.[35]

On the other hand, protests over American policy appeared early and grew noticeably more vocal with the passage of time. Above all else, Britons wanted no part of the fighting, and some opposition to Washington's policies reflected concern lest the United Kingdom be dragged into the conflict, either as a result of American pressure or through an escalation of the war. At the official level, differing assessments of China's role in the war divided the two allies. Whitehall simply did not see the Chinese threat to Southeast Asia that Washington claimed as a principal justification for American policy in Indochina. Finally, as the fighting dragged on, Britons in growing numbers came to doubt that the United States could win and concluded that the destruction in Indochina no longer made sense. Demonstrations against American policy turned increasingly ugly; in late 1967, London police labeled one attempt to storm the American embassy as the worst riot in memory.

Even so, the Wilson government gave general political backing to the American effort in Vietnam. Were the United States driven ignominiously from Indochina, the Foreign Office cautioned, this would encourage an American isolationism that would then demand a pullback from Europe. London hastened to add that its own substantial commitment in Malaysia precluded tangible assistance to the United States. But on the whole, American officials grudgingly conceded that the Wilson government was probably about as supportive as could reasonably be expected. Making Wilson's task easier, until 1968 at any rate, was Hanoi's apparent unwillingness to sit down with the Americans at the negotiating table.

Of course, an individual as strong-willed as Lyndon Johnson was hardly satisfied with anything less than full-throated support, including the dispatch of British troops to Vietnam. David Nunnerley quotes an unnamed White House aide to the effect that London's refusal to contribute even a token force—a "platoon of bagpipers," in the phrase of the day—put Britain "almost in the position of France, of withdrawing to all practical purposes from the SEATO treaty."[36] Wilson has recalled that at one point he ventured to advise Johnson on the war's conduct, only to be greeted with "an outburst of Texan temper" and a presidential ultimatum: "I won't tell you how to run Malaysia and you don't tell us how to run Vietnam."[37] Nor was Johnson alone in his resentment of British aloofness or his desire for a more concrete British contribution. "What I would like to say" to the British, McGeorge Bundy observed in 1965, "is that a British Brigade in Vietnam would be worth a billion dollars at the moment of truth for Sterling [sic]."[38] Despite stories to the contrary, no evidence supports the contention that the United States used Britain's financial need to exact British support for Washington's policy. Still, even if American officials exercised restraint in this fashion, they frequently did so with ill humor. "All we needed was one regiment," an exasperated Dean Rusk bitterly remarked to a British journalist. "The Black Watch would have done. Just one regiment, but you wouldn't. Well don't expect us to save you again."[39]

When an American attack on the port of Haiphong damaged a British ship, most Americans waved off British protests with the response that the British had gotten no more than they deserved for refusing to halt trade with North Vietnam. On another occasion, the British ambassador informed American officials that while his country was only too happy to sell the United States bombs and other munitions, London preferred that it not be announced that these weapons were to be used in Vietnam. Such comments hardly made Washington decisionmakers receptive to British concerns about American policy. Indeed, hard-liners in the Johnson administration tended to view British anxieties as symptomatic of a larger British loss of will. Reminding the president that Whitehall had also sought to avoid confrontation during the Berlin crisis a few years earlier, national security adviser Walt Rostow warned Johnson that "we are up against an attitude of mind which, in effect, prefers that we take losses in the free world rather than the risks of sharp confrontation."[40]

The American decision in mid-1966 to bomb oil storage facilities near Hanoi and Haiphong created a serious left-wing revolt within his party for Wilson. The prime minister, ignoring Foreign Office pleas for caution, immediately "dissociated" the British government from American actions. But he pointedly refused to accept the demands of his backbenchers for a full disavowal of American policy in Vietnam. Wilson and his defense minister also issued a series of confusing statements in the House of Commons to the effect that the United Kingdom had not and would not sell arms to the United States for use in Indochina. As a description of past British practices this was patently false, while as a guideline for future action, it incensed American officials, who eventually persuaded Wilson to back off from such an unequivocal stand.

As in America, the communist Tet offensive in early 1968 provoked intense debate in Great Britain about the wisdom of Washington's Vietnam policies. Opposition leader Edward Heath called upon Wilson to reassure Johnson of British backing at this moment of crisis. But the dramatic events in Vietnam led many former defenders of American policy to reassess their positions. Peregrine Worsthorne, up to then a vigorous Johnson supporter, publicly withdrew his backing from the war in a widely discussed article in the *Sunday Telegraph*.[41] The *Times* declared that the offensive demonstrated once and for all that the United States, for all its might, could not win the war.[42]

Many Britons feared that the Americans would retaliate by escalating the conflict. Wilson, who happened to be in Washington at the height of the fighting, used the occasion of a White House after-dinner speech, normally a time for innocuous platitudes about Magna Carta and the World War II collaboration, to urge Johnson publicly not to bow to the demands of American hawks for further escalation.

To perhaps a surprising degree, Wilson viewed the war in Vietnam in deeply personal terms, at one point calling it "the greatest human tragedy of the postwar world."[43] The prime minister also saw the conflict in Indochina as an opportunity for Britain to play an important mediating role. As one of the two co-chairmen of the 1954 Geneva conference—the Soviet Union was the other—Britain would assume the mantle of the honest broker. But to carry out this role, Wilson concluded, he could not too openly criticize either of the major combatants, Washington or Hanoi. Few Britons, however, felt inclined to criticize Hanoi, whereas growing numbers came to believe that the United States deserved condemnation. This inevitably made Wilson appear, at least in the eyes of those critical of American policy, as an apologist for Washington. "[T]his is the central issue," one of Wilson's left-wing colleagues wrote in 1968. The prime minister judged that "standing close to the Americans is the price" he must pay in order to mediate, while the prime minister's opponents believed just as fervently that "we really can't play any part in peace-making precisely because we have not been able to denounce the Americans."[44]

Anxious to find a diplomatic solution to the conflict, Wilson shuttled back and forth between Washington and Moscow. Never enthusiastic about these efforts, and not fully trusting Wilson to protect American interests, Johnson nonetheless tolerated the prime minister's initiatives—in part because they seemed the price required to maintain Wilson's public support for American policy. But without a true meeting of the minds between Washington and London, and with so much at stake for an increasingly beleaguered president, it was only a matter of time before a real misunderstanding occurred. This, of course, is precisely what happened, in February 1967, during a London visit by Soviet Premier Alexei Kosygin. Johnson would later claim that Wilson misrepresented the American position to Kosygin. The British, on the other hand—and in this they were supported by American officials in London—came to believe that Johnson had backed off from his own peace plan after Wilson had conveyed it to the visiting Soviet leader. To make matters worse, LBJ refused to extend an American bombing pause for a few extra days in order to give Kosygin an opportunity to convey the latest American offer to Hanoi. Wilson, feeling betrayed and humiliated, angrily told the House of Commons that a diplomatic solution had been within reach. Based on what we now know about the course of subsequent negotiations, the prime minister was almost certainly incorrect in this contention. Even so, ill feeling abounded on all sides, leading some veterans of the Suez debacle to conclude that British–American ties had returned to their 1956 nadir. Wilson's anger only increased when he accidentally discovered that Johnson, without informing him, was also using other secret intermediaries to deal with Hanoi. In his memoirs, the president limited himself to the observation that had the British stationed a brigade along the demilitarized zone separating North and South Vietnam, their general approach to the war and to finding a peaceful solution would have been considerably different.[45] This was true, of course, but also rather irrelevant.

NEW PLAYERS AND A MORE DISTANT RELATIONSHIP

Few individuals in British political and diplomatic circles were sorry to see the Johnson administration draw to a close. During Lyndon Johnson's last two years in the White House, bilateral Anglo–American ties sank to their lowest point since the 1930s. The Suez crisis had represented a more serious threat to the bonds of amity and alliance linking the two nations, but Macmillan and Eisenhower had speedily moved to repair the breach. Wilson, however, was no Macmillan, nor Johnson an Eisenhower.

Even when the two countries worked in tandem—as in the weeks leading up to the Six-Day War in June 1967—it no longer seemed all that important. Of course, from the British point of view, this collaboration, even though ultimately unsuccessful in averting war, was far preferable to the incomprehension and lack of communication that had preceded the previous conflict in the Middle East eleven years earlier. Nonetheless, some of his advisers urged the prime minister to keep Britain out of the crisis altogether. The United Kingdom, they cautioned, no longer had the power to affect events, so why needlessly involve Britain and jeopardize London's remaining Middle East interests? Others warned the prime minister that it was precisely such extra-European activities as this that lent substance to de Gaulle's claims that Britain was not sufficiently Europe-oriented.

But in spite of these occasions when Washington and London worked closely together, Great Britain, for many Americans, increasingly appeared a drain and a drag. Politically, Bonn, Paris, and Toyko had matched London's importance for the United States. Strategically, Britain's declining power and reduced global presence made the United Kingdom less critical for the maintenance of American security. Diplomatically, London had failed to give the United States the support in Vietnam Washington believed its policies deserved. Economically, Whitehall, even after the 1967 devaluation, displayed little of the capability or the will required to reverse the malaise that rotted British vitality. This was "a steady—a workmanlike—but not a particularly golden moment in Anglo–American relations," Walt Rostow observed in 1969, in what might be considered a valedictory statement for the Johnson years. "Between the two countries there remain sturdy strands of interdependence. . . . But there are no great common adventures or challenges to make us exploit to the hilt the storehouse of common values that are still there."[46]

Thus, while Richard Nixon was not a popular figure in Britain, most British observers greeted his inauguration with the hope common to new beginnings. In his memoirs, Wilson goes to great pains to assert that Nixon, from the earliest days of his administration, sought a close partnership with the United Kingdom. In the abstract this is probably accurate. The president, for instance, in referring to ties between the two allies, deliberately resurrected the phrase "special relationship," a formulation that had largely fallen from favor during the Johnson years. In doing so, he publicly sided against those in the State Department who sought, in the interests of European unity, to soft-pedal London's special position in Washington.

Henry Kissinger, who as national security adviser and then secretary of state was to have an extraordinary influence over the creation and conduct of American foreign policy during the next eight years, brought to the White House an equally developed appreciation of Anglo–American ties. For Kissinger, the "special relationship" meant "a pattern of consultation so matter-of-factly intimate that it became psychologically impossible to ignore British views." Advising the president a few weeks after Nixon took office, Kissinger observed that "we do not suffer in the world from such an excess of friends that we should discourage those who feel that they have a special friendship with us."[47] For his own part, Kissinger writes that while he served as national security adviser, he kept the Foreign Office "better informed and more closely engaged" than he did the State Department.[48] Even if one doubts the literal accuracy of this statement, its underlying message is suggestive.

But neither Nixon nor Kissinger could alter the shifts in the global power structure of the past twenty years. From the beginning, both Americans acted as if Britain were irrelevant to their larger purposes. Almost from its first day, a rather yawning gap developed between the new administration's rhetorical allegiance to the closest of ties with the United Kingdom and its actual practices of secrecy, unilateralism, and, some Britons complained, duplicity.

Vietnam continued to be an irritant, and the Republican Nixon proved no more receptive than his Democratic predecessor to British moralizing on the war. With a new administration in Washington, Wilson seems to have largely abandoned his hopes of brokering a political settlement of the conflict. But late in 1969, reports of the massacre at My Lai revived all the bitterness that Nixon's inauguration and initial troop withdrawals had dampened. The House of Commons devoted the better part of a day to debating the war shortly after the first credible reports about My Lai surfaced. Wilson urged the M.P.s to withhold judgment on the rumored atrocities until all the facts were in. But the *New York Times* reported that the sense of the Commons was more accurately reflected by the member who stated that the war had reached the point where "it is destroying the very principles and values in which we all believe."[49]

Edward Heath's surprise victory in June 1970 secretly elated Nixon. It was not merely that the new prime minister was a conservative, or a man who, like himself, valued individual responsibility, self-reliance, and a minimum of government control. In addition to these political and philosophical similarities, Nixon no doubt recalled that the British statesman had carefully cultivated the former vice president during the bleak mid-1960s when no one in his own country paid Nixon any mind.

In many respects, the two men were from the same mold. Each wore a stiffness and a grim humorlessness, as befit one surrounded by an unfriendly world. Neither was prepared to open up, to lower his guard. Neither displayed the gregariousness or the ease with people associated with democratic politics of the late twentieth century. Each the product of an economically difficult childhood, both men seemed driven by deeply buried insecurities that called for constant vigilance lest they find themselves toppled from positions to which they had had no right to aspire in the first place. Lacking warmth themselves, neither fully understood how personal relationships could be turned to larger ends.

But one overriding difference distinguished the two men. Nixon saw Heath's election as an opportunity to establish the close personal ties he had never enjoyed with Wilson, whereas Heath wanted nothing of the sort. For the prime minister, policy complemented personality. Heath's electoral triumph in 1970 brought to 10 Downing Street for the first time in thirty years a prime minister who held few emotional attachments to, or expectations for, the special relationship. While not anti-American, the new prime minister, who had served as Britain's chief negotiator during its first attempt to secure EEC membership, believed that his nation's future lay in Europe. As Kissinger has written, Heath largely accepted the Gaullist argument that London's special ties to the United States rendered Britain insufficiently European. As a consequence, he viewed the special relationship as "an obstacle to the British vocation in Europe." Not only was Heath content to have Washington treat him as simply another ally, Kissinger later marveled, "he came close to *insisting* on receiving no preferential treatment."[50]

Unlike his predecessors stretching back to 1951, Heath made no effort to arrange a meeting with the American president soon after taking office. Transatlantic telephone conversations were rare, although Nixon issued special instructions that his proscription against unscreened calls did not apply to the prime minister. "His relations with us were always correct," Kissinger was to recall, "but they rarely rose above a basic reserve that prevented . . . the close coordination with us that was his for the taking." Determined to avoid "any whiff of Anglo–American collusion," Heath dealt with Washington "with an unsentimentality totally at variance with the 'special relationship.' "[51] And in so doing, he saw to it that the objectives of the State

Department Europeanists whom Nixon had deliberately thwarted were largely achieved after all. The result, Kissinger writes, was that the close consultation that had characterized relations between the British prime minister and the American president for three decades "was reduced to formal diplomatic exchanges."[52]

Yet not even Heath's deliberate turn toward Europe could obscure the fact that on many major international questions, a substantial similarity of perceptions and harmony of interests still bound the two Atlantic democracies. Kissinger underestimates the element of self-interest guiding earlier prime ministers when he writes that Heath was different from his predecessors in that he "based his policy toward the United States not on sentimental attachments but on a cool calculation of interest." But he is closer to the mark when he adds that Heath's convictions "so nearly coincided with ours that close collaboration would result from that self-interest."[53] Moreover, Heath's foreign secretary, former Prime Minister Douglas-Home, and the career officials at the Foreign Office remained committed to the idea of a special relationship and succeeded in softening the impact of Heath's expressed preference for a more standoffish approach toward the Americans. Douglas-Home was "an unconditional friend of the United States. . . . There was quite literally no one whom we trusted more," Kissinger recalls.[54]

That Heath argued vigorously against a hasty withdrawal from Vietnam, for fear of encouraging the Soviets to test Western resolve in Europe, was also duly noted and appreciated in Washington. Indeed, despite the gradual emergence of detente, the Soviet Union retained something of its old adhesive influence on British–American ties. Kissinger developed an especially fruitful working relationship with Sir Thomas Brimelow, the Foreign Office's senior Soviet expert. In his memoirs, Kissinger gives Brimelow credit for drafting American documents for use in negotiations with Moscow and adds that the "British were so matter-of-factly helpful that they became a participant in internal American deliberations, to a degree probably never before practised [sic] between sovereign nations."[55] Here again, one can overlook the hyperbole without dismissing the underlying point. Collaboration on intelligence matters also continued to distinguish the Anglo–American relationship from those either nation enjoyed with any third country. Finally, the British ambassador had easier access to the White House than any foreign diplomat except the Israeli and Soviet ambassadors.

Nonetheless, none of this could fully compensate for the coolness that marked the relationship at its senior-most level. And in fact, this less intimate partnership coincided nicely with the preferred Nixon-Kissinger modus operandi. Nixon's dramatic announcement in July 1971 that he was to go to China, after a diplomatic silence of nearly a quarter century, took Whitehall totally by surprise. In not tipping London off ahead of time, the Americans treated Britain no differently from any of their other allies—just as Heath had desired. There were those in Whitehall, however, who believed that London's willingness to swallow its reservations and follow the American lead on China for better than two decades had created certain obligations that at the least demanded the courtesy of an advance warning. Making matters worse was the fact that Britain was then negotiating with the Chinese to upgrade Sino–British ties. Kissinger's trip and the sudden thaw in Sino–American relations undercut the British negotiating position and forced Whitehall to accept a less favorable settlement than it had anticipated. Thus, while London applauded the new tone in the Sino–American relationship, both for itself and because it promised to remove an irritant from Anglo–American relations, the circumstances of its inception exacerbated frictions between Washington and London.

Nixon's controversial economic moves of 15 August 1971 followed this same pattern of unilateral American action. In levying a 10 percent surcharge on all imports and ending the convertibility of the dollar into gold, the United States took actions that would inevitably have a substantial bearing on British interests. Here again, however, there had been no consultation, no deliberations, no prior notice. Washington failed to appreciate the impact of its decisions on its friends, British officials complained. Still, Heath received exactly that degree of preferential treatment he had requested—none.

During the strategic arms limitation talks (SALT) that produced the 1972 agreement, Britain's role was once more that of an outsider. Wilson later claimed that London made a useful contribution by helping to resolve the anxieties of the European allies, who feared that Washington, in its eagerness for a deal, might give short shrift to Europe's concerns.[56] This may well be true, but it was a far cry from earlier days, when Washington and London coordinated on all major initiatives touching on relations with Moscow. If nothing else, the arms control negotiations of the 1970s demonstrated just how little distinction American officials now made between Britain and their other European partners.

Finally, as the United Kingdom moved closer to Common Market membership, Washington officialdom began to rethink the assumption that Britain-in-Europe would automatically advance American interests. And the less likely it appeared that economic integration would be accompanied by increasing political cohesion, the more extensive American doubts became. American commercial, financial, and agricultural interests worried about an enlarged Common Market that accorded preferential trade arrangements to many of the former colonies of its member states. On Capitol Hill, these anxieties fueled support for a protectionist trade bill pushed by Wilbur Mills, the powerful chairman of the House Ways and Means Committee. And American concerns were in no way assuaged by Heath's assurances that an enlarged European community would be merely "competitive" rather than "confrontational."[57]

The net result, according to the well-connected journalist Henry Brandon, was that by the time Nixon and Heath met for two days of discussions in

Bermuda at the end of 1971, neither even tried to pretend that any part of the relationship was still special.[58] Undoubtedly, this acknowledgment corresponded to Heath's desire and, if not to Nixon's preference, at least to his temperament. More fundamentally, it reflected some of the differences between the world of 1951 and that of 1971. Certainly it made it easier for Britain to gain entry to the EEC, as it would do barely a year later.

An old alliance, like an old marriage, has to be worked at, editorialized the *New York Times* in reviewing the Bermuda summit.[59] But here as well matters had changed over the past quarter century. The will to "work at" the relationship had substantially diminished; the urge to preserve and strengthen the partnership was no longer as compelling as it once had been. On the eve of Britain's entry into the Common Market, one British historian wrote of the Anglo–American relationship that "the whole thing seems so much less sentimental, so out of date, so unimportant." Like two aging spouses, Great Britain and the United States had gradually discovered that the interests and the passions that had originally drawn them together were no longer sufficient to keep them together. A few voices protested—quite accurately—that no divorce had occurred, nor even an irreconcilable separation. Nonetheless, it was impossible to ignore the fact, as David Nunnerley observed, that "few of the trappings of a masquerade are any longer maintained. . . . [T]he great love affair . . . has finally come to an end."[60]

Whether either nation was well served by this cooling of ardor is ultimately unanswerable, probably irrelevant, and quite possibly ahistorical. Given the idiosyncracies of Wilson and Johnson, Nixon and Heath—and more important, given the realities of power and influence in the world—it was inevitable.

chapter 6

ALLIANCE ESTRANGED: 1973–1980

The year 1973 dawned in both Washington and London full of the promise of new beginnings. Richard Nixon, fresh from one of the largest electoral triumphs in American history, prepared to begin his second term with the sort of personal vindication that only democratic politicians can fully savor. Before January was over, the Paris peace accords with Hanoi mercifully freed the United States from the drag Vietnam had represented. The administration's attention could now be directed toward other pressing issues, including the somewhat tattered relations with the European allies. The end of the war also removed one of the most divisive issues between Washington and its European friends. As the *Times* acknowledged shortly after the Paris accords, it had been difficult to feel a sense of common purpose with the United States, and more difficult still for politicians to declare one, as long as American troops were committed to a war that was widely unpopular in Europe.[1]

On the first day of 1973, the United Kingdom at long last became a full-fledged member of the EEC and took its place at the European table. After years at the window peering in, the British were now called upon to determine precisely what Common Market membership meant. And the casual American assumption that Britain-in-Europe would incidentally promote American interests—long a premise of U.S. foreign policy—would now be tested.

C. L. Sulzberger, longtime political writer for the *New York Times*, reflected a view widely held in the United States when he predicted that Britain's entry into the EEC should little disturb Anglo–American relations. After all, he explained, that relationship was based "on a commonality of ties and a joint experience rather than an artificially or distinctly special and consequently preclusive understanding."[2] Others were less confident. "The special relationship between America and Britain will be finished at last," wrote Anthony Lewis, also of the *New York Times*. "To put it bluntly, that means that American governments will no longer be able to expect almost automatic support from a pliant ally." A Britain-inside-Europe, for instance, would never have been as patient about Vietnam. Life, Lewis concluded, would soon be far more complicated for American policymakers.[3]

The year began with a Washington meeting between the president and the prime minister. Nixon pointedly noted that of all the European allies, only Heath had refrained from public criticism during the highly controversial bombing of North Vietnam—the so-called Christmas bombing—that had preceded by a month the peace accords ending the Vietnam War. "What you did," a grateful Nixon told his British guest, "did not go unnoticed and what others did, did not go unnoticed either."[4]

Acknowledging America's newfound freedom from Asian entanglements, and implicitly conceding a previous neglect, Kissinger dubbed 1973 the "Year of Europe." In a widely discussed address in April, the national security adviser spelled out Washington's interest in an updated relationship with its allies more in line with current power ratios. He restated American support for European unification. He pledged that the United States would not withdraw its troops from Europe unilaterally. He sought to allay fears that Washington would sacrifice the interests of its friends in pursuit of detente with the Soviet Union. Finally, he challenged the European allies to draw up "a new Atlantic charter" to guide alliance relations.[5]

Behind these expressions of shared interests, however, lay a host of pressing concerns. By the early 1970s, the cold war preoccupations of earlier decades had given way to new problems of money, trade, and agriculture—far more prosaic matters not necessarily conducive to a sense of partnership. In this altered international environment, new voices in Washington warned that the political and security advantages of a united Europe might soon be overshadowed by the economic and commercial disadvantages. This was all the more true in light of what George Ball referred to as the "lamentable tendency in high places [in Europe] to reduce the European Community to the level of a commercial arrangement."[6] Many American officials openly complained of what to them seemed a European willingness to accept American military protection without feeling any reciprocal obligation to take into account American economic and political interests. Faced with mounting economic problems, Washington thought it only fair that a rebuilt Europe pay a larger share of the costs of keeping American troops on the Continent. But the relaxation of East–West tensions made it unlikely that European parliaments or publics would be so disposed. The United States was also anxious for trade negotiations that would reduce steep EEC tariffs, particularly on agricultural products, and better enable American goods to compete in European markets. Here as well, the administration found its European partners distinctly less than enthusiastic. Reflecting these difficulties, the *Wall Street Journal* noted in early 1973 that "relations between the U.S. and Europe are widely agreed to be the worst since World War II."[7]

With these frictions as the backdrop, Europeans were inclined to suspect that Kissinger's call for a new Atlantic charter masked deeper motives. While Whitehall's initial response to the speech was positive, second doubts took hold within days. Some commentators interpreted Kissinger's address to mean that the United States intended to use its troop commitment to Europe to barter for a greater sharing of the allied security burden and freer access to European markets. Others saw it as a subtle attempt to break up the EEC. Many detected a patronizing tone in Kissinger's call for a "Year of Europe" and doubted that the United States was prepared to deal with its allies on a basis of equality. The French put out the word that Kissinger's plea for fuller transatlantic consultations was in reality a disguised demand for a veto power over European decision-making, sought in order to perpetuate American domination of Europe. Kissinger's words, the London *Sunday Times* informed its readers, could constitute "the opening shots in a new Battle of the Atlantic."[8]

Kissinger denied that he envisioned a direct linkage between the security aspects of the alliance and political, monetary, or trade issues. But many Europeans questioned the sincerity of these denials. At any rate, few Britons or any of the other allies were prepared to make concessions in the field of trade and finance in order to retain the American defense commitment, a point Douglas-Home gently made several days after Kissinger's speech.

THE YOM KIPPUR WAR

The outbreak of war in the Middle East in October 1973 and the Arab oil embargo that followed put to rest the Year of Europe concept. In the face of initial Arab victories, the United States launched a massive airlift of supplies to Israel. Then, once the Israelis turned the military tide, American intelligence picked up signs that the Soviets might dispatch an armed force to the Middle East to save the Egyptians. On the evening of 24 October, Moscow delivered a blunt ultimatum to Washington, threatening to send Soviet troops to Egypt with or without American concurrence. A few hours later, Nixon ordered American nuclear forces, including those based in Britain, to Defcon 3, one step below a full war alert. Roughly three-quarters of an hour later, Kissinger informed the British ambassador of American actions.

The 1973 Middle East war demonstrated once and for all the divergence that had developed between American and British definitions of the common security. Like its European partners, London was noticeably cool to American initiatives in the United Nations during the early stages of the conflict. Britain also refused to allow the use of American bases in the United Kingdom to resupply the Israelis. (Washington was never formally denied this permission. As Kissinger has related, it was made plain that the Americans should not seek it.) In addition, Heath withheld permission for American SR-71 reconnaissance aircraft engaged in intelligence-gathering flights over the Middle East battlefields to refuel at British bases in Cyprus.

In distancing themselves from American policy, the British adopted a stance held by most of the other European allies, who were also skeptical of being drawn into the conflict. But more so than the other allies, the British were angered by the American nuclear alert, especially the fact that Washington had taken this step without consulting London. Since the alert included aircraft based on British soil, it implicitly associated the United Kingdom with Washington's move. James Callaghan, the shadow foreign secretary and normally quite well disposed toward the United States, pointedly reminded the Americans that they occupied bases in the United Kingdom only with British consent. Former prime minister Wilson spoke publicly of "the humiliation of the American alert" and declared that Washington's failure to consult London beforehand was an "outrage."[9]

Americans, in turn, were angered by the reaction of their European friends. In Washington, the London *Times* reported, "the old Dullesian pliant 'agonizing reappraisal' is being revived."[10] American officials had hoped that British membership in the EEC would make the European community more outward looking. Instead, Britain appeared to be leading the chorus of condemnation. An embittered Kissinger acidly remarked that America's NATO partners were acting as if no alliance existed. To the British reminder that NATO was, after all, a regional alliance whose obligations and responsibilities did not extend to the Middle East, Kissinger replied that his allies were acting "like clever lawyers." Washington's expectation of support from its friends, he would later write, "was based not on a legal claim but on the imperatives of common interests."[11] After all, Europe, including Great Britain, also had vital interests in the Middle East, he said. And London's complaints about a lack of consultation were gratuitous. Britain had received more notification, further in advance, than any of the other allies. And yet, the British had been among the least cooperative of America's security partners.

Such comments only suggested that the American did not appreciate that, for London, the issue was not one simply of adequate notification, after the important decisions had already been made. True, Kissinger blithely conceded, allies should be consulted in advance of the decision-making whenever possible. But in an emergency, "the chief protector of free world security" cannot be "hamstrung by bureaucratic procedure." Besides, he was to write in an admission more candid than diplomatic, "imminent danger did not brook an exchange of views and, to be frank, we could not have accepted a judgment different from our own."[12]

Some months later, Douglas-Home tried in a letter to Kissinger to amplify the British perspective. The United States would not place much value on the United Kingdom either as a friend or an ally, the foreign secretary wrote, if London blindly supported American policy even when Whitehall thought it misguided. But apparently this is exactly what Washington expected. Once the war broke out, Kissinger later argued, the question of the wisdom of American policy ought not to have been the issue. He believed Europe's public carping only encouraged intransigence in Moscow and the Arab world, which might have prolonged the war, further endangered Europe's oil supplies, and undermined European interests in general. Ultimately, such detachment from American policy would tempt the Soviets "to play the Western allies off against one another, imperiling the security of all free peoples."[13]

But here as well, London dissented. Again like their European partners, the British strongly doubted that the crisis was the Soviet–American test of will Washington described. They believed the Mideast conflict should be seen as a regional crisis, requiring a regional solution. American complaints were poor thanks for London's support, alone among the Europeans, during the Christmas bombing of Hanoi. Kissinger, ran the refrain in Whitehall, was more imperious with his friends than with his adversaries, prepared to grant indulgences to his enemies but not his allies.

Nineteen seventy-three was 1956 in reverse, David Owen later wrote, but this time it was the Americans who felt let down.[14] Indeed, recollections of that earlier Mideast crisis bore heavily on the participants in 1973. As Heath remarked to several American correspondents, "I don't want to raise the issue of Suez but it's there for many people."[15] As in 1956, one party was absolutely convinced that it was acting in the interests of the entire alliance, while the other vehemently denied this was the case. No amount of consultation could erase this fundamental difference in how each side defined the problem and its bearing on Western interests.

EEC plans to open talks with the Arab states on Europe's energy needs further widened the rift between the United States and its allies. To Kissinger, the proposal seemed to cut across American attempts to organize a common response to the oil shortages on the part of all petroleum consumers. It threatened, moreover, to disrupt his intricate diplomatic maneuvers toward a political settlement of the Arab-Israeli dispute. An angry Kissinger declared that America's biggest foreign policy problem was dealing not with its enemies but its friends, "in an atmosphere of constant strife and endless competition."[16] A few days later, Nixon himself entered the fray, telling a Chicago audience that it was time for Americans and their European partners to "sit down and determine that we are either going to go along together on both the security and the economic and political fronts or we will go separately." The president warned that Congress would not be willing to keep American troops in Europe if it came to feel that the United States could expect nothing but economic confrontation and hostility from its allies in return. "[T]he day of the one-way street is gone," he bluntly stated.[17] Although much of Nixon's ire was directed at France, he refused to single out any one country and lashed out at Europe and Europeans in general.

British papers trumpeted that Nixon was threatening to withdraw American troops from Europe. At issue, wrote the *Economist,* was "whether a coherent European foreign policy can be squared with the political survival of the Atlantic community." Probably understating the role played by the Heath government, the magazine's editors sought to blame Paris for the malaise that currently gripped the Western alliance. "The French are trying to define the contrived distinctness of the European community in a way that rules out any real consultation with America on matters that affect major American policies. The only end to that road is the breaking of the special relationship between the United States and western Europe that has been a central feature of the world's politics since 1917: the breaking, indeed, of the Atlantic community."[18] One could not avoid noticing that, for the editors of the *Economist,* the special relationship was no longer a uniquely Anglo–American tie, but one between Washington and Western Europe.

Even before this flurry, Douglas-Home had sought to reassure Kissinger on the fundamental soundness of British–American ties. "We are firmly alongside the United States on East/West issues which could lead to serious confrontation," he wrote. "In any case of uncertainty the benefit of doubt would weigh decisively on the American side of the scales." Their present objective, Douglas-Home concluded, "should be to restore the old intimacy and I can see no reason why this should not be possible."[19]

But it would not be up to Douglas-Home to effect that restoration, for early the following year Harold Wilson and his Labour party returned to power. Unlike the previous occasions when Labour had turned out a Conservative government, many American officials were quietly pleased. In Kissinger's understated phrase, Wilson and his associates possessed a "more subtle view of the requirements of European unity," one that did not demand Heath's standoffishness from the United States.[20] Indeed, Wilson consciously set out to ease the strain that had marked British–American relations under his predecessor. His foreign secretary, James Callaghan, was a warm admirer of the United States and quickly developed a close friendship with Kissinger. One of Callaghan's first actions upon taking office was to inform his European partners that Britain would not take part in an energy conference with the Arab countries unless Washington was brought in on the preparations. When France refused, plans for the conference quietly disappeared.

Nineteen seventy-four also saw a change of governments in the United States. In Homeric contrast to the sweeping nature of Nixon's electoral triumph in 1972, the following twenty-one months brought spreading scandal, an eroding presidency, and ultimately the unprecedented resignation of the president of the United States. Britons watched in fascinated horror as the world's most powerful nation fed upon itself. Occasionally, they gave way to flights of fancy, as when the *Times'* American correspondent, writing in the wake of the "Saturday night massacre," reported that as the FBI moved in to seal off the office of the Watergate prosecutor, "the whiff of the Gestapo was in the clear October air. Some of the soberest men in government and out are now privately expressing anxiety that the military might now intervene—either to back the President or throw him out. It seems the stuff of nightmares, but too much has happened this year for men to disbelieve anything they hear when they are awake."[21]

Generally, British reporting on political developments in Washington was not this lurid. The British had never held any particular warmth for Nixon and were inclined to accept the possibility that he was guilty of much of what his enemies accused him. But as the crisis dragged on, concern mounted over the implications of an America paralyzed by indecision, headed by a president lacking the moral authority to lead. Callaghan, for one, has decried the fact that the administration's preoccupation with its domestic crisis precluded vigorous American action either prior to or after the Turkish invasion of Cyprus in the summer of 1974.[22] In the end, Nixon's resignation came as a relief for Whitehall. British analysts viewed Gerald Ford with noticeable condescension, but generally conceded that the new president's integrity and human qualities made him well-suited for restoring the confidence of the American people in their government. And despite their resentment about the way Kissinger took the allies for granted, most commentators expressed considerable satisfaction that Kissinger would remain in office to guide the inexperienced president.

THE "BRITISH DISEASE"

For Anglo–American relations, these mid-decade years were a time of introspection and uncertainty rather than of high drama or bold initiatives. Attempts—not always successful—to hammer out joint strategy on the international energy crisis, the global economic recession, the Middle East, and, as always, relations with the Soviet Union set the dominant tone for the relationship.

Through much of the 1970s, the entire industrialized world coped with the most severe economic recession since the Great Depression forty years earlier. The United Kingdom, however, had less of a margin than most of its security partners to cushion the hard times. Since the mid-1950s, the British economy had grown less than 3 percent annually, while most other industrialized economies had expanded at rates of at least twice this figure. Other nations—notably Japan and West Germany—had built new factories to better compete in world markets, but British industry had resisted innovation and clung to antiquated methods at a time of rapid technological change. The inevitable result was declining productivity and a shrinking share of the world's commerce. Whereas in the mid-1950s Britain had supplied 30 percent of the manufactured goods sold on world markets, twenty years later its share was less than 8 percent. Fewer exports in combination with large overseas expenditures made Britain the world's largest borrower. In March 1976, the once-proud pound dipped below $2 for the first time in history. By May it had fallen another 15 percent. Domestically, things were bleaker still. By the autumn of 1975, unemployment had climbed over the million mark for the first time since the 1930s. A year later it was nearly one and a half million. Inflation soared above 25 percent. Industrial tensions mounted and strikes proliferated as unions raced to keep wages ahead of rising prices. Amidst this chaos, the governing Labour party, riven by fierce ideological divisions, appeared incapable of decisive action. Worn down by the never-ending stream of crises, Wilson unexpectedly resigned early in 1976.

American admirers of the United Kingdom watched in horrified dismay. Commentators spoke of "the British disease," a malady supposedly characterized by drabness, lethargy, and a resigned acceptance of irreversible decline. Many drew the conclusion that the policies of a succession of British governments were responsible for Britain's current plight. "Britain's undoing is its own doing," Vermont Royster wrote in the *Wall Street Journal.* Its present situation was the direct result of three decades of welfarism, coupled with a refusal to pay for government services through higher taxes. The United Kingdom, Royster declared, "offers a model study in how to bring to ruin a once vigorous nation."[23] Syndicated columnist Joseph Alsop was equally blunt. "Britain today is about where Weimar Germany was in the 1920s only 10 months or so before every German needed a suitcase full of paper marks to buy a decent breakfast," he wrote in mid-1975.[24] Many American officials concurred in this analysis. Britain's "crumbling financial and fiscal condition" had created "a very dangerous situation," the chairman of the Council of Economic Advisers wrote the president. "The frightening parallels, with a lag, between the financial policies of the U.S. and those of the U.K. should give us considerable pause."[25] President Ford defended his opposition to federal financial aid for New York City by pointing to Great Britain, where, he claimed, government subsidies had led to economic disaster. In a valedictory interview shortly before leaving office, Ford again pointed to Britain as an example to be shunned. "It would be tragic for this country if we went down the same path and ended up with the same problems that Great Britain has."[26]

But once more the story had another side. In spite of their doubts about British policies, Washington officials continued to view Britain as a deserving friend and a credible risk. In mid-1976, the United States joined the world's other major industrialized democracies to provide Britain with $5.3 billion in standby credits to stop the latest slide of the pound. The American share of this aid package was $2 billion, a hefty sum in light of the substantial financial problems the United States itself faced in 1976. But still the value of the pound plummeted. By autumn, for the first time in history, it fell below $1.60. With his own party in open revolt, Callaghan, who had succeeded

Wilson as prime minister, seemed a good bet to fall. The Labour party's National Executive Committee voted 13–6 against the government's economic belt-tightening, but the International Monetary Fund called for further cutbacks in public spending in return for its support. In November, Ford received Harold Lever as a personal emissary from the prime minister to discuss Britain's distress. Lever found the president supportive of London's request before the IMF, although Ford was quick to add that the United States could not provide additional unilateral assistance. Two months later, Britain received its rescue package.

Analysts with a long memory marveled at the spirit in which the two countries confronted these difficulties. Faced with the gravest economic threat since the 1930s, Washington and London adopted an approach dramatically different from the beggar-thy-neighbor policies that had been their response to the Great Depression. Sharing many of the same problems of inflation, unemployment, stagnation, escalating energy prices, budgetary deficits, and international payments imbalances, officials of the two nations assumed an interdependence directly contrary to the attitudes prevalent during the 1930s. Both sets of officials accepted the necessity of concerting their policies if they were successfully to combat the common threats. To cite but one example, Arthur Burns, chairman of the Federal Reserve Board, and Sir Leslie O'Brien, governor of the Bank of England, maintained a constant stream of correspondence, punctuated by frequent meetings both formal and informal. With this continual communication came a greater appreciation in Washington for British sensitivities. *"[I]t is important to avoid criticism of the British Government's past or present economic policies in any public remarks you may make,"* National Security Adviser Brent Scowcroft warned a colleague.[27] The United States "can ill afford to view Great Britain's trouble as distant or remote from our own interests and concerns," the AFL-CIO's George Meany wrote the president in 1976. "The fate of Britain, her economy and her democratic society, is strongly and irrevocably linked to that of the United States and, indeed, of all the world's remaining free democracies." Meany went on to urge Ford to authorize "whatever guarantees, loans, or other programs of aid that may be required" to assist the British in restoring their economy, so that the United Kingdom could resume "its proper role as a great asset to the universal cause of human progress and freedom."[28]

THE SEARCH FOR A PROPER PLACE IN WORLD AFFAIRS

In addition to dealing with the economic turmoil of these years, each country was absorbed with introspective concerns that reflected an underlying uncertainty about its position in the world. Hovering over much of the decade were sweeping questions about America's role in global affairs in the wake of Vietnam. It took some time, moreover, for Americans to sort out the meaning and repercussions of a president's disgrace. Many observers, at home and abroad, worried about America withdrawing into itself, about a post-Vietnam hesitancy to exercise power or accept responsibility. These anxieties inevitably spilled over into the Anglo–American partnership. For one thing, Whitehall was concerned that the American withdrawal from Southeast Asia could lead to a reduction in American commitments in other parts of the world, notably Europe. Callaghan accurately summed up British attitudes when he observed that "[i]f America loses its self-confidence, then the Western world is in bad shape."[29]

For its part, Great Britain began to second guess its entry into the Common Market at almost the same time it gained admission. The governing Labour party was badly split over the question of whether Britain should stay in the EEC and, anxious to avoid making a decision, placed the matter before the country in an unprecedented national referendum. The government's divisions inevitably precluded vigorous leadership in addressing either the economic malaise engulfing the country or any of the other difficulties that plagued the United Kingdom in these years—a virtual civil war in Northern Ireland; growing industrial tensions, frequently class-ridden in nature and manifesting themselves in bitter strikes; a resurgence of nationalism in Scotland and Wales. "Britain is drifting slowly toward a condition of ungovernability," CBS commentator Eric Sevareid told his television audience in 1975. "It is now a debatable question whether Parliament or the great trade unions are calling the political tune."[30] So it was that Washington cheered the results of the EEC referendum, which produced a 2–1 margin for remaining in the Community. Perhaps the British might now end the querulous debate that had hampered efforts to address their other pressing problems.

Instead, the focus of that debate merely shifted somewhat. In 1976, Callaghan directed the Central Policy Review Staff to conduct a study of Britain's overseas interests and requirements. The report that resulted the following year was noticeably pessimistic, some even said defeatist. The United Kingdom "no longer has the influence to play a decisive part in solving international disputes," the Review Staff concluded.[31] In a single generation, Britain had gone from being a major imperial power and one of the two undisputed leaders of the West to a position roughly on par with the three other medium-sized countries in the European community. In 1945, "there was hardly an international problem in which the UK was not a major participant. . . . That has changed; there are now comparatively few international political situations in which the UK is both a major participant and has the power to determine the outcome."[32]

In the present world, the report went on, "a country's power and influence are basically determined by its economic performance. Inevitably therefore the UK's ability to influence events in the world has declined and there is very little that diplomatic activity and international public relations can do to disguise the fact." Indeed, "it is misleading and dangerous to think that the UK can maintain its position in the world by keeping up appearances. . . . If it maintains pretensions to a world role which is palpably beyond its power or will to sustain, the UK is more likely to convince influential foreigners that we are still prey to delusions of post-imperial grandeur than to give them confidence that we are headed for early recovery."[33]

The Review Staff then called for a "more realistic and modest concept" of Britain's role in the world, including "a switch of emphasis from what we can teach foreigners to what we can learn from them." The European community "is increasingly the channel through which the UK voice is heard in the world, whether on political or economic issues," the report observed. "If the UK is to be able to influence events, it will probably be increasingly through the contribution it makes to the formation of a collective European policy."[34]

Such findings enraged many Britons. The government released a white paper taking issue with the report's conclusions. Lord George-Brown, Harold Wilson's foreign secretary a decade earlier, complained that the report was shot through with "little Englandism."[35] A Commons committee expressed "deep scepticism" about the validity of the assumptions underpinning the analysis, specifically charging that the study confused the nature of power and influence by placing too much emphasis on economic strength.[36] Instead, Britain's historical ties, diplomatic skills, geographical position, ideology, and—significantly—its English language all ensured the United Kingdom a continuing influence in international affairs. The committee then endorsed the advice of Foreign Secretary David Owen that Britain needed to develop "a greater degree of self-confidence and buoyancy and a willingness to promote some of the things we are good at."[37] Reflecting this counsel, the parliamentary committee formally adopted, as one of the five broad objectives of British foreign policy, the need "to promote the English language and British culture."[38]

The intensity of the debate set off by the Review Staff report is highly suggestive. It indicates, first of all, the uncertainty about Britain's proper place in world affairs that persisted in Whitehall and Westminster. It illustrates the extent to which the strains of the preceding years had sapped the confidence of many members of Britain's foreign policy establishment. Just as much, it demonstrates a continued reluctance on the part of many in that establishment to concede that the United Kingdom was now closer in power to Italy than to the two superpowers. And finally, the emphasis of the M.P.s on the importance of the English language hints at a hope that Britain might yet use some undefined Anglo–American grouping to wield influence out of proportion to its inherent military and economic strength.

The nostalgic call for a British–American combine is also revealing. As the cold war antipathies cooled in the late 1960s and early 1970s, the rationale for a special partnership binding Washington and London also diminished. Nixon's policy of seeking detente with Moscow and Beijing, while enthusiastically endorsed in London, had the unintended effect of undermining the special relationship. Indeed, by the mid-1970s, relatively little of major import, at least in American eyes, remained of a strictly bilateral nature. The United States shared many of the same problems and concerns as the world's other industrialized democracies—economic recovery, inflation, secure and affordable sources of energy. Security, defense, and economic issues had all become multilateral. "Interdependence" was the watchword, downgrading bilateral relationships.

Moreover, Britain's obvious disabilities made it less attractive as a security partner for the Americans. Indeed, in an unguarded moment the chairman of the U.S. Joint Chiefs of Staff let slip that Britain and its military forces were "pathetic. . . . All they've got are generals and admirals and bands. . . . [I]t makes you sick to see their forces."[39] Things were hardly better in the diplomatic sphere. Most major foreign policy issues, the *New York Times* bluntly observed in 1976, "tend to bypass Britain."[40] Almost alone among the senior officials in the American government, Henry Kissinger continued to value especially close links with the British, though even he admitted that no one any longer tried to resurrect the "special relationship" label.

As was invariably the case, the British could not afford to write off Anglo–American ties quite so easily. Whitehall, for instance, quickly saw that EEC membership neither automatically solved Britain's economic problems nor eliminated the need for American support. And Britain could not expect to regain its economic vitality until the United States did so. General agreement existed that significant British improvement could come only in conjunction with substantial American gains. In the diplomatic, political, and military spheres as well, London still looked to Washington for the lead. And indeed, important vestiges of the former intimacy remained. Officials of the two nations maintained their habit of close consultation at all levels on most political and economic matters. Collaboration in the intelligence field remained highly developed. Finally, for all the American disparaging remarks about British military capabilities, close ties between the two defense establishments persisted. In the mid-1970s, the Ministry of Defence maintained seventy-five front-line staff officers in Washington, compared with seven in Bonn and ten in Paris. Moreover, a steady stream of military visitors flowed across the Atlantic; in 1976, there were 2,700 official Ministry of Defence visits to the United States.

Six weeks into his new government, Prime Minister Callaghan, in response to a question about the special relationship, briskly replied: "Of course it is special." Then, in the very next breath, he denied that he was "claiming a relationship with the U.S. that France or Germany do not have." Here again was the *Economist*'s refrain that the special relationship bound not just two nations, but the entire Western alliance. But Callaghan was apparently uncomfortable with having written off the bilateral relationship so easily, because he immediately sought to reestablish its uniqueness: "[T]o me, the special relationship is that I sit down with an American and can discuss matters from a common viewpoint. I think that's one of the reasons Henry

[Kissinger] and I got on so well. He used to say to me that when he came to London he got a sort of world outlook as he did in Washington. That is bound to create a special relationship between us."[41] Alastair Buchan, one of the wisest of commentators on British–American ties, said much the same thing when he wrote shortly before his death in 1976 that "[h]ot lines and frank exchanges . . . are no substitute for shared political values in a hostile world or a common language in an increasingly lazy one." Duly noting Britain's new relationship with Europe, Buchan nonetheless added: "The Gulf Stream of common intercourse at every level, cultural, educational, economic, official, shows no sign of diminishing its two-way flow, however intense the cross-Channel traffic may become."[42]

As they celebrated their nation's two hundredth birthday in 1976, Americans, however fleetingly or superficially, were given an opportunity to reconsider those political values they had inherited from Britain and in which Buchan placed such great stock. Quite sensibly, the British approached the frequently gaudy festivities not with any lingering resentment of long-ago losses, but in wholehearted appreciation of two centuries of American independence. The British staged an array of exhibitions and cultural exchanges to commemorate the national anniversary and, not incidentally, to reaffirm the common heritage. The Royal Ballet, the Royal Shakespeare Company, and the King's College (Cambridge) choir toured the United States as part of the celebration. British Airways enticed American tourists to the British Isles with the slogan "Come back, all is forgiven." And in one of the most highly publicized events of the year-long celebration, Queen Elizabeth and Prince Philip made a wildly successful five-day state visit to the former colonies. The state dinner in their honor was broadcast live on prime-time American television, the first time TV cameras had been allowed inside the White House for such an occasion. In Philadelphia the queen told an enthusiastic audience that American Independence Day should be celebrated as much in Great Britain as in the United States, inasmuch as the Declaration of Independence was a "great act in the cause of liberty."[43] Traveling on to New York, this great-great-great-great granddaughter of George III shopped in Bloomingdales and was made an honorary citizen of New York City.

THE CARTER ADMINISTRATION

The inauguration of a new administration in Washington six months later had little immediate impact on British–American ties. Jimmy Carter's election had raised eyebrows in some British quarters, and concern about his inexperience in foreign affairs was guardedly but persistently voiced. The new president's evident determination to accord human rights a central position in his foreign policy struck many as another instance of the typical American naivete in international affairs. Not, of course, that Britain opposed human rights, British commentators observed, but a great power was obligated to balance morality with reality. Many openly worried whether the president's willingness to challenge the Soviet Union on its human rights practices represented the proper balance.

Somewhat to its surprise, however, the Callaghan government soon discovered in the Georgian a friend and partner. Callaghan skillfully cultivated Carter, to the point where, according to National Security Adviser Zbigniew Brzezinski, the prime minister became Carter's favorite allied leader.[44] Callaghan once jokingly explained their obvious regard for each other by pointing out that they shared a Baptist religion, a naval background, and the same initials. Cyrus Vance, Carter's secretary of state, and David Owen, Callaghan's foreign secretary (whose wife was American), enjoyed similarly cordial relations.

Several working assumptions influencing the Carter administration promoted this revitalized sense of camaraderie. First was a general recognition that there existed limits on what the United States could do by itself, and that allies, therefore, could be useful. Second was a far greater acknowledgment than in the Nixon/Ford/Kissinger years that many of the most serious problems confronting the Western world required close and continued coordination with the other major industrialized nations, including, of course, Great Britain. Finally, there was a general feeling within the administration that in the past, the sensibilities of American allies had been needlessly ruffled by Washington's indifference to their interests and their perspectives on problems of joint concern. "Although of importance, US–Soviet issues should not be permitted to so dominate our foreign policy that we neglect relationships with our allies and other important issues, as has been the case in the past," Vance cautioned Carter in a memorandum outlining the foreign policy tasks facing the new administration. "Early attention must be directed to concrete suggestions . . . as to how one might improve the coordination and cooperation with our allies and the European Community. . . . We should not give our European colleagues a proposed plan on which we expect them to sign off. To do so would be to repeat the errors of the 'Year of Europe.' . . . We must avoid the appearance of forcing our views down their throats."[45] After the high-handedness instinctive to Kissinger, such an attitude, even if not always carried out in practice, found a welcoming audience in Whitehall.

Of course, the fact that Washington and London continued to hold a common outlook on most major international questions also had much to do with the cordiality of the personal ties. The British, for instance, were greatly relieved when, after several initial challenges to Moscow, the Carter administration settled down to a policy of cautious accommodation with the Soviets, highlighted by continued negotiations for a follow-up to the SALT I treaty. In Whitehall, preserving and advancing the detente of the early 1970s was a priority of considerable importance. London lobbied for a comprehensive test ban treaty, a reduction in Central European conventional forces, a second strategic arms accord, restraints on weapons transfers to sensitive areas around the globe, and any other measure that promised to ease East–West tensions. After Moscow dismissed Carter's sweeping SALT proposals in the spring of 1977, Callaghan, stressing the Kremlin's desire for an agreement, pressed the president to continue the dialogue with the Soviet Union. "Britain took a leading role in striking a balance between the often conflicting imperatives of arms control and human rights," Foreign Secretary Owen has recalled with some pride.[46]

Similarly, Carter's obvious commitment to a strong NATO buttressed by an active American presence in Europe reassured the British in the wake of Vietnam. London, despite its hopes for detente, viewed a vigorous military posture in Central Europe as an essential ingredient for world stability. As a consequence, Callaghan faithfully followed Carter's lead as the president first decided to move ahead with the politically sensitive neutron bomb and later cancelled its production. The prime minister also persuaded a reluctant Cabinet to endorse Carter's call for a 3 percent yearly increase in spending on conventional arms. Finally, the British readily agreed to allow the United States to double the number of its nuclear-capable F-111s stationed in the United Kingdom.

Yet Callaghan's critics persisted in asking what Britain got out of all this cooperation. London's ties with the Americans aroused European suspicions, and, under Callaghan, Britain's relations with its EEC partners grew visibly strained, with public quarrels over farm prices, fish, energy, and monetary matters. What Britain obtained from America that would justify the heightened friction with Europe was less immediately obvious. Carter's inability to solve America's economic ills—in fact, they worsened during his administration—deeply worried the British, who realized that their own recovery inevitably depended upon an economic upturn in the United States. Indeed, an underlying current of resentment and recrimination over American economic and financial policies ran not far beneath the apparently close political and diplomatic ties between the two nations.

What was widely perceived in Europe as Carter's erratic conduct of foreign policy caused equal dismay. On one occasion, the president flirted with the idea of issuing a statement that to British ears came perilously close to implying a "no first use" nuclear strategy. Ignoring for a moment the implications of such a strategy—and many people sincerely committed to arms control believed that this policy would enhance rather than diminish the chances of nuclear war—London rightly recognized that a unilateral American declaration of this sort would completely unhinge the strategic consensus that had held NATO together for thirty years. An alarmed Callaghan fired off an urgent caution to the president, who ultimately decided this was one brouhaha he did not need. Still, the incident "was a searing experience," David Owen recalled. "The near-crisis over 'no first use' gave me my first vivid realization of the fact that Europe cannot put its whole defence strategy, and the execution of it, solely in the hands of the United States. . . . To those of us who knew about it at the time, it was a permanent lesson to be very careful in our nuclear relationship with the Americans."[47] Stung by a succession of such incidents, Callaghan finally took it upon himself to send Carter a letter reporting concerns about American foreign policy allegedly held by German Chancellor Helmut Schmidt and Soviet leader Leonid Brezhnev, but doubtless by Callaghan as well. It was, depending upon one's perspective, either a mark of extreme intimacy, or of great presumption.

For all the newfound cordiality between London and Washington, in dealing with two of the world's hotspots, the Middle East and southern Africa, each ally preferred going it alone. Carter's exclusion of the British from any substantial role in the negotiations leading to the Camp David accords is perhaps understandable. London and Washington, after all, had seldom been able to act in harmony on Mideast affairs. Even so, the absence of any British role in the process was still novel enough to occasion the observation from Lord Home (formerly Sir Alec Douglas-Home) that it "would have been inconceivable a short time ago that we would not have been in on any talks connected with a settlement in the Middle East."[48]

More surprising was the manner in which Carter deferred to the British in seeking a settlement that would lead to majority rule in Rhodesia. On the surface, this issue seemed tailor-made for Carter, whose selection of Andrew Young as United Nations ambassador underscored his administration's empathy with Third World struggles for economic, social, and racial justice. Indeed, for two years Carter and especially Vance, usually (though not invariably) working closely with Foreign Secretary Owen, devoted considerable effort to finding a compromise that would end the bloodshed in Rhodesia. Nonetheless, after meeting nothing but failure and frustration, Carter encouraged London to take the initiative on the issue, even in the face of warnings from National Security Adviser Brzezinski that the British were "leading us by the nose."[49] When in the autumn of 1979 the British at last succeeded in getting all parties to accept the Lancaster House agreement, which opened the way for majority rule in Rhodesia (soon to be renamed Zimbabwe), Washington's role had been limited to watching from the sidelines.

In May 1979, the Conservatives, led by Margaret Thatcher, toppled Callaghan's government in an election that turned largely on Labour's inability to stem Britain's economic decline and industrial strife. Thatcher's victory had been widely expected, and was thought to presage no important change in British foreign policy. Although Thatcher and her party were more inclined than the Labourites to be suspicious of the Soviets, the Conservatives harbored no more enthusiasm than Labour for significantly increasing Britain's defense spending. Few observers recognized in the new prime minister a force that would revitalize the British–American relationship. Indeed, informed opinion held that the Carter administration had been privately rooting for a Labour upset. Most speculation in the United States suggested that Thatcher would try to repair Britain's strained ties with Europe, which might cause some loosening of the bonds between London and Washington. That the new prime minister waited seven months before visiting the American capital seemed to confirm this speculation.

Thatcher's election was followed within weeks by the signing of a second strategic arms limitation treaty between the United States and the Soviet Union. Despite its keenness for East–West cooperation and for arms control, London had followed the progress of the SALT II talks with some anxiety. British strategists worried that the negotiations covered only those long-range weapons capable of reaching the United States and would have preferred the talks to include shorter-range Soviet weapons, such as the SS-20 missile and the Backfire bomber, targeted against Western Europe. In addition, British defense planners feared that SALT restrictions might prevent them from modernizing Britain's strategic forces through the acquisition of the American Trident submarine-launched ballistic missile. Prodded by concerns expressed in London and Bonn, Vance took special pains to bring the allies more fully into the process by which American negotiating positions were formulated. Moreover, the administration gave the British private assurances that a strategic arms treaty with the Soviets would not preclude subsequent British acquisition of American nuclear systems. In the end, Thatcher warmly endorsed Senate ratification of SALT II.

True to its word, the Carter administration agreed to sell London the Trident as a replacement for the Polaris. When completed, the purchase would more than double the number of Britain's strategic warheads. Moreover, the preferential terms it got from the United States pleased the Thatcher government immensely. As Defence Minister John Nott observed, "The Americans have been absolutely splendid over nuclear cooperation. Their support and help—morally, financially and logistically—on [nuclear] modernisation were more than you would have expected from your greatest friend."[50]

While Nott's statement was accurate enough, it was also misleading as a description of British–American relations in the final year of the Carter presidency. The last fourteen months of Carter's tenure in the White House found the administration besieged by a succession of crises, whose cumulative impact ultimately convinced the American electorate that the Carter team did not merit a second term. In November 1979, Iranian students inspired by a radical ideology and a fundamentalist mullah seized the American embassy in Tehran and held fifty-two Americans captive for better than a year. In December, the Soviet army stormed into Afghanistan, prompting widespread fears in the United States about a Soviet thrust into the strategic Persian Gulf region. Carter's manifest inability to secure the release of the hostages or to do anything other than fume at the Soviets increased his already serious political vulnerability. By the spring of 1980, he faced substantial challenges not only from a resurgent Republican party but from within his own party as well.

Beset by adversaries on all fronts, Carter found little support from his European allies, including his "greatest friend" in the United Kingdom. Like the Germans and the French, the British worried about a precipitant use of force by the Americans against Tehran. But their counsel of restraint and endorsement of diplomacy in dealing with the Iranians became increasingly irrelevant to a besieged president criticized for indecision and weakness. Ultimately, London went along with American economic sanctions against the Iranians, more because this seemed the least Britain could do to support the senior member of the alliance than because anyone thought sanctions would compel Tehran to release the American captives. The attempt to rescue the hostages, however, agitated many Britons, especially since the EEC had only days earlier adopted economic sanctions against Iran largely to forestall an American military move. Thatcher was eloquent in her public support for the failed rescue, even declaring "absurd" the complaints that Washington should have consulted Whitehall ahead of time.[51] (Learning that the British had picked up rumors about the impending action, Carter had dispatched an emissary a few days before the rescue attempt to brief the prime minister on American plans. But the American envoy had been careful not to ask her for any comment.) A week later, however, Thatcher's foreign secretary journeyed to Washington with the message that further military actions would not find support in allied capitals.

Unlike the Americans, London was apt to see the crisis in Afghanistan more in regional than global terms. Thatcher publicly supported Carter's castigation of the Soviets for their invasion. But again, the gap between rhetoric and actions was readily apparent. As part of his policy of isolating the Soviet Union, Carter proposed a boycott of the 1980 Summer Olympics in Moscow. While Canada, Japan, and West Germany honored the president's request to stay away from the games, Britain chose to compete (as did France, Italy, and several of the smaller NATO countries). The American call for economic sanctions against the Soviets generated no greater enthusiasm from the British.

Finally, Carter lost the backing of his allies for the diplomatic initiative of which he was most proud—the Camp David peace process. Instead of whole-heartedly supporting the president's approach, the British and the other EEC nations announced an alternative strategy for the Middle East in the Venice Declaration of 1980. By calling for a larger role for the Palestinian Liberation Organization in any Arab–Israeli peace negotiations, the Europeans publicly parted company with Carter and, in effect, legitimized a position that was anathema to the United States and to its good friends the Israelis.

"It is now beyond doubt that the Atlantic alliance is in the worst disarray of its history," declared the *Guardian* in the spring of 1980. Skepticism about

Carter's leadership and judgment was universal. "President Carter is lurching down a road of his own choosing while his allies run after him, trying both to stop him and to appear to support him, and failing on both accounts," the *Times* wrote that same month.[52] Nor were the reservations all on one side, for in the view of many Americans, every time the United States needed support, its friends stumbled all over themselves in their haste to back away from Washington. It was little wonder, then, that when Harold Brown, Carter's defense secretary, asked his readers two years after leaving office to "think about national security," he spent 280 pages without a single hint of any relationship, much less a special relationship, between the United States and the United Kingdom.[53] To experienced observers, it appeared that those ties distinguishing postwar British–American relations from all other bilateral relationships had at last been severed.

chapter 7

ALLIANCE RENEWED: 1981–1988

The special relationship between the United States and the
United Kingdom has been buried a thousand times. And a thousand times it
has arisen, phoenixlike, to reclaim its place as an important dimension in
world affairs. So it was in the 1980s. Largely written off as an irrelevant relic
of the past by the end of the Carter years, the unique relationship linking
Britain and America reemerged in a revitalized form in the following decade,
as Ronald Reagan and Margaret Thatcher deliberately reforged personal ties
that had not existed since Macmillan's retirement and Kennedy's death nearly
twenty years earlier.

In many respects, Reagan and Thatcher were an unlikely pair. Deeply suspicious of the East Coast establishment that had frequently promoted close ties
with Britain, Reagan swept into office espousing a unilateralism and a willingness to employ American muscle that suggested that allied sensibilities would
not weigh heavily within the decision-making circles of his administration. For
her part, Thatcher had entered Number 10 Downing Street with an outlook
more attentive to Europe than the Atlantic—a predisposition that working
with Carter did nothing to diminish. In personal terms, Thatcher had little of
the warmth and charm that gained Reagan such great popularity at home.
Thatcher was a prodigious worker, Reagan anything but. Thatcher relished
detail, Reagan was notoriously oblivious to all but the broadest of strokes. As
one British observer remarked, "Clearly Mrs. Thatcher likes Ronald Reagan a
lot. The funny part is that a man like Ronald Reagan, of limited intellect and
limited capacity for work, wouldn't last six weeks in a Thatcher Government,
would he?"[1]

And yet the two forged a personal relationship that many deemed "the deepest and most successful between a British prime minister and an American president since the wartime partnership of Churchill and Roosevelt."[2] In part, their affinity was ideological, for the two shared a remarkably similar set of core beliefs—so much so that the *Economist* took to referring to "Ronald Thatcherism."[3] In the domestic sphere, both valued the virtues of self-reliance, individual enterprise, the free market, private ownership, and a noninterventionist government. Both assumed office determined to wean their countrymen from dependence on the state. In foreign policy each preached—and practiced—national resurgence, traditional patriotism, tough anticommunism, and strong defense.

Moreover, Thatcher was an unabashed admirer of the United States. She greatly esteemed the entrepreneurial values, the dynamism, and the competitive spirit she saw in the United States. She praised American-style initiative and energy, and compared it favorably to what she feared was a British inability or unwillingness to shed the cozy security of government paternalism. Determined, as Geoffrey Smith has written, that Britain not "lapse into mediocrity with graceful gentility," she quite consciously held the United States up to her countrymen as worthy of emulation.[4]

But a similarity of beliefs and the prime minister's admiration for the United States cannot alone explain the warmth Reagan and Thatcher developed for each other. Deliberate calculation on the part of the prime minister must also be taken into account. Disabused of her initial hopes of using London's ties to Europe to promote British interests around the world, she seems to have viewed Reagan's election in 1980 as offering an alternative strategy. Thereafter, she based much of her government's foreign policy on revitalizing the "specialness" of ties between Washington and London. And she did this especially by cultivating the new and inexperienced American president.

Thatcher first met Reagan in 1975, shortly after she successfully challenged Heath for leadership of the Conservative party. There had been instant rapport between the two. Five years later, as soon as the election returns confirmed that Reagan had defeated Carter, she fired off what the *Times*'s political editor called "an exceptionally warm" message of congratulations.[5] Over the following eight years, Thatcher seldom wavered from her strategy of promoting the closest possible ties with the Americans, even when such a course cost her political support at home.

As a result of these efforts, she won for herself the role each of her postwar successors had sought and failed to attain: that of conduit or go-between between Europe and America. "I would like to think that I can interpret the Americans to the Europeans, and the Europeans to the Americans," she once explained.[6] In turn, the other alliance leaders looked to her to keep Reagan within the bounds of allied consensus.

And this, it turned out, was often a challenging assignment. Repeatedly during his years in the White House, Reagan voiced sentiments, pursued policies, and took actions—in Grenada, Libya, and Central America; in arms control and dealings with the Soviets; at Reykjavík and with his Strategic Defense Initiative—that severely strained alliance cohesion. British officials privately ascribed to many of Thatcher's frequent trips to Washington the need to head off possible administration blunders on important international issues. As the *Economist* explained near the end of Reagan's second term, the prime minister "feels strongly that one of her roles is to prevent Mr. Reagan [from] making mistakes, and to limit the damage when they are made."[7] According to the *Washington Post*'s Lou Cannon, "There have been many summits when Thatcher finished Reagan's lines for him and other summits when she gently dragged him to a waiting limousine before he created an international incident by saying whatever came into his head."[8] Of all the allied leaders, a State Department official conceded, "she is the only one who can lean on him."[9]

No doubt there was a large element of calculation in her cultivation of the president. Thatcher, according to an informed British observer, was "very consciously trying to use Ronald Reagan to serve Britain's purposes."[10] A former member of the prime minister's cabinet recalled, "She gets very irritated with the man, and with Americans in general. I've seen her beside herself with frustration. But she's quite right not to let him see it."[11] Most observers thought they detected more than a little patronizing in her handling of the president. "Poor dear, there's nothing between his ears," she is supposed to have said.[12] True or not, the fact remains that Thatcher developed a standing with Reagan that was out of all proportion to her country's importance in world affairs.

THE PRESIDENT'S BEST FRIEND

Such a status did not come easily. In 1986, when Reagan dispatched American warplanes to punish Libya for the bombing of a West Berlin nightclub that took the life of an American serviceman, Thatcher stood virtually alone among Washington's principal allies in supporting the president's actions. But more than merely rhetorical backing, she gave concrete assistance to the president by permitting British-based American F-111s to participate in the raid. France, in pointed distinction, refused even to allow American planes to transit its airspace. The prime minister certainly was not obligated to permit the use of British bases for such a purpose. Nor had the British government been consulted until after the decision to punish the Libyans had been made—and even then Whitehall was simply informed of Washington's intentions and requested to allow the use of the F-111s.

For Thatcher, granting Reagan's request entailed considerable risks. Undoubtedly, this would place British hostages held by pro-Libyan terrorist groups in Lebanon in added danger. It could well lead to new kidnappings.

Moreover, the prime minister could anticipate that a decision to help the Americans would be unpopular with her countrymen. Indeed, after the strike the British public, the press, the opposition, and even most of her own Cabinet overwhelmingly and vehemently decried both the bombings and Thatcher's role in facilitating them. One poll found that only 25 percent of Britons believed that Thatcher should have allowed the Americans to use the air bases in Britain, while 71 percent felt the decision had been wrong.[13] Two former prime ministers, Heath and Callaghan, claimed they would have refused the Americans permission to use British-based planes. Thatcher, so a common taunt had it, had once and for all demonstrated that she was nothing more than Reagan's "pet poodle."

All this the prime minister could have anticipated. And, for that matter, she was not necessarily convinced that an air strike was the best way to handle Libya. Nonetheless, she went along with the president not because of Libya—not even, as has been suggested, because of Reagan's stalwart support for Britain during its war over the Falklands—but because of the special relationship. At a time when Washington's other European friends would likely be scurrying to distance themselves from America's actions, she wished to demonstrate to the Americans that Britain was an ally that could be counted on. And in this she succeeded admirably. British consulates in the United States were deluged with grateful telephone calls.

Nor was Libya an isolated case. At the Ottawa and Versailles economic summits and on other occasions in Reagan's early years, Thatcher was conspicuous as the only allied leader to refrain from criticizing the president's economic policies of high interest rates and higher budget deficits, though they worried Britain as much as its European partners. Thatcher followed the United States in withdrawing Britain from UNESCO (the United Nations Economic, Social, and Cultural Organization) despite substantial objections from within her own government. Finally, the prime minister was generally supportive, in a distant sort of way, of the president's policies in Central America. Whitehall doubted that the various conflicts in the region could be resolved by force and questioned the wisdom of aiding the Nicaraguan contras. Thatcher understood, however, that on this matter little would be gained by bucking the Americans. While London quietly refused to support the American trade embargo against the Sandinista regime in Managua, the British generally left the issue to the Americans to work out for themselves. In each of these instances, muffling British reservations and demonstrating solidarity with the United States seemed to Thatcher a more pressing objective than debating the merits of American actions.

Then there was "star wars," the Strategic Defense Initiative (SDI), so dear to Reagan's heart. Privately, many Britons regarded the president's vision of a nuclear-free world as silly and even reckless. Indeed, many experts feared that Reagan's avowed goal of rendering nuclear weapons obsolete would only accelerate the arms race. Moreover, British analysts could not see how a space-based defensive shield over the United States would protect Europe. They were, however, all too conscious that a Soviet antimissile defense could nullify any lingering value of Britain's own deterrent force. In a widely noted speech in March 1985, Foreign Secretary Geoffrey Howe compared SDI to the Maginot Line, the infamous French system of fortifications that in 1940 had so utterly failed to protect France from the German onslaught.

Once the extent of Reagan's commitment to SDI became apparent, however, Thatcher arranged an invitation to Camp David in order to voice European concerns that Reagan's vision of a world without nuclear weapons not serve to isolate Europe from the United States. At Camp David she secured a statement reaffirming that SDI's purpose was to enhance, not abandon, deterrence, and a commitment from Reagan that deployment of any defense system would take place only after further negotiations with Moscow. Publicly thereafter, Thatcher called SDI research a necessary countermeasure to Soviet efforts in space-based defense systems and supported Reagan's plan more explicitly than any other allied leader. While the depth of her own commitment to SDI remained problematic, she appears to have concluded that she would be better able as a partner than a critic to keep Reagan from moving SDI too far beyond the Western defense consensus.

Britain was the first country to sign a memorandum of understanding with the United States establishing the conditions under which British companies would participate in SDI-related research. Even here, however, it is notable that the negotiations dragged on for many months before agreement could be reached. Britain was also the most active ally in soliciting SDI research contracts, although this did not necessarily indicate a lessening of British concerns about the wisdom of the entire enterprise. Nor were British reservations diminished once it became apparent that the payoff for British participation would be disappointingly low. By the end of 1988, Britain had received seventy SDI contracts, but their total value was only $56 million—a far cry from the $1.5 billion commitment Whitehall tried to secure from Washington at the time London agreed to participate in the program.

As with the Libyan air strike and SDI, Thatcher deliberately risked the loss of domestic support by backing the president's weapons modernization program. The early 1980s witnessed the resurgence of a revitalized peace movement in both Europe and the United States, spawned in large measure by the Reagan administration's belligerent rhetoric toward the Soviet Union, its greatly expanded defense budgets, its perceived lack of interest in arms control, and its willingness, in Grenada, Central America, and elsewhere, to use force. In Britain, the antiwar and antinuclear movement recalled the heyday of the Campaign for Nuclear Disarmament in the late 1950s. There was a certain irony to this reinvigorated activism. For most of the period since World War II, Britain had worried about the United States maintaining its commitment to Europe. Now added to this traditional anxiety were new voices that wished to see that commitment reduced. Many Britons, of course, continued to believe an American military presence in Europe essential to their security. But many others came to feel that presence constituted the chief threat to their security.

This new wave of uneasiness expressed itself most openly in opposition to a 1979 NATO decision to deploy 108 Pershing II intermediate-range missiles and 464 cruise missiles in Europe unless the Soviets agreed to dismantle the mobile and highly accurate SS-20s that Western analysts considered particularly destabilizing. Widely reported protests at Greenham Common and elsewhere met the first cruise missile deployments in 1983, following several years of fruitless negotiations between Washington and Moscow. The anti–cruise missile movement was perhaps louder than it was large, but it did reflect a wider discontent with Britain's reliance on the American nuclear umbrella. It also signified that a small but vociferous minority of Britons viewed its chief ally with greater alarm than its primary antagonist. Many Britons were especially troubled by the fact that unlike the Thors stationed in the United Kingdom a quarter century earlier, Britain had no control over arming or launching the cruise missiles. Injudicious statements from the Reagan administration about nuclear "warning shots" and "winning" nuclear wars aggravated the situation further. But when the Thatcher government sought a new agreement that would ensure Britain some voice in any decision to use the cruise missiles, Washington refused. In the end, what had been designed to strengthen the Western alliance proved instead an extremely divisive force.

No doubt, the protestors at Greenham Common and elsewhere were far more radical and anti-American than the British population as a whole. Nonetheless, British fears about the judgment, competence, and intentions of the Reagan administration extended far beyond the small group of activists who captured the headlines. A British poll taken in the fall of 1985 asked which superpower represented a greater threat to peace in Europe. Thirty-three percent named the Soviet Union, 32 percent the United States, and 28 percent found both equally responsible. In other words, 60 percent of the British respondents believed that the United States had a responsibility for world tensions as large as or larger than the Soviet Union.[14] A year and a half later, a Harris poll revealed that Britons claimed to trust Mikhail Gorbachev more than they did Ronald Reagan.[15]

Labour tried to capitalize on these anxieties, though with a marked lack of success. Thatcher had been "sycophantic" in her dealings with Reagan, Labour leader Neil Kinnock charged.[16] Britain under the Tories had become nothing more than America's fifty-first state. Forsaking the middle course of the Wilson and Callaghan governments, the Labour party in the early 1980s adopted policies that challenged Britain's entire postwar defense strategy. A Labour government, party leaders pledged, would get rid of the American cruise missiles, scrap the Trident program, abandon the British nuclear deterrent, and negotiate the withdrawal of American nuclear bases. Americans—and not just the administration—were appalled. In the runup to the 1987

British election, Reagan departed from the traditional stance of neutrality to label Labour's defense policies "grievous errors."[17] But the Conservative victory suggested that the British electorate was not ready for such sweeping changes either.

Thatcher's success in holding off the Labour radicals only increased her prestige in Washington. During Reagan's second term she exercised an influence over American policy toward the Soviet Union not enjoyed by any other postwar prime minister. Of course, her own hard-line views gave her a cachet with the Reagan team, and with the president himself, from the very beginning. Moreover, she faithfully supported Reagan during the difficult period when arms control talks with the Soviets broke down completely. Later, once negotiations resumed and it appeared possible that one or several treaties might actually be concluded, she again publicly stood by her friend in the White House, lending him important support in the face of accusations from his conservative friends that their champion had grown soft. (Reportedly, Senate minority leader and presidential candidate Robert Dole telephoned her to make sure that she backed the intermediate-range nuclear forces [INF] treaty before announcing his own support.)

Like the other European allies, Thatcher was badly shaken by Reagan's performance at the Reykjavík summit, when the president nearly accepted Soviet leader Mikhail Gorbachev's proposal to abolish all nuclear weapons. In her view, Gorbachev's demarche placed at risk Western Europe's only protection from Soviet superiority in conventional forces. After the summit, she hurriedly traveled to Washington, where, according to her closest aides, she "put Reagan back on track" and elicited from him assurances that nuclear weapons still had a role to play in Western defenses.[18] In Reagan's final year, in the wake of the INF agreement, she also pushed hard for a modernization of the alliance's remaining nuclear arms and pressed the president not to ignore the need for reductions in chemical weapons and conventional forces. Of course, it is difficult to gauge with any accuracy how much her counsel may have influenced American policy. But the evidence suggests that Reagan found compelling Thatcher's argument that the British and French nuclear systems should not be lumped in with the American nuclear arsenal in his arms control negotiations with Moscow.

It was not simply a matter of geographic convenience that led Reagan to stop in London on his way home from the 1988 Moscow summit. He wished to give Thatcher a firsthand report, and he knew that she would then spread the word to the other allies. But Reagan was not the only superpower leader to seek Thatcher's advice. Gorbachev visited the prime minister in London on his way to the 1987 summit in Washington, and would have again immediately after his December 1988 New York meeting with the president had he not been forced to cut short his trip because of a major earthquake in Soviet Armenia. As the *Washington Post* observed, Thatcher "frequently cautions that there are only two superpowers, modestly noting that Britain is not one of them. But increasingly these days, neither Gorbachev nor Ronald Reagan takes a step toward the other without first checking the time, and the temperature, with Maggie."[19] To the extent that this was true—and one must be careful not to overstate matters—this constituted an extraordinary achievement for the leader of a nation so markedly inferior in strength and influence to the world's two superpowers. It also represented an impressive dividend for her loyalty to the president.

THE FALKLANDS WAR

But loyalty is a two-way street. To an important degree Thatcher's sense of solidarity with Reagan arose out of the support the United States had given Britain at the time of its South Atlantic war with Argentina in 1982. Occurring early in the Reagan-Thatcher era, the Falklands war was pivotal in solidifying Thatcher's conviction that close ties with the United States were a necessary precondition for Britain to influence events beyond its borders.

The Argentine invasion of the Falkland Islands in April 1982 turned out to be a godsend for Margaret Thatcher, although this is far clearer in retrospect than it was at the time. Determined to revive Britain's financial fortunes, the prime minister had followed a policy of economic retrenchment that had severely pinched millions of Britons, and public opinion samplings in the early months of 1982 suggested that Thatcher would likely be a one-term prime minister. Then came the Argentine attack and Britain's measured advance southward through the Atlantic, culminating in the successful wresting back from Buenos Aires of what, under any other circumstances, would have been viewed as little more than insignificant flyspecks amidst an ocean far from British shores. The war with Argentina was sufficiently bloody to persuade British citizens that they had been in a real fight, but not so costly or lengthy as to induce widespread war weariness. The conflict's decisive outcome gave the British a rare lift after nearly twenty-five years of more or less continual setbacks. Thatcher parlayed the ensuing national pride into a second electoral triumph, which bought her time to address the country's economic doldrums her policies had accentuated. Her partial successes on this score over the next several years can be measured by the fact that her triumph at the polls in 1987 made her the only British prime minister in this century to win three consecutive elections. And in an important respect, all this was possible only because of the British victory over Argentina, which in turn had been achieved only because of the United States. In her moment of need, Ronald Reagan was there, and Margaret Thatcher was not one to forget debts.

When the Falklands crisis first broke, many Americans found it difficult to take seriously. The press, the public, and even the State Department, Secretary of State Alexander Haig has recalled, tended to view the hostilities as "a

Gilbert and Sullivan battle over a sheep pasture between a choleric old John Bull and a comic dictator in a gaudy uniform."[20] Reagan came under intense pressure from some of his key advisers, notably United Nations ambassador Jeane Kirkpatrick, to follow a strictly neutral course. Washington initially tried to avoid choosing between a NATO ally and a Latin American friend with whom relations had become increasingly cordial. Haig undertook a highly publicized mediation effort, shuttling back and forth between London and Buenos Aires in an effort to resolve the dispute amicably. In Britain, Haig's efforts seemed not simply inappropriate but offensive, since most Britons saw the issue as a clearcut case of unprovoked aggression. American attempts to stave off full-scale conflict in the South Atlantic raised dark suspicions, particularly on the Right, of another Suez.

But British anger was completely forgotten in the wake of the aid Washington eventually offered London. The Americans made their airstrip on Ascension Island available to the British, who otherwise would have faced nearly insurmountable logistical problems in supplying a task force in the South Atlantic. Washington provided British forces with aviation and marine fuel, antiaircraft and antiradar missiles, and endless equipment and spare parts. "I abolished all the inbaskets between the British embassy and my desk," American Defense Secretary Caspar Weinberger later recalled. "We fulfilled requests usually within 24 hours, whereas the usual chain would have taken weeks and weeks."[21] Particularly crucial was the communications and intelligence help Washington furnished. A satellite was specially repositioned to provide London important information on Argentine fleet movements, while American authorities cooperated on signals intelligence as well. At one point, Washington even let it be known that the United States was prepared to lend the Royal Navy an aircraft carrier should that become necessary. "To those intimately involved, it seemed at times as if the two navies were working as one," reported the Economist. The British operation in the South Atlantic "could not have been mounted, let alone won, without American help."[22]

The Falklands war and Washington's role during the crisis provide compelling evidence of the continued importance—for both countries—of the Anglo–American relationship. The Reagan administration was loathe to antagonize the Argentines, both because of its desire to improve relations with Latin America and more immediately because Argentina was assisting Washington in creating a guerrilla force to oppose the Marxist regime in Nicaragua. Moreover, from Washington's vantage, fighting over the Falklands was a classic case of the wrong war at the wrong time in the wrong place against the wrong enemy—a distraction from Britain's primary responsibility of shoring up NATO defenses.

But once it became apparent that London was determined to contest the issue, American neutrality was impossible. The Argentine attack against the British position in the Falklands had been too blatant. As a nation of laws, Haig subsequently wrote, the United States "could not have one rule with regard to the use of force for its friends and another for the Soviet Union and its proxies."[23] Nor was it principle alone that was at issue. At bottom, American authorities concluded, Western resolve was being tested. Buenos Aires did not believe the British would fight. This Argentine miscalculation had to be exposed as a fundamental mistake, "lest it be made by a greater power over a greater issue, with far graver consequences."[24] Finally, the British could not be allowed to perform poorly. Washington worried that an indifferent British military showing would raise questions about NATO defense capabilities. Of course, it helped immensely that Reagan liked and respected Thatcher, and that Caspar Weinberger was as Anglophiliac as any American official in memory. Nonetheless, beyond these personal links were long-range calculations of principle and interest.

And beyond even these calculations of principle and interest lay one further and all-important consideration: Margaret Thatcher must not be toppled from power, for the likely alternative—a Labour government dominated by the antinuclear wing of the party—would spell disaster for the Western alliance. This conviction that American interests required the preservation of a particular government drove American policy during the Falklands crisis as it perhaps had never done before.

Yet the British response to the American invasion of Grenada eighteen months later demonstrated that there were limits even to Thatcher's gratitude for American aid during the Falklands war. When it came to Grenada, Britain was not exactly an uninterested bystander. The small Caribbean nation was a member of the Commonwealth and recognized the queen as head of state. Even so, the British were barely consulted about American plans, and British objections were cavalierly ignored. Indeed, Washington did not inform London of its decision to intervene in Grenada until eleven o'clock on the evening preceding the invasion. Reportedly, Thatcher was irate, swearing that Anglo–American relations could never again be the same. In the days that followed she publicly questioned all Reagan's justifications for the invasion and pointedly observed that Britain and the rest of the Commonwealth had been able to live with a communist prime minister in Grenada. As for the president's argument that Grenada's proximity to the United States gave Washington a special responsibility for the island's affairs, she icily replied that Grenada was no nearer the United States than Cairo to London.

The Reagan administration clearly felt let down after the help it had given Thatcher in the Falklands. "When she needed us we were there," a State Department official bitterly remarked.[25] If the prime minister could not loyally support the United States, the least she might have done was to remain quiet. As it was, her opposition gave the lead to a nearly unanimous European condemnation of the American military action.

Even on East–West issues there were limits to the Reagan–Thatcher partnership. Thatcher may have been the most right-wing British prime minister of the postwar era, but she nonetheless refused to allow the harshly ideological anti-Soviet view characterizing Reagan's first term to shape British foreign policy. Washington and London quarreled bitterly over whether Western companies should help the Soviet Union construct a natural gas pipeline from Siberia. Great Britain (along with other Western European states) would not permit British manufacturers to heed Reagan's attempts to restrict sales for the project and then blocked the president's effort to punish those companies, ultimately forcing him to back down. On arms control issues as well, maintaining a unanimity was seldom possible for long. British officials, including those in the Ministry of Defence, were skeptical about Reagan administration accusations that the Soviet radar at Krasnoyarsk violated the 1972 ABM treaty and disputed Washington's contention that Soviet actions removed any obligation for the United States to continue complying with the treaty. The Thatcher government also insisted that work on SDI remain within the "strict" interpretation of the ABM treaty and encouraged a reluctant Reagan to abide by the terms of the unratified SALT II agreement.

But these were the exceptions. Overall, the 1980s brought a renewed sense of partnership to the alliance, at least at official levels. As an American diplomat explained, "Both sides have gotten, in baldest terms, support on the major crucial security issues as they've proceeded, whether it's the Falklands or Libya. When the chips are down, she's been prepared to stand with us and vice versa."[26]

AN ERA DRAWS TO A CLOSE

At the same time, and even somewhat paradoxically, public support in Britain for a special relationship with the Americans clearly declined during the eight years that Ronald Reagan held sway in Washington. The far more moderate rhetoric and policies of Reagan's second term never erased the uneasiness occasioned by the president's strident language toward the Soviet Union and apparent eagerness to heat up the cold war characteristic of his earlier years. His readiness to use force alienated many Britons. The general impression that he was not particularly acute or energetic made it easy to ridicule him. Even Thatcher's willingness to go along with what many of her countrymen deemed unwise policies served to undermine support for a British–American partnership markedly different from the relationship London enjoyed with Paris, Bonn, and the other European capitals.

As a consequence, and despite their obvious pleasure at the general tenor of the past eight years, British officials were not sorry to see the Reagan era draw to a close. The administration had become exhausted, physically and intellectually, many Britons believed. The Iran–contra affair had undercut Reagan's credibility abroad as well as at home. Like the Watergate scandal during the Nixon years, the Iran–contra fiasco had been followed in Britain with a mixture of bemusement and shock. Thatcher, at least in public, had stoutly defended the president. But that she felt less sanguine about the sorry spectacle in private is not to be doubted. Many Britons found mystifying if not actually distasteful the respect, even reverence, accorded Lieutenant Colonel Oliver North in some American political circles. Beyond that, the highly publicized hearings into Colonel North's clandestine, not to say illegal, activities highlighted the incoherent nature of the decision-making process under Ronald Reagan that so offended and exasperated the British.

As Reagan's stock dropped during his last two years in office, Thatcher's seemed to rise correspondingly. Well before the end of Reagan's second term, commentators and analysts were writing that she was in the process of replacing the president as the preeminent figure in the Western alliance. Margaret Thatcher, observed the *Times* in mid-1987 following a Washington meeting with Reagan, spoke very much with the authority of "a senior partner in the firm."[27] Things had turned around, Deputy Prime Minister Lord Whitelaw explained a few months later. "She needed him very much earlier on. Now, I think, he needs her."[28]

Many American observers were saying much the same thing. One *Washington Post* writer in early 1988 remarked that Thatcher was "well positioned . . . to become the 'caretaker' of alliance interests in this American election year, and perhaps beyond."[29] An editorial in the *Dallas Times Herald* offered the startling observation that "to Americans, frightened by the lassitude of Ronald Reagan, Mrs. Thatcher looks like the foremost defender of the free world. Indeed, she may be the most important leader on the planet, aside from Mikhail Gorbachev."[30] The general unimpressiveness of either candidate in the 1988 presidential race did little to moderate these sentiments. "British officials work hard to allay the impression that Mrs. Thatcher will regard any new President as a beginner who, in a fairer world, would be her understudy in the Western alliance," the *New York Times* reported. "Her advisers insist that she understands that even an inexperienced President automatically assumes the leadership of the West."[31] But many who read these lines were not convinced, and found their mere expression suggestive.

As the Reagan years wound down, there was considerable speculation in the United States about the end of the American era. A succession of much-discussed books, most notably Paul Kennedy's *The Rise and Fall of the Great Powers*, postulated that the days of American dominance in world affairs were coming to an end because Washington had unwisely overextended itself around the globe. Analysts drew analogies with the decline of the British empire over the preceding seventy-five years, and several called for America to look to Britain's example in order to manage its own decline as gracefully as possible. Even many who ridiculed the America-in-decline thesis found Britain something of a model to emulate, in notable contrast to the conventional wisdom a dozen years earlier. According to the *Washington Post*, Britain under Thatcher's stewardship "has shed the image of a strike and debt-ridden disaster area and gained a reputation worldwide for prudent and parsimonious management."[32] The *New Republic* wrote of "the enormous creativity and flair that the British economy now shows" and suggested that Harold Macmillan's famous expectation that Britain would play the wise Greek to America's vigorous Roman might well be reversed over the following decade, with Britain now the more dynamic of the two.[33]

Yet despite diminishing confidence in America's ability to deal with world problems and specific uneasiness over Reagan's rhetoric and policies, the average Briton continued to regard America and Americans with considerable affection. A 1986 public opinion survey revealed that Britons expressing a liking for Americans outnumbered those voicing a dislike by a 4–1 margin.[34] They also trusted Americans and expected the United States to side with Britain in any true emergency. Anti-Americanism, as distinct from anxiety about Reagan and his policies, is clearly a diminished force in British life. British socialists seldom view American capitalism any longer as the personification of all that is evil in industrialized society. British intellectuals no longer see American ideas only as an inferior branch of European civilization. British students flock to American universities; nearly one-third of those studying abroad do so in the United States, more than in any other nation.

Britons also like things American—film and fashion, hamburgers and soft drinks, computers and precision machinery. The British citizen cannot escape the pervasive American influence even if he tries, for it is manifested not only by cruise missiles and high interest rates, but by music groups, television programs, and a host of consumer perishables that permeate everyday British life. Michael Jackson, Bruce Springstein, and "Dallas" have played an Americanizing role in the lives of today's British youth comparable to that which Coca-Cola and "I Love Lucy" played for their parents. In 1985, there were 197 McDonald's restaurants in the United Kingdom. American films fill British theaters; one study found that the United States holds 92 percent of the movie market in Britain. American news competes with domestic stories; usually between one-fifth and one-eighth of the *Economist*'s newshole is devoted to articles from or about the United States.[35]

Not surprisingly, substantial majorities worry that Britain's industry, economy, politics, defense policy, television, and even sports are all too heavily influenced by the United States. Denis Healey, Labour's spokesman for foreign affairs, has openly complained of a general "sell-out to American pressure which is corrupting every area of our public life, both at home and abroad."[36] According to one British filmmaker, the domestic market "is not important anymore. We figure 70% or 80% of gross revenues from any film we make have to be earned in the States," which ensures that British movies are designed with primarily American tastes in mind.[37] When a British golfer edged an American to capture the 1987 British Open, one would have thought, to judge by the popular and press enthusiasm, that Great Britain had achieved a major battlefield triumph. Large numbers also profess to believe that America unduly influences British morality. And commentators during the 1987 general election noted, with considerable distaste, that the British were beginning to import American polling and public relations techniques for their electoral campaigns.

Apprehensions about American economic, cultural, and intellectual dominance also go far to explain the difficulties Thatcher experienced in the Westland and British Leyland imbroglios in 1986. In the Westland case, the point at issue was whether Britain's only helicopter manufacturer should be rescued from bankruptcy by an American company or by a consortium of European corporations. The British Leyland case revolved around the question of whether the government should be permitted to sell the last major British-owned auto manufacturer to the American giants Ford and General Motors. To the average Briton, however, both disputes touched on issues far more profound than the future of two individual companies. Instead, they raised questions about Britain's place in the world, its prospects of regaining an independent economic standing, its ability to avoid foreign domination. Both controversies reflected, if not anti-Americanism per se, at least a profound British fear of being swallowed up by huge American multinationals. In such a climate, pointing out that British investment in the United States surpassed American investment in the United Kingdom had little impact. Nor, in the Leyland case, did it do any good to remind worried Britons that most analysts believed that economic logic dictated selling the British firm to its American rivals. Instead, the issues were framed as a choice between collaboration with Europeans and colonization by American multinationals.

Northern Ireland remained a sore point in Britain as well. Many Britons found it impossible to credit the interest American politicians displayed in Northern Ireland as anything other than an unprincipled toadying to popular prejudices. The *Economist* spoke for virtually the entire British population when it observed that "Northern Ireland attracts a certain class of American politician as an open wound attracts flies, and for the same reason: they can feed on it."[38] Equally upsetting was the tolerance Americans displayed toward the fund-raising and, many maintained, gun-running activities of the Irish Republican Army in the United States. Acceptance of the MacBride principles—a voluntary code of corporate conduct aimed at fighting discriminatory employment practices in Northern Ireland—by several American states and a number of important American corporations seemed to many Britons not a high-minded attempt to combat anti-Catholic prejudice, as MacBride proponents claimed, but rather as unfair and heavy-handed interference in matters that were rightly of no concern to the United States.

THE FUTURE OF THE PARTNERSHIP

And what of the future? As long as Thatcher remains in power, it is probable that Whitehall will continue to place a premium on close ties with Washington. If Labour forms the next government, things are less certain. A Labour government would almost surely keep Britain in NATO, the sine qua non for any meaningful British–American relationship. Labour leader Kinnock, tired of losing elections, is currently trying to draw his party's defense policies closer to the postwar consensus, although his chances of succeeding are uncertain. And so long as this remains in doubt, Washington will view the prospects of a Labour government with considerable alarm. Of course, a Labour victory, even in the absence of a firm reassertion of a more mainstream defense program, would not inevitably spell disaster for Anglo–American ties. Governments, even Labour governments, have been known to moderate their programs once handed the burdens of responsibility. Nonetheless, the defection of many centrists to the Liberal-Social Democratic Alliance, accelerated by changes in the way Labour selects its parliamentary candidates, has apparently opened the way for continued left-wing domination of the party.

Even so, a number of factors suggest that close links between the two countries will be maintained. Britain still provides important defense and intelligence facilities for the Americans. The United States has eight major air bases in the United Kingdom, plus dozens of lesser communications and intelligence installations, command centers, and reserve bases. While some of these facilities are part of the NATO defense structure, a good number are not committed to the alliance but are reserved exclusively for American use. Lakenheath air base in Suffolk, where the nuclear-capable F-111s are housed, is the largest American air base in Europe. Mildenhall airfield is home to the high-flying SR-71, successor to the U-2. American ballistic missile submarines operate out of Holy Loch in Scotland. The National Security Agency has facilities scattered around Britain to intercept and decode the secret electronic communications of foreign nations. In addition to providing crucial intelligence information to the United States, these various installations offer important operational and logistic support for American military forces in Europe and the Atlantic. Ultimately, of course, they also serve as a forward line of defense for the United States itself.

The militaries of the two nations maintain the collaborative relationship they never entirely gave up after the war. They regularly engage in bilateral exercises and joint operations in the Atlantic and Germany. The two navies work particularly closely in a dangerous underwater game of detection and evasion with Soviet submarines. Joint Anglo–American programs work to develop ever more sophisticated weapons—the second-generation Harrier aircraft, for example. Formal and informal agreements allow the Americans to use British facilities on Ascension Island, Bermuda, Cyprus, and Diego Garcia, thereby enabling the United States to deploy its forces worldwide more efficiently. Indeed, in recent years the British-owned island of Diego Garcia, located a thousand miles south of India, has been developed into a major American naval base, with important intelligence and communications facilities as well. Britain is "different" from the other NATO members, conceded an American official. "If you don't have this intimate military relationship" between Britain and America, "you do not have NATO."[39]

Nuclear collaboration continues unabated as well. The United Kingdom remains the only nuclear power in the world to which the United States provides missiles. In fact, Britain relies heavily on Washington for virtually all aspects of its nuclear arsenal. The Americans furnish the British with highly enriched uranium, nuclear designs, launching platforms, navigation systems, and target intelligence. Britain has tested its warheads and delivery systems exclusively at American test sites in Nevada since 1962. British nuclear weapons are targeted in accordance with American strategic war plans. At the tactical level, Britain is completely dependent on the United States for nuclear artillery shells, short-range missiles, nuclear depth bombs, and atomic land mines. The actual warheads for these weapons remain in American custody and require American permission before the British can use them. A 1979 study for the House of Commons put the matter bluntly: Britain's "independent" nuclear deterrent had never been independent. Indeed, "its major function and justification was to serve as an alliance force, and operate as a dependent adjunct of United States strategic forces."[40] According to one London official, the Anglo–American nuclear partnership remains so close that "even if we wanted to, we would find it almost impossible to collaborate with a third party on warheads."[41]

In other respects as well, Britain is still a more important ally for the United States than its size and strength would suggest. As one of only five announced nuclear weapons states, the United Kingdom is a member of what still remains, forty-odd years after Hiroshima, a very exclusive club. NATO continues to serve as the foundation of Britain's defense and security policies, and 95 percent of Britain's defense budget goes, directly or indirectly, toward NATO missions. Aside from the United States, Britain is the only NATO member to contribute to all three elements of the alliance's defense structure—strategic and theater nuclear weapons and conventional forces. The British Army on the Rhine is, after the American contingent, the largest non-German force in the Federal Republic. The British navy and air force are each the fourth largest in the world. Britain still possesses strategically placed bases in Belize, Cyprus, Gibraltar, Hong Kong, Brunei, the South Atlantic, and the Indian Ocean. As a permanent member of the United Nations Security Council, the United Kingdom retains an important voice on international issues not directly touching on its own interests, while its Commonwealth ties give British diplomats special entrée to nearly fifty states around the globe. Finally, Britain's political stability constitutes a valuable asset in a world where instability and surprise often seem the norm.

The willingness of the Thatcher government to maintain high defense expenditures relative to Britain's size also makes the United Kingdom an attractive security partner for the United States. In the late 1980s, "burden-sharing" has once again become a staple of political debate in the United

States. But the United Kingdom has remained largely unscathed, for its defense expenditures are still proportionally higher than those of most of the other allies. Statistical measures vary according to who uses what standards, but all agree that the United Kingdom is third among the NATO members in defense expenditures as a percentage of gross domestic product. Britain spends a larger share of its GDP on defense—5.1 percent in 1988—than any other European ally except Greece. The United States, in comparison, spent 6.8 percent in 1988, France 3.9 percent, West Germany 3.1 percent, and Italy 2.2 percent. Measured in terms of total military expenditures, the United States in 1988 spent ten times the amount of any of its allies, with France, Germany, and Britain all spending approximately $27–$28 billion. Measured by per-capita defense expenditures, the United Kingdom, at $481 per person, ranks fourth among the sixteen NATO allies, behind the United States ($1,164), Norway ($520), and France ($514), but ahead of Germany ($454), Italy ($235), Turkey ($54), and the other alliance members.[42]

Indeed, Britain's reliability as an ally appears all the more pronounced compared to many of Washington's security partners. France has withdrawn from the military side of NATO and expelled American forces from French soil. Norway and Denmark do not permit American bases on their territory. Spain has closed the Poseidon base at Rota and the F-16 airfield outside Madrid, while Britain has volunteered to accept some of the aircraft expelled from Spain. Greece withdrew from NATO for six years in the 1970s and periodically threatens to shut down all American bases in the country. Ankara insists on new restrictions on American bases in Turkey. The United States pays well over $1 billion each year for the use of bases in Greece, Turkey, Spain, and Portugal—but nothing for its equally important and far more numerous facilities in the United Kingdom. So by many measures, Washington has good reason to view the British with special favor. The Anglo–American connection, the *Economist* judged in 1984, "forms the emotional core of the Atlantic alliance."[43]

British officials and diplomats exploit these collaborative links skillfully. The United Kingdom continues to enjoy exceptional access, influence, and occasionally leverage in Washington, usually exercised through a web of contacts in the United States government matched by no other foreign nation, with the possible exception of Israel. Of all America's friends, a former U.S. secretary of the navy has observed, only Great Britain possesses those day-to-day contacts "where you pick up the phone to call somebody at the other end and he's been at your home and you've been at his home, and you know him by his first name and you know his children's names and that kind of thing. I mean it's a different kind of a relationship."[44] Indeed, the existence of these informal, personal ties is a far better guarantee of the continued vitality of British–American relations than merely formal treaties or obligations.

In other ways as well, links between the two countries remain many, varied, and frequently intimate. Britain, with better than $70 billion in direct investments in the United States at the end of 1987, is far and away America's leading foreign investor, with a portfolio more than twice that of the Japanese, and three and a half times that of the Germans. To cite one example—in the influential advertising industry—three of America's seven largest ad agencies, including the legendary J. Walter Thompson, are owned by British firms. American investors continue to find British companies attractive as well. In 1987, American investment in the United Kingdom stood at $44.7 billion; only Canada drew more American dollars. Indeed, Americans invest more in Britain than in all of Latin America. Trade ties are similarly robust. In 1985, Americans bought $15.6 billion worth of products from the United Kingdom. Britain is still the fourth largest market for American-made goods, surpassed only by Canada, Japan, and Mexico. (But in contrast to earlier years, Britain now sells more to Americans than it buys from them; in 1985, the difference came to $4.3 billion. The crossover occurred in 1981.)

In short, many elements of a special relationship between the United Kingdom and the United States remain, even if one seldom hears the phrase "special relationship" invoked on any but ceremonial occasions. Moreover, these unique bonds are likely to persist for the foreseeable future, bound by the glue of common interest: the need to maintain Western security while simultaneously working for a more stable, less confrontational relationship with the Soviets; a desire to promote and preserve democracy in the Third World; the necessity of avoiding a breakdown in the international financial system.

At the same time, the movement toward greater European unity is probably irreversible. The British, French, and West Germans are currently discussing various avenues for closer military cooperation. Britain, along with Italy, Spain, and the Federal Republic, is part of a $37 billion European Fighter Aircraft project. London and Paris have explored the possibility of jointly developing a new air-to-surface missile, which would mark the first time London has worked on nuclear armaments with any country other than the United States. While the missile project has been abandoned, at least temporarily, the pressures on the defense budgets of all the allies suggest that similar proposals are likely to receive more favorable treatment in the years to come. Complementing these military ties are increasingly close economic links. By 1 January 1993, the twelve nations of the EEC will have achieved a barrier-free customs market. Already, British exports to the Community are three and a half times as large as British sales to the United States.

Moreover, for all their continuing close ties, the fact remains that Britain is simply not as important to the United States as it once was. As recently as 1960, the United Kingdom still possessed the third largest GNP in the world. Today it is in sixth place, and in danger of being bumped still lower by Italy. Similarly, the past quarter century has seen the size of Britain's military forces shrink not only absolutely, but more important, in relation to those of other countries. By the mid-1980s, the entire British armed forces were no larger than the number of American troops stationed in Europe. Strategically, Britain's relative decline is even more striking. The acquisition of Polaris in the 1960s gave the United Kingdom approximately one-sixth as many nuclear warheads as the United States possessed. Today, the British do not have one-sixtieth as many as either the United States or the Soviet Union. Even the American bases in Britain have lost some of their old value, since the far-ranging Trident II submarine has little need for the Holy Loch base, while increasingly sophisticated intercontinental ballistic missiles have made the Air Force bases in the United Kingdom less essential.[45] Finally, no matter how expertly the British manage their affairs, Britain in the early 1990s will face a set of budgetary pressures certain to widen the present gap between available resources and projected defense requirements. This shortfall will inevitably force upon whatever British government happens to hold power unwanted decisions that will further reduce Britain's military usefulness to Washington.

The new element in the bilateral relationship, however, is that the United States may no longer be as important to Britain as in former days. Few anticipate an outbreak of war, which somewhat diminishes London's dependence on the American security guarantee. No longer the world's towering economic power, the United States is less able to sustain the British economy through difficult times than it was a generation ago. Britain's recent economic revival has reduced that need anyway. Psychologically, Britain appears at last to have accepted that it is more a European than a global power, which makes it less dependent upon day-to-day American support in the world outside Europe. Finally, today's Foreign Office official draws his bearings not from the Anglo–American partnership during World War II, but from Suez, Vietnam, and the British entry into the EEC. He (and increasingly, she) is less inclined automatically to feel special ties to the Americans.

As David Watt has rightly observed, the most pressing questions for British diplomats in the years to come are likely to have little to do with special relationships. Instead, they will revolve around the extent to which European and American interests diverge, and how to manage that divergence.[46] Henry Kissinger has made much the same point in identifying "the perennial questions of all alliances": How much unity do we need? How much diversity can we stand?[47] In seeking solutions to these questions, Watt cautions, the exceptional character of postwar Anglo–American relations will not prevent the United Kingdom, more often than not, from lining up with its European friends against the Americans.

That this should be the case is inevitable. The special relationship between London and Washington was the product of a particular and specific set of circumstances arising out of the wreckage of World War II. It was not foreordained by history—indeed, the record of Anglo–American ties over most of the past two centuries would have led one to expect anything but a special relationship. Nor was it destined to remain an immutable part of the global order. As the circumstances that spawned it gradually changed, so too did the special relationship, until it lost much of what had heretofore made it special. It was, in short, a unique and temporary response to a particular moment in world history that is not likely to be repeated.

Still, the historian must avoid the temptation simply to write off Anglo–American ties as of no further consequence. In the decades since 1945, the special relationship between Britain and America has demonstrated, if nothing else, a remarkable resiliency. It has been denounced, deplored, and decried. At times it has been conspicuously, even spectacularly, ignored. Its dissolution has been repeatedly proclaimed. That it ever existed has been denied. And yet it has survived, very much a comfortable, ordinary, everyday feature of the diplomatic landscape, and proving again the perspicacity of Edmund Burke, who two hundred years ago saw that the bonds holding the two nations together, "though light as air, are as strong as links of iron."[48] And like those links, the Anglo–American relationship, once forged, has proved uncommonly enduring. It would be the foolish bettor who wagered on its imminent demise.

CHRONOLOGY

1945	August: United States drops atomic bombs on Hiroshima and Nagasaki. Japan surrenders, ending World War II. President Harry S. Truman terminates lend-lease.
	September–December: British–American negotiations on a U.S. credit for the United Kingdom.
1946	March: Winston Churchill delivers his "iron curtain" speech at Fulton, Mo.
	July: Congress approves the credit to Great Britain.
1947	March: Truman Doctrine speech announces that the United States will take over British responsibilities in Greece and Turkey.
	June: Secretary of State George Marshall proposes a reconstruction plan for the war-torn nations of Europe.
	July: Britain, in accordance with the terms of the American credit, makes sterling freely convertible. The run on the

pound that follows proves ruinous, and within weeks
London has to suspend convertibility.

1948   July:
                U.S. B-29s arrive in Britain at the height of the crisis
                occasioned by the Soviet blockade of Berlin.

1949   April:
                NATO created.

                September:
                Devaluation of the British pound by 30 percent.

1950   June:
                North Korean troops invade South Korea. Within days
                    American troops are sent to South Korea, and the
                    United Nations approves the dispatch of a peace-
                    keeping force to Korea.

                December:
                Prime Minister Clement Attlee meets with Truman in
                    Washington in the wake of reports that the United
                    States is considering using the atomic bomb in Korea.

1952   October:
                Britain tests its first atomic bomb, thereby becoming the
                    third member of the nuclear club.

                November:
                The United States detonates the world's first hydrogen
                    bomb.

1954   Spring:
                Crisis in Indochina, culminating in the fall of the French
                    garrison at Dien Bien Phu. Eisenhower briefly contem-
                    plates U.S. intervention to save the French, but Prime
                    Minister Churchill makes it clear Britain will have no
                    part in any such scheme.

                Fall:
                France vetoes the European Defense Community. British
                    Foreign Minister Anthony Eden then brokers an agree-
                    ment under which West Germany is permitted to rearm
                    and join NATO.

1956   July:
Nasser nationalizes the Suez Canal following an American announcement that the United States is withdrawing its earlier offer to help finance the Aswan Dam project.

29 October:
Israel invades the Sinai. Within days Britain and France have dispatched troops to Egypt as well, diverting world attention from the Soviet Union's brutal suppression of the revolt in Hungary.

6 November:
Britain accepts a cease-fire in Egypt, having failed to topple Nasser or achieve any of its other objectives. Anglo–American relations sink to a postwar low.

1957   March:
Prime Minister Harold Macmillan and President Dwight D. Eisenhower meet in Bermuda to patch up the damage caused by the Suez fiasco. Eisenhower agrees to provide Britain with sixty Thor intermediate-range missiles capable of carrying nuclear warheads.

May:
Britain tests its first hydrogen bomb.

October:
The Soviet Union launches the world's first satellite, which touches off widespread fears in the United States about American strategic vulnerability.

1958   July:
Congress amends the McMahon Act to permit the sharing of nuclear information with the United Kingdom. Wholesale nuclear collaboration follows almost immediately.

1960   February:
Macmillan's "wind of change" speech heralds a new British sensitivity toward the national aspirations of the United Kingdom's African possessions.

March:
Washington agrees to sell the Skybolt air-to-surface missile to Britain. In return, Britain will allow the United States to base its Polaris nuclear submarines at Holy Loch.

May:

Big Four summit in Paris falls apart in aftermath of Soviet downing of an American U-2 reconnaissance plane.

1961   June:

President John F. Kennedy meets with Soviet leader Nikita Khrushchev in Vienna. Badly shaken by Khrushchev's rude intransigence, Kennedy stops off in London on the way home, where Macmillan, playing the avuncular role to the hilt, lays the foundation for what would become a close personal relationship with the young American president.

August:

Macmillan announces that the United Kingdom will seek EEC membership.

1962   October:

Cuban missile crisis.

December:

Skybolt crisis, defused by Kennedy's agreement at Bermuda to sell Britain the submarine-launched Polaris missile.

1963   January:

France's President Charles de Gaulle vetoes British entry into the EEC.

July:

Limited Test Ban Treaty signed by the United States, the United Kingdom, and the Soviet Union, the world's three nuclear weapons states.

November:

Kennedy assassinated. With Macmillan's retirement five weeks earlier, Anglo–American ties enter a period where personal links between presidents and prime ministers are far less intimate, and overall U.S.–U.K. relations far less central to world politics.

1965   February:

President Lyndon Johnson orders continuous bombing of North Vietnam. A month later the United States sends its first combat troops to South Vietnam. As the years pass, the war in Indochina will increasingly draw Washington's interest away from Europe.

1967   February:
               Soviet Premier Alexei Kosygin in London. Prime Minister
                  Harold Wilson attempts to broker a settlement to the
                  conflict in Vietnam, only to be rebuffed by the Ameri-
                  cans.

               July:
               The British announce their intention to withdraw from
                  Singapore and Malaysia.

               November:
               The British pound is devalued by 14.3 percent. De Gaulle
                  for the second time vetoes British entry into the Com-
                  mon Market.

1968   January:
               Britain announces an accelerated withdrawal from east of
                  Suez.

               January–February:
               Tet offensive convinces many Washington officials that
                  the war in Vietnam cannot be won and leads Lyndon
                  Johnson to cap America's escalation and withdraw from
                  the presidential race.

               July:
               Nuclear Non-Proliferation Treaty signed. Hereafter, the
                  conduct of nuclear arms control negotiations will be a
                  bilateral affair between the United States and the So-
                  viet Union.

1970   June:
               The Conservative victory at the polls brings to 10 Down-
                  ing Street the first prime minister since Neville Cham-
                  berlain who deliberately seeks to downplay British–
                  American relations.

1971   July:
               President Richard M. Nixon announces that he plans a
                  trip to China. The absence of any warning to the Brit-
                  ish illustrates the distance that has crept into British–
                  American ties.

               August:
               Nixon surprises the world with a series of controversial
                  economic moves, including an import surcharge and an
                  end to the dollar's convertibility. Once again, Britain is
                  given no advance notice.

1972

December:
Highly controversial American bombing of Hanoi and other North Vietnamese cities. Of all America's allies, only Britain defends the United States.

1973

1 January:
Britain becomes a member of the EEC.

27 January:
Peace accords signed in Paris, bringing American ground combat in Indochina to an end. Later in the year, Congress will mandate an end to the air war as well.

April:
National Security Adviser Henry Kissinger calls for a new Atlantic Charter as part of the Year of Europe.

October:
Yom Kippur War, followed by U.S. nuclear alert and Arab embargo on oil supplies to the West, reveals how deeply split the United States and the United Kingdom have become.

1975

June:
British referendum endorses U.K. membership in the EEC by a 2–1 margin.

1976

July:
Queen Elizabeth makes a wildly successful state visit to the United States as part of the American bicentennial celebration.

1979

November:
U.S. hostages seized in Tehran.

December:
NATO dual-track decision to deploy Pershing II and cruise missiles in Europe while simultaneously seeking substantial reductions in the nuclear forces of both alliances. The Soviet Union invades Afghanistan. Britain and America's other allies refuse to participate in the full range of sanctions President Jimmy Carter wants to wield against Moscow.

1980   July:
Britain, ignoring Carter's call for a boycott, participates in the Summer Olympics in Moscow.

1981   20 January:
Ronald Reagan becomes president. He and Prime Minister Margaret Thatcher begin to reforge the close personal ties that have been lacking in the British–American relationship for almost twenty years.

1982   2 April:
Argentina invades the Falkland Islands. After some indecision, the United States strongly backs the British effort to retake the islands.

14 June:
Argentina surrenders.

1983   23 March:
Reagan calls for the development of a space-based defensive shield that would make nuclear weapons "impotent and obsolete."

October:
American troops invade Grenada, a member of the British Commonwealth.

November:
First cruise missile deployments in Great Britain touch off widespread protests.

1984   December:
Thatcher hosts Soviet heir apparent Mikhail Gorbachev in London, declares the West "can do business" with him. Reagan–Thatcher statement from Camp David affirms that "star wars" defenses would be deployed only after negotiations with Moscow.

1986   Winter–spring:
Westland and British Leyland affairs demonstrate the prevalence of British fears about being swallowed up by huge American multinationals.

April:
British-based U.S. warplanes bomb Libya, prompting an

immense outpouring of anti-American sentiment in the
United Kingdom.

October:
Reagan–Gorbachev summit at Reykjavík ends in failure.
Thatcher then travels to Washington to seek public reas-
surance that the United States has not unilaterally re-
nounced NATO strategic doctrine concerning the importance of nuclear weapons for Western defenses.

1987   June:
The Conservatives win a third straight election, making
Margaret Thatcher the longest-serving British prime
minister in the twentieth century.

December:
Reagan and Gorbachev sign the INF treaty eliminating all
intermediate-range nuclear missiles.

1988   December:
Thatcher returns to Washington as Reagan's last official
visitor, thus ending one of the warmest president–prime
minister relationships in the history of British–
American relations.

NOTES AND REFERENCES

introduction

1. Kenneth Harris, *David Owen* (London: Weidenfeld & Nicolson, 1987), 138–39.

2. Richard H. Ullman, "America, Britain, and the Soviet Threat in Historical and Present Perspective," in William Roger Louis and Hedley Bull, eds., *The "Special Relationship": Anglo-American Relations Since 1945* (Oxford: Clarendon Press, 1986), 103.

3. Ernest R. May and Gregory F. Treverton, "Defence Relationships: American Perspectives," in Louis and Bull, *"Special Relationship,"* 181.

4. *New York Times,* 11 December 1963, 46.

5. D. Cameron Watt, *Succeeding John Bull: America in Britain's Place, 1900–1975* (Cambridge: Cambridge University Press, 1984), 3.

chapter 1

1. Quoted in H. G. Nicholas, *The United States and Britain* (Chicago: University of Chicago Press, 1975), 9.

2. Ibid., 74.

3. Winston S. Churchill, *Their Finest Hour,* vol. 2 of *The Second World War* (Boston: Houghton Mifflin, 1949), 409.

4. Quoted in Christopher Thorne, *Allies of a Kind: The United States, Britain, and the War against Japan, 1941–1945* (New York: Oxford University Press, 1978), 453.

5. H. C. Allen, "Anti-Americanism in Britain," *Contemporary Review* 200 (December 1961): 625.

6. Minute by J. C. Donnelly, 7 November 1944, AN 4213/20/45, F.O. 371, Public Record Office, Kew.

chapter 2

1. Quoted in *The* (London) *Times*, 2 July 1945, 3.

2. "The Effect of Our External Financial Position on Our Foreign Policy," September 1944, UE 615/169/53, F.O. 371.

3. Winston S. Churchill, *Triumph and Tragedy*, vol. 6 of *The Second World War* (Boston: Houghton Mifflin, 1953), 429.

4. *Vital Speeches of the Day* 12 (15 March 1946): 329–32.

5. Henry Norweb to H. Freeman Matthews, 7 February 1946, 711.41/2-746, RG 59, State Department Records, National Archives, Washington, D.C.

6. Halifax to Bevin, 12 December 1945, AN 3853/35/45, F.O. 371.

7. W. Averell Harriman and Elie Abel, *Special Envoy* (New York: Random House, 1975), 509.

8. Halifax to Bevin, 12 December 1945, AN 3853/35/45, F.O. 371.

9. Keynes to Walter Lippmann, 29 January 1946, Walter Lippmann Papers, Yale University, New Haven, Conn.

10. Quoted in Caroline Anstey, "The Projection of British Socialism: Foreign Office Publicity and American Opinion, 1945–50," *Journal of Contemporary History* 19 (July 1984): 436.

11. Quoted in Daniel Yergin, *Shattered Peace: The Origins of the Cold War and the National Security State* (Boston: Houghton Mifflin, 1977), 445.

12. Quoted in Alistair Horne, "The Macmillan Years and Afterwards," in Louis and Bull, *"Special Relationship,"* 88.

13. *Economist*, 23 February 1946, 282.

14. *New York Times*, 31 May 1946, 8.

15. Nicholas, *The United States and Britain*, 130.

16. U.S. Department of State, *Foreign Relations of the United States* [hereafter cited as *FRUS*], 1945, vol. 2 (Washington, D.C.: U.S. Government Printing Office, 1967), 48.

17. *FRUS: The Conference at Quebec, 1944* (1972), 493.

18. Harry S. Truman, *Year of Decisions*, vol. 1 of *Memoirs* (Garden City, N.Y.: Doubleday, 1955), 539.

19. Francis Williams, *Twilight of Empire: Memoirs of Prime Minister Clement Attlee* (New York: Barnes, 1962), 118.

20. *New York Times*, 30 May 1948, p. E5.

21. *FRUS, 1947* (1972), 3:269.

22. Hugh Dalton, *High Tide and After: Memoirs, 1945–1960* (London: Frederick Muller, 1962), 74–75.

23. Minute by J. C. Donnelly, 23 October 1945, AN 3224/4/45, F.O. 371.

24. Halifax to Eden, 3 December 1945, Halifax Papers, Churchill College, Cambridge.

25. Keynes to Dalton, 1 October 1945, Keynes Papers, Treasury Records 247, Public Record Office, Kew.

26. This paragraph draws heavily from Anstey, "The Projection of British Socialism."

27. Quoted in Victor Rothwell, *Britain and the Cold War, 1941–1947* (London: Jonathan Cape, 1982), 284.

28. Alastair Buchan, "Mothers and Daughters (or Greeks and Romans)," *Foreign Affairs* 54 (July 1976):659.

29. *Vital Speeches of the Day* 14 (1 February 1948):226–34.

30. *New York Times*, 16 September 1948, 18.

31. Ibid.

32. Aneurin Bevan, "Britain and America at Loggerheads," *Foreign Affairs* 36 (October 1957): 63.

33. *FRUS, 1948* (1974), 3:1113.

34. George H. Gallup, ed., *The Gallup International Public Opinion Polls: Great Britain, 1937–1975*, vol. 1 (New York: Random House, 1976), 161, 179, 226.

35. Quoted in Leon D. Epstein, *Britain—Uneasy Ally* (Chicago: University of Chicago Press, 1954), 24.

36. Anthony Adamthwaite, "Britain and the World, 1945–9: The View from the Foreign Office," *International Affairs* 61 (Spring 1985):231.

37. *FRUS, 1950* (1977), 3:855.

38. Ibid., 869–81 and passim.

39. Ibid., 875.

40. Ibid.; *FRUS, 1950* (1980), 4:591–92.

41. *FRUS, 1950*,3:875, 878, 880.

42. Acheson interview, Memoirs File, Post-Presidential Files, Truman Papers, Independence, Mo.

43. Alan Bullock, *Ernest Bevin: Foreign Secretary, 1945–1951* (London: Heinemann, 1983), 88.

chapter 3

1. *Public Papers of the Presidents, 1950* (Washington, D.C.: U.S. Government Printing Office, 1965), 727.

2. This is an argument persuasively advanced by Rosemary Foot in "Anglo–American Relations in the Korean Crisis: The British Effort to Avert an Expanded War, December 1950–January 1951," *Diplomatic History* 10 (Winter 1986).

3. Attlee to Bevin, 10 December 1950, AU 1053/19, F.O. 371.

4. Robert H. Ferrell, ed., *Off the Record: The Private Papers of Harry S. Truman* (New York: Harper & Row, 1980), 203.

5. Quoted in Foot, "Anglo–American Relations in the Korean Crisis," 53.

6. William Roger Louis, "American Anti-Colonialism and the Dissolution of the British Empire," in Louis and Bull, *"Special Relationship,"* 278.

7. See J. William Fulbright to R. B. McCallum, 21 March 1957, BCN 105, F54, J. William Fulbright Papers, Fayetteville, Ark.

8. Richard Goold-Adams, *John Foster Dulles: A Reappraisal* (New York: Appleton-Century-Crofts, 1962), 298.

9. Quoted in Alfred Grosser, *The Western Alliance: European–American Relations since 1945* (New York: Vintage, 1982), 121.

10. Duncan Campbell, *The Unsinkable Aircraft Carrier: American Military Power in Britain* (London: Michael Joseph Ltd., 1984), 118.

11. David Reynolds, "A 'Special Relationship'?: America, Britain and the Inter-

national Order since the Second World War," *International Affairs* 62 (Winter 1985/86): 11.

12. House of Commons, *Parliamentary Debates*, 5th series, 537 (2 March 1955): 2182.

13. Ibid., 568 (1 April 1957): 71.

14. *FRUS, 1952–54* (1983), 5:1721.

15. Quoted in Henry Brandon, *The Retreat of American Power* (Garden City, N.Y.: Doubleday, 1973), 159–60.

16. William E. Leuchtenburg et al., *Britain and the United States: Four Views to Mark the Silver Jubilee* (London: Heinemann, 1979), 67, his italics.

17. Robert H. Ferrell, ed., *The Diary of James C. Hagerty: Eisenhower in Mid-Course, 1954–1955* (Bloomington: Indiana University Press, 1983), 75.

18. Lord Harlech, "Suez SNAFU, Skybolt SABU," *Foreign Policy* 2 (Spring 1971): 39.

19. Anthony Eden, *Full Circle: The Memoirs of Anthony Eden* (Boston: Houghton Mifflin, 1960), 512.

20. Unsigned, undated minute [ca. 23 November 1956], AU 1057/2, F.O. 371.

21. *Public Papers of the Presidents, 1956* (1958), 720.

22. On this point consult F. S. Northedge, *Descent from Power: British Foreign Policy, 1945–1973* (London: George Allen & Unwin, 1974), 136.

23. Emmet John Hughes, *The Ordeal of Power: A Political Memoir of the Eisenhower Years* (New York: Atheneum, 1963), 217.

24. Quoted in Louis, "American Anti-Colonialism and the Dissolution of the British Empire," 277.

25. Eden, *Full Circle*, 628.

26. Quoted in Stephen E. Ambrose, *Eisenhower: The President* (New York: Simon & Schuster, 1984), 373.

chapter 4

1. Bruce to Secretary of State, 13 December 1961, National Security Files, John F. Kennedy Papers, John F. Kennedy Library, Boston.

2. Dwight D. Eisenhower, *Waging Peace, 1956–1961*, vol. 2 of *The White House Years* (Garden City, N.Y.: Doubleday, 1965), 124.

3. *FRUS, 1955–1957* (1986), 4:610.

4. Quoted in H. A. DeWeerd, "British Defense Policy: An American View," 3 August 1961, P-2390, Harvey A. DeWeerd Papers, George Marshall Library, Lexington, Va.

5. Marquess of Salisbury, "Anglo–American Shibboleths," *Foreign Affairs* 36 (April 1958): 401, 407.

6. Allen, "Anti-Americanism in Britain," 625.

7. *FRUS, 1955–1957*, 4:615.

8. Ferrell, *The Diary of James C. Hagerty*, 35.

9. Ibid., 66.

10. H. C. Allen, "The Anglo-American Relationship in the Sixties," *International Affairs* 39 (January 1963):41.

11. *Executive Sessions of the Senate Foreign Relations Committee*, Historical Series, vol. 13, part 1 (Washington, D.C.: U.S. Government Printing Office, 1984), 25.

12. Allen, "Anti-Americanism in Britain," 629.

13. Gorer quoted in "Six Britons Debate Anti-Americanism," *New York Times Magazine*, 22 July 1962, 57.

14. Northedge, *Descent from Power*, 348

15. David Nunnerley, *President Kennedy and Britain* (New York: St. Martin's, 1972), 35.

16. *Economist*, 5 May 1962, 7.

17. Horne, "The Macmillan Years and Afterwards," 92.

18. George Ball memorandum for the president, 7 August 1961, National Security Files, Kennedy Papers.

19. Memorandum of George W. Ball recording conversation with Walter Hallstein, 8 December 1962, National Security Files, Kennedy Papers.

20. Diaries of David K. E. Bruce, 3, 9 August 1961, Virginia Historical Society, Richmond, Va.

21. George Ball memorandum for the president, 10 December 1962, National Security Files, Kennedy Papers.

22. *Vital Speeches of the Day* 28 (1 August 1962):628.

23. "European Strategy Discussion with Mr. Peter Thorneycroft," memorandum of conversation, 13 September 1962, National Security Files, Kennedy Papers.

24. Sir H. Caccia to Foreign Office, 1 January 1957, AU 1051/2B, F.O. 371.

25. *The* (London) *Times*, 24 February 1958, 3.

26. Henry Brandon, "Skybolt," (London) *Sunday Times*, 8 December 1963, 31.

27. Horne, "The Macmillan Years and Afterwards," 96.

28. Brandon, "Skybolt," 31.

29. Arthur M. Schlesinger, Jr., *A Thousand Days: John F. Kennedy in the White House* (New York: Fawcett, 1965), 790.

30. Nunnerley, *Kennedy and Britain*, 155.

31. Harold Macmillan, *At the End of the Day, 1961–1963* (London: Macmillan, 1973), 358.

32. George W. Ball, *The Discipline of Power: Essentials of a Modern World Structure* (London: Bodley Head, 1968), 102.

33. Richard E. Neustadt, *Alliance Politics* (New York: Columbia University Press, 1970), passim.

34. (London) *Sunday Times*, 23 December 1962, 3.

35. On this see Northedge, *Descent from Power*, 287.

36. Nunnerley, *Kennedy and Britain*, 79.

37. Ibid., 75.

38. Ibid., 76.

39. *New York Times*, 11 December 1963, 46.

40. Bruce to secretary of state, 1 December 1963, filed with Bruce Diaries.

41. (London) *Sunday Times*, 24 November 1963, 14.

42. Nunnerley, *Kennedy and Britain*, 231.

43. *New York Times*, 30 March 1963, 6.

44. (London) *Sunday Times*, 24 November 1963, 14.

chapter 5

1. *Vital Speeches of the Day* 29 (1 January 1963): 162–66.

2. *Yorkshire Post* quoted in American Embassy (hereafter cited as Amembassy), London, to White House, 8 December 1962, box 170A, National Security Files, Kennedy Papers.

3. The (London) *Times,* 7 December 1962, 12.

4. Macmillan statement in Bruce to secretary of state, no. 2140, 7 December 1962, box 170A, National Security Files, Kennedy Papers.

5. White House to secretary of state, 7 December 1962, box 170A, National Security Files, Kennedy Papers.

6. Secretary of state to the White House, 8 December 1962, National Security Files, Kennedy Papers.

7. Walter Heller memorandum for the president, 9 November 1964, EX CO 305, box 75, White House Central Files, Lyndon Baines Johnson Library (hereafter cited as LBJL), Austin, Texas.

8. *New York Times,* 27 March 1963, 6.

9. David K. E. Bruce oral history, LBJL.

10. Author's interview with Walt Rostow, 8 January 1988.

11. ONE staff memorandum no. 26–65, "Britain's Economy and Its Implications," 25 June 1965, country file: United Kingdom, National Security Files, LBJL.

12. Fowler memorandum for the president, 14 July 1966, National Security Files, LBJL.

13. Draft memorandum for the president, 1 June 1965, attached to D. K. memorandum to McGB, 1 June 1965, folder: Trendex, National Security Files, LBJL.

14. Harold Wilson, *A Personal Record: The Labour Government, 1964–1970* (Boston: Little, Brown, 1971), 6.

15. James Callaghan, *Time and Chance* (London: Collins, 1987), 159.

16. George Ball, "British Sterling Crisis," 6 August 1965, country file: United Kingdom, National Security Files, LBJL.

17. Francis M. Bator memorandum for the president, 1 June 1967, folder: Visit of PM Harold Wilson, 6/2/67, National Security Files, LBJL.

18. Bundy memorandum for the president, 28 July 1965, folder: Trendex, National Security Files, LBJL.

19. "British Sterling Crisis," 6 August 1965, National Security Files, LBJL.

20. Quoted in Northedge, *Descent from Power,* 297.

21. Amembassy, London, to Department of State, no. A-2843, 23 May 1966, country file: United Kingdom, National Security Files, LBJL.

22. Ball memorandum for the president, 22 July 1966, National Security Files, LBJL.

23. Lyndon Baines Johnson, *The Vantage Point: Perspectives of the Presidency, 1963–1969* (New York: Holt, Rinehart & Winston, 1971), 315.

24. *New York Times,* 21 July 1967, 30.

25. Ball memorandum for the president, 22 July 1966, country file: United Kingdom, National Security Files, LBJL.

26. Memorandum of conversation, 10 May [1966], attached to letter, Henry Owen to Walt Rostow, 1 June 1966, National Security Files, LBJL.

27. Ball memorandum for the president, 22 July 1966, National Security Files, LBJL.

28. Bruce to secretary of state, no. 9217, 8 May 1967, National Security Files, LBJL.

29. Letter, Bundy to Sir Burke Trend, 3 November 1965, National Security Files, LBJL.

30. Amembassy, London, to Department of State, no. A-2843, 23 May 1966, National Security files, LBJL.

31. Ibid.

32. *New York Times*, 14 May 1967, E3.

33. Herb Gunn, "The Continuing Friendship of James William Fulbright and Ronald Buchanan McCallum," *South Atlantic Quarterly*, 83 (Autumn 1984): 429.

34. *The* (London) *Times*, 6 August 1964, 8, 9.

35. John P. Roche memorandum for the president, 10 January 1967, EX CO 305, box 76, White House Central Files, LBJL (polling data may be found in Leonard H. Marks memorandum for the president, 19 June 1967, EX CO 305).

36. Nunnerley, *President Kennedy and Britain*, 227.

37. Wilson, *A Personal Record*, 80.

38. Bundy memorandum for the president, 28 July 1965, folder: Trendex, country file: United Kingdom, National Security Files, LBJL.

39. Quoted in Nunnerley, *President Kennedy and Britain*, 227.

40. Rostow memorandum for the president, 28 July 1966, folder: PM Wilson Visit Briefing Book, 7/29/66, country file: United Kingdom, National Security Files, LBJL.

41. Worsthorne article discussed in Rostow memorandum for the president, 12 June 1968, EX FO 6-3, box 63, White House Central Files, LBJL.

42. *The* (London) *Times*, 16 February 1968, 11.

43. Wilson, *A Personal Record*, 206.

44. Richard Crossman, *The Diaries of a Cabinet Minister*, vol. 3 (New York: Holt, Rinehart & Winston, 1977), 236.

45. Johnson, *The Vantage Point*, 255.

46. W. W. Rostow, "The Anglo-American Situation," *The American Oxonian* 56 (July 1969): 105.

47. Henry Kissinger, *White House Years* (Boston: Little, Brown, 1979), 90–91.

48. Henry A. Kissinger, "Reflections on a Partnership: British and American Attitudes to Postwar Foreign Policy," *International Affairs* 58 (Autumn 1982): 577.

49. *New York Times*, 9 December 1969, 17.

50. Kissinger, *White House Years*, 933, italics in original.

51. Henry Kissinger, *Years of Upheaval* (Boston: Little, Brown, 1982), 140–43.

52. Ibid., 141.

53. Kissinger, *White House Years*, 938.

54. Kissinger, *Years of Upheaval*, 516.

55. Ibid., 281–82; Kissinger, "Reflections on a Partnership," 577.

56. Wilson, *A Personal Record*, 689.

57. Kissinger, *White House Years*, 964.

58. Brandon, *The Retreat of American Power*, 166–67.

59. *New York Times*, 24 December 1971, 24.

60. Nunnerley, *President Kennedy and Britain*, 2.

chapter 6

1. *The* (London) *Times,* 25 April 1973, 19.
2. *New York Times,* 14 January 1973, E17.
3. Ibid., 22 May 1971, 3.
4. Kissinger, *Years of Upheaval,* 137.
5. *Vital Speeches of the Day* 39 (15 May 1973): 452–55.
6. Leuchtenburg, *Britain and the United States,* 54.
7. *Wall Street Journal,* 1 February 1973, 20.
8. (London) *Sunday Times,* 29 April 1973, 16.
9. *The* (London) *Times,* 1 November 1973, 18.
10. Ibid., 10 December 1973, 16
11. Kissinger, *Years of Upheaval,* 711.
12. Ibid., 713.
13. Ibid., 711, 721.
14. Leuchtenburg, *Britain and the United States,* 74.
15. Kissinger, *Years of Upheaval,* 720.
16. *Economist,* 16 March 1974, 43.
17. *Public Papers of the Presidents, 1974* (1975), 276.
18. *Economist,* 23 March 1974, 12–13.
19. Kissinger, *Years of Upheaval,* 721.
20. Ibid., 933.
21. *The* (London) *Times,* 22 October 1973, 14.
22. Callaghan, *Time and Chance,* 339ff.
23. *Wall Street Journal,* 20 August 1975, 14.
24. *Washington Post,* 19 June 1975, A18.
25. Alan Greenspan memorandum for the president, 23 April 1975, CO 160, box 56, White House Central Files, Gerald R. Ford Library, Ann Arbor, Mich.
26. Quoted in Dennis Kavanagh, *Thatcherism and British Politics: The End of Consensus?* (Oxford: Oxford University Press, 1987), 1.
27. Scowcroft memorandum for Alan Greenspan, 24 February 1976, CO 160, box 57, White House Central Files, Ford Library (emphasis in original).
28. Letter, George Meany to the president, 30 September 1976, folder: CO 160 10/1/76–11/30/76, White House Central Files, Ford Library.
29. *Time,* 24 May 1976, 29.
30. Eric Sevareid comment for CBS, "Backlash Building in Britain," 6 May 1975, folder: 7.49 Great Britain (1), box 24, Charles H. McCall Files, Ford Library.
31. United Kingdom, Central Policy Review Staff, *Review of Overseas Representation* (London: Her Majesty's Stationery Office, 1977), 9.
32. Ibid., 111.
33. Ibid., ix, 10.
34. Ibid., 8, 10.
35. United Kingdom, House of Commons, Defence and External Affairs Sub-Committee, *Fourth Report from the Expenditure Committee,* House of Commons Paper 286-I (1978), xxv.
36. Ibid., cxxv.
37. Ibid.
38. Ibid., xxiv.

39. *Washington Post*, 19 October 1976, A12.

40. *New York Times*, 29 May 1976, 2.

41. *Time*, 24 May 1976, 29.

42. Buchan, "Mothers and Daughters (or Greeks and Romans)," 669.

43. *New York Times*, 7 July 1976, 1.

44. Zbigniew Brzezinski, *Power and Principle: Memoirs of the National Security Adviser, 1977–1981* (New York: Farrar, Straus & Giroux, 1983), 291.

45. Cyrus Vance, *Hard Choices: Critical Years in America's Foreign Policy* (New York: Simon & Schuster, 1983), 445–46.

46. Harris, *David Owen*, 135.

47. Ibid., 138.

48. House of Commons, *Fourth Report from the Expenditure Committee*, xxv.

49. Brzezinski, *Power and Principle*, 141.

50. *Economist*, 11 June 1988, 56.

51. *The* (London) *Times*, 1 May 1980, 2.

52. Both assessments are in Coral Bell, *President Carter and Foreign Policy: The Costs of Virtue?* (Canberra: Australian National University, 1980), 81.

53. Harold Brown, *Thinking About National Security: Defense and Foreign Policy in a Dangerous World* (Boulder, Colo.: Westview, 1983).

chapter 7

1. Quoted in the *New York Times*, 2 June 1988, A9.

2. *Economist*, 11 June 1988, 55.

3. Ibid., 1 June 1985, 3.

4. Geoffrey Smith, "The British Scene," *Foreign Affairs* 64 (Summer 1986): 924.

5. *The* (London) *Times*, 6 November 1980, 10.

6. Ibid., 1 May 1980, 2.

7. *Economist*, 11 June 1988, 55.

8. *Washington Post*, 8 June 1987, A2.

9. Ibid., 21 December 1984, A23.

10. *New York Times*, 2 June 1988, A9.

11. Quoted in the *Economist*, 11 June 1988, 55.

12. *New York Times*, 2 June 1988, A9.

13. Martin Holmes et al., *British Security Policy and the Atlantic Alliance: Prospects for the 1990s* (Washington, D.C.: Pergamon-Brassey's, 1987), 115.

14. Jonathan Dean, *Watershed in Europe: Dismantling the East-West Military Confrontation* (Lexington, Mass.: D.C. Heath, 1987), 14.

15. *Washington Post*, 29 May 1987, A27.

16. *Wall Street Journal*, 24 November 1986, 34.

17. *Washington Post*, 29 May 1987, A27.

18. Ibid., 8 December 1987, A30.

19. Ibid., 3 January 1988, B1.

20. Alexander M. Haig, Jr., *Caveat: Realism, Reagan, and Foreign Policy* (New York: Macmillan, 1984), 266.

21. Quoted in the *Economist*, 11 June 1988, 56.

22. Ibid., 3 March 1984, 29–30.

23. Haig, *Caveat*, 276.

24. Ibid., 267.

25. Quoted in the *Economist*, 11 June 1988, 56.

26. Quoted in the *New York Times*, 2 June 1988, A9.

27. *The* (London) *Times*, 20 July 1987, 11.

28. Whitelaw quoted in the *Washington Post*, 3 January 1988, B4.

29. Ibid., 2 March 1988, 2.

30. *Dallas Times Herald*, 7 January 1988, A10.

31. *New York Times*, 2 June 1988, A9.

32. *Washington Post*, 3 January 1988, B1.

33. Michael Elliott, "Sammy and Rosie Get Paid," *New Republic*, 15 February 1988, 18.

34. (London) *Sunday Times*, 23 February 1986, 31.

35. *Public Opinion* 9 (February–March 1986).

36. Quoted in Holmes, *British Security Policy and the Atlantic Alliance*, 88.

37. Quoted in the *Wall Street Journal*, 4 March 1986, 15.

38. *Economist*, 16 April 1988, 70.

39. Quoted in the *Washington Post*, 29 September 1986, A1.

40. Quoted in Campbell, *The Unsinkable Aircraft Carrier*, 94.

41. Quoted in the *Washington Post*, 22 December 1987, A16.

42. All figures from U.S. Department of Defense, found in the *New York Times*, 20 May 1988, A14.

43. *Economist*, 3 March 1984, 29.

44. Quoted in David Dimbleby and David Reynolds, *An Ocean Apart: The Relationship Between Britain and America in the Twentieth Century* (New York: Random House, 1988), 335–36.

45. On these points, see May and Treverton, "Defence Relationships," 169–73.

46. David Watt, "Introduction: The Anglo–American Relationship," in Louis and Bull, "*Special Relationship*," 14.

47. Kissinger, "Reflections on a Partnership," 585.

48. James Callaghan quoted Burke in the *New York Times*, 27 May 1976, 8.

BIBLIOGRAPHIC ESSAY

There is no better place to begin exploring British–American relations than H. C. Allen, *Great Britain and the United States* (London: Odhams Press, 1954). While thirty-five years old, Allen's volume remains indispensable for anyone interested in the underlying forces shaping Anglo–American ties. From Allen one should then proceed to two more recent studies. The scope of David Dimbleby and David Reynolds's *An Ocean Apart: The Relationship between Britain and America in the Twentieth Century* (New York: Random House, 1988) is indicated by its subtitle. Reflecting its authors' British backgrounds, the volume draws extensively on interviews with prominent British and American officials originally conducted for the BBC television series of the same name. For the post–World War II period, these two volumes should be supplemented by William Roger Louis and Hedley Bull, eds., *The "Special Relationship": Anglo-American Relations since 1945* (Oxford: Oxford University Press, 1986), an immensely useful compilation of recent scholarship by historians, journalists, and practitioners of British–American diplomacy.

As is the case with virtually any topic in American diplomatic history since 1861, the annual volumes of *Foreign Relations of the United States*, the State Department's documentary series, contain a wealth of information on Anglo–American relations. Other helpful studies of the British–American relationship include A. C. Turner, *The Unique Partnership: Britain and the United States* (New York: Pegasus, 1971); D. Cameron Watt, *Succeeding John Bull: America in Britain's Place, 1900–1975* (Cambridge: Cambridge University Press, 1984), which laments the results of the transfer of power from the United Kingdom to the United States over the past seventy-five years; Kenneth N. Waltz, *Foreign Policy and Democratic Politics: The American and British*

Experience (Boston: Little, Brown, 1967); H. G. Nicholas, *The United States and Britain* (Chicago: University of Chicago Press, 1975); Bruce M. Russett, *Community and Contention: Britain and America in the Twentieth Century* (Cambridge, Mass.: MIT Press, 1963); and Alastair Buchan, "Mothers and Daughters (or Greeks and Romans)," *Foreign Affairs* 54 (July 1976): 645–69. Allan Nevins, ed., *America through British Eyes* (New York: Oxford University Press, 1948), illustrates the ambivalence with which the British viewed their American offspring even in the years before the United States replaced Great Britain as the world's preeminent power. Nevins should be read in conjunction with Henry Steele Commager, ed., *Britain through American Eyes* (New York: McGraw-Hill, 1974). Daniel Snowman, *Britain and America: An Interpretation of Their Culture, 1945–1975* (New York: Harper & Row, 1977), is a comparative social and cultural study.

There are several valuable studies of British–American ties during the early years of the new republic, including Samuel F. Bemis, *Jay's Treaty: A Study in Commerce and Diplomacy* (New York: Macmillan, 1923); Alfred L. Burt, *The United States, Great Britain, and British North America from the Revolution to the Establishment of Peace after the War of 1812* (New Haven: Yale University Press, 1940); Bradford Perkins, *The First Rapprochement: England and the United States, 1795–1805* (Philadelphia: University of Pennsylvania Press, 1955); Bradford Perkins, *Prologue to War: England and the United States, 1805–1812* (Berkeley: University of California Press, 1961); and Reginald Horsman, *The Causes of the War of 1812* (Philadelphia: University of Pennsylvania Press, 1962).

For the nineteenth century, see Charles S. Campbell, *From Revolution to Rapprochement: The United States and Great Britain, 1783–1900* (New York: Wiley, 1974), a brief but very useful overview; Kenneth Bourne, *Britain and the Balance of Power in North America, 1815–1908* (Berkeley: University of California Press, 1967); Frank Thistlethwaite, *The Anglo–American Connection in the Early Nineteenth Century* (Philadelphia: University of Pennsylvania Press, 1959); Bradford Perkins, *Castlereagh and Adams: England and the United States, 1812–1823* (Berkeley: University of California Press, 1964); J. Fred Rippy, *Rivalry of the United States and Great Britain over Latin America, 1808–1830* (Baltimore: Johns Hopkins University Press, 1929); Dexter Perkins, *The Monroe Doctrine, 1823–1826* (Cambridge: Harvard University Press, 1927); Wilbur D. Jones, *The American Problem in British Diplomacy, 1841–1861* (Athens: University of Georgia Press, 1974); Frank L. Owsley, *King Cotton Diplomacy: Foreign Relations of the Confederate States of America*, 2nd ed. (Chicago: University of Chicago Press, 1959); and Adrian Cook, *The Alabama Claims, American Politics and Anglo–American Relations, 1865–1872* (Ithaca, N.Y.: Cornell University Press, 1975).

For the emergence of America as a world power, one should see Alexander E. Campbell, *Great Britain and the United States, 1895–1903* (London: Longmans, 1960); Charles S. Campbell, *Anglo–American Understanding, 1898–*

1903 (Baltimore: Johns Hopkins University Press, 1957); Bradford Perkins, *The Great Rapprochement: England and the United States, 1895–1914* (New York: Atheneum, 1968); and Ernest R. May, *American Imperialism: A Speculative Essay* (New York: Atheneum, 1968). George Monger, *The End of Isolation: British Foreign Policy 1900–1907* (London: Nelson, 1963), contains useful material on British–American relations in the Far East. The extent of the Anglo–American rapprochement at the turn of the century can only be understood by appreciating the rampant Anglophobia felt by many Americans of the period. On this, consult Edward Crapol, *America for Americans: Economic Nationalism and Anglophobia in the Late Nineteenth Century* (Westport, Conn.: Greenwood Press, 1973).

Helpful studies of the World War I period include Patrick Devlin, *Too Proud to Fight: Woodrow Wilson's Neutrality* (New York: Oxford University Press, 1975); Ernest R. May, *The World War and American Isolation, 1914–1917* (Cambridge: Harvard University Press, 1959); Kathleen Burk, *Britain, America and the Sinews of War, 1914–1918* (London: George Allen & Unwin, 1985); Wilton B. Fowler, *British–American Relations, 1917–1918: The Role of Sir William Wiseman* (Princeton: Princeton University Press, 1969); Seth P. Tillman, *Anglo–American Relations at the Paris Peace Conference of 1919* (Princeton: Princeton University Press, 1961); and Lloyd C. Gardner, *Safe for Democracy: The Anglo–American Response to Revolution, 1913–1923* (New York: Oxford University Press, 1984).

For the years between this century's two global wars, see Michael J. Hogan, *Informal Entente: The Private Structure of Cooperation in Anglo–American Economic Diplomacy, 1918–1928* (Columbia: University of Missouri Press, 1977); Roger Dingman, *Power in the Pacific: The Origins of Naval Arms Limitation, 1914–1922* (Chicago: University of Chicago Press, 1976); Christopher Hall, *Britain, America, and Arms Control, 1921–37* (New York: St. Martin's, 1987); Robert Dallek, *Franklin D. Roosevelt and American Foreign Policy, 1932–1945* (New York: Oxford University Press, 1979), the standard account of FDR's diplomacy; David Reynolds, *The Creation of the Anglo–American Alliance, 1937–41: A Study in Competitive Co-operation* (Chapel Hill: University of North Carolina Press, 1982), a splendid monograph; Ritchie Ovendale, *"Appeasement" and the English Speaking World: Britain, the United States, the Dominions, and the Policy of "Appeasement," 1937–1939* (Cardiff: University of Wales Press, 1975); C. A. MacDonald, *The United States, Britain, and Appeasement, 1936–1939* (New York: St. Martin's, 1981); and James R. Leutze, *Bargaining for Supremacy: Anglo–American Naval Collaboration, 1937–1941* (Chapel Hill: University of North Carolina Press, 1977).

There now exists a wealth of solid studies on the Anglo–American connection during World War II. One would have to start with Winston Churchill's magisterial six-volume history entitled *The Second World War* (Boston: Houghton Mifflin, 1948–53). Three older studies that have retained their usefulness are William H. McNeill, *America, Britain, and Russia: Their Cooperation and*

Conflict, 1941–1946 (London: Oxford University Press, 1953); Sir Llewellyn Woodward, *British Foreign Policy in the Second World War* (London: Her Majesty's Stationery Office, 1962); and Herbert Feis, *Churchill—Roosevelt—Stalin: The War They Waged and the Peace They Sought* (Princeton: Princeton University Press, 1957). In addition to Dallek's biography of Franklin Roosevelt mentioned earlier, one should see James MacGregor Burns, *Roosevelt: The Soldier of Freedom* (New York: Harcourt Brace Jovanovich, 1970). For Churchill, Martin Gilbert's *Road to Victory: Winston S. Churchill, 1941–1945* (New York: Houghton Mifflin, 1986) is likely to remain the definitive work for many years to come. The extraordinary personal relationship between Roosevelt and Churchill can be explored in Warren F. Kimball, ed., *Churchill and Roosevelt: The Complete Correspondence,* 3 vols. (Princeton: Princeton University Press, 1984). Other helpful studies include Theodore A. Wilson, *The First Summit* (Boston: Houghton Mifflin, 1969), on the 1941 Placentia Bay meeting; Joseph P. Lash, *Roosevelt and Churchill, 1939–1941: The Partnership that Saved the West* (New York: Norton, 1976), which examines the genesis of the personal relationship between FDR and Churchill; Warren F. Kimball, *The Most Unsordid Act: Lend-Lease, 1939–1941* (Baltimore: Johns Hopkins University Press, 1969), on the origins of lend-lease; Alan P. Dobson, *US Wartime Aid to Britain, 1940–1946* (New York: St. Martin's, 1986), on lend-lease; Margaret Gowing, *Britain and Atomic Energy, 1939–1945* (New York: St. Martin's, 1964), on the wartime Anglo–American nuclear collaboration; Richard G. Hewlett and Oscar E. Anderson, Jr., *A History of the United States Atomic Energy Commission,* vol. 1: *The New World, 1939/1946* (University Park: Pennsylvania State University Press, 1962); Robert Beitzell, *The Uneasy Alliance: America, Britain, and Russia, 1941–1943* (New York: Knopf, 1972); Herbert Feis, *Between War and Peace: The Potsdam Conference* (Princeton: Princeton University Press, 1960); Christopher Thorne, *Allies of a Kind: The United States, Britain, and the War against Japan, 1941–1945* (New York: Oxford University Press, 1978); and William Roger Louis, *Imperialism at Bay: The United States and the Decolonization of the British Empire, 1941–1945* (New York: Oxford University Press, 1978).

General studies of British–American ties since World War II, in addition to the valuable Louis and Bull compilation mentioned earlier, include Coral Bell, *The Debatable Alliance: An Essay in Anglo–American Relations* (London: Oxford University Press, 1964); chapter 10 of Henry Brandon, *The Retreat of American Power* (Garden City, N.Y.: Doubleday, 1973); Alan P. Dobson, *The Politics of the Anglo–American Economic Special Relationship, 1940–1987* (New York: St. Martin's, 1988), which despite its title explores the economic side of the special relationship only up to 1967; Lionel M. Gelber, *America in Britain's Place: The Leadership of the West and Anglo–American Unity* (New York: Praeger, 1961); and David Reynolds, "A 'special relationship'?: America, Britain and the International Order since the Second World War," *International Affairs* 62 (Winter 1985–86): 1–20. F. S. Northedge, *Descent from*

Power: British Foreign Policy, 1945–1973 (London: George Allen & Unwin, 1974), provides an overview of British foreign policy in the postwar period. C. J. Bartlett, *The Long Retreat: A Short History of British Defence Policy, 1945–70* (London: Macmillan, 1972), offers a useful summary and should be used in conjunction with John Baylis, *Anglo–American Defence Relations, 1939–1984*, 2nd ed. (London: Macmillan, 1984). R. N. Rosecrance, *Defense of the Realm: British Strategy in the Nuclear Epoch* (New York: Columbia University Press, 1968), is especially good on British defense planning in the decade after Hiroshima. Andrew J. Pierre, *Nuclear Politics: The British Experience with an Independent Strategic Force, 1939–1970* (London: Oxford University Press, 1972), is very helpful on British–American cooperation and conflict. Timothy J. Botti, *The Long Wait: The Forging of the Anglo–American Nuclear Alliance, 1945–1958* (New York: Greenwood, 1987), offers a detailed look at the process by which Britain and the United States forged their nuclear partnership. Margaret Gowing, *Independence and Deterrence: Britain and Atomic Energy, 1945–1952*, 2 vols. (New York: St. Martin's, 1974), covers much the same ground. Lawrence S. Kaplan, *NATO and the United States: The Enduring Alliance* (Boston: Twayne, 1988), places Anglo–American ties into their larger context. Duncan Campbell, *The Unsinkable Aircraft Carrier: American Military Power in Britain* (London: Michael Joseph Ltd., 1984), while colored by its skepticism about the value of British–American military ties, offers a wealth of detail about the defense, nuclear, and intelligence links between Britain and the United States. The ties between the intelligence communities of the two nations can also be explored in Jeffrey T. Richelson and Desmond Ball, *The Ties That Bind: Intelligence Cooperation between the UKUSA Countries* (Boston: Allen & Unwin, 1985).

A vast number of studies have sought to explain the origins of the cold war. Among the most helpful are John Lewis Gaddis, *The United States and the Origins of the Cold War* (New York: Columbia University Press, 1972); Thomas G. Paterson, *On Every Front: The Making of the Cold War* (New York: Norton, 1979); Daniel Yergin, *Shattered Peace: The Origins of the Cold War and the National Security State* (Boston: Houghton Mifflin, 1977); Robert A. Pollard, *Economic Security and the Origins of the Cold War, 1945–1950* (New York: Columbia University Press, 1985); and Robert L. Messer, *The End of an Alliance: James F. Byrnes, Roosevelt, Truman, and the Origins of the Cold War* (Chapel Hill: University of North Carolina Press, 1982).

The transition from hot war to cold war as it affected, and was affected by, British–American relations is detailed in Robert M. Hathaway, *Ambiguous Partnership: Britain and America, 1944–1947* (New York: Columbia University Press, 1981); Terry H. Anderson, *The United States, Great Britain, and the Cold War, 1944–1947* (Columbia: University of Missouri Press, 1981); Robin Edmonds, *Setting the Mould: The United States and Britain, 1945–1950* (New York: Norton, 1986); Ritchie Ovendale, *The English-Speaking Alliance: Britain, the United States, the Dominions, and the Cold War, 1945–1951* (London:

George Allen & Unwin, 1985); Henry B. Ryan, *The Vision of Anglo-America: The US–UK Alliance and the Emerging Cold War, 1943–1946* (Cambridge: Cambridge University Press, 1987); and Richard A. Best, Jr., *"Cooperation with Like-Minded Peoples": British Influences on American Security Policy, 1945–1949* (Westport, Conn.: Greenwood Press, 1986).

Richard N. Gardner, *Sterling-Dollar Diplomacy*, expanded ed. (New York: McGraw-Hill, 1969), is the best study of the 1945 "British loan." Sir Richard Clarke, *Anglo–American Economic Collaboration in War and Peace, 1942–1949*, Sir Alec Cairncross, ed. (Oxford: Clarendon Press, 1982), reproduces some of the British documents pertaining to the loan negotiations. Churchill's famous "iron curtain" speech is examined in Fraser J. Harbutt, *The Iron Curtain: Churchill, America, and the Origins of the Cold War* (New York: Oxford University Press, 1986). Elaine Windrich, *British Labour's Foreign Policy* (Stanford: Stanford University Press, 1952), is dated but still worth consulting, especially in conjunction with Kenneth O. Morgan, *Labour in Power, 1945–1951* (Oxford: Clarendon Press, 1984). Also useful is Elisabeth Barker, *The British between the Superpowers, 1945–50* (Toronto: University of Toronto Press, 1983). William Roger Louis, *The British Empire in the Middle East, 1945–1951: Arab Nationalism, the United States, and Postwar Imperialism* (Oxford: Clarendon Press, 1984), is absolutely first-rate. William C. Mallalieu, *British Reconstruction and American Policy, 1945–1955* (New York: Scarecrow Press, 1956), documents the intense strain on the British economy in the postwar years. Michael J. Hogan, *The Marshall Plan: America, Britain, and the Reconstruction of Western Europe, 1947–1952* (New York: Cambridge University Press, 1987), is a superb study of American efforts to rebuild Britain and the rest of Western Europe after World War II. The same subject is also ably explored in Alan S. Milward, *The Reconstruction of Western Europe, 1945–51* (London: Methuen, 1984). Martin H. Folly offers a helpful analysis of the British role in the creation of NATO in "Breaking the Vicious Circle: Britain, the United States, and the Genesis of the North Atlantic Treaty," *Diplomatic History* 12 (Winter 1988): 59–77. Events in the Far East in the years immediately after World War II can be followed in Rosemary Foot, *The Wrong War: American Policy and the Dimensions of the Korean Conflict, 1950–1953* (Ithaca, N.Y.: Cornell University Press, 1985); Edwin W. Martin, *Divided Counsel: The Anglo–American Response to Communist Victory in China* (Lexington: University Press of Kentucky, 1986); and Nancy Bernkopf Tucker, *Patterns in the Dust: Chinese–American Relations and the Recognition Controversy, 1949–1950* (New York: Columbia University Press, 1983).

Memoirs and biographies of some of the key decisionmakers in the early cold war years include Clement R. Attlee, *As It Happened* (New York: Viking, 1954); Kenneth Harris, *Attlee* (New York: Norton, 1982); Alan Bullock, *Ernest Bevin: Foreign Secretary, 1945–1951* (London: Heinemann, 1983), which supersedes all earlier biographies of this important statesman; Hugh Dalton, *High Tide and After: Memoirs, 1945–1960* (London: Muller, 1962);

Harry S. Truman, *Memoirs*, 2 vols. (Garden City, N.Y.: Doubleday, 1955–56); Robert J. Donovan, *Conflict and Crisis: The Presidency of Harry S. Truman, 1945–1948* (New York: Norton, 1977), and *Tumultuous Years: The Presidency of Harry S. Truman, 1949–1953* (New York: Norton, 1982); Roy Jenkins, *Truman* (New York: Harper & Row, 1986), a sympathetic biography by a prominent British politician; Dean Acheson, *Present at the Creation: My Years in the State Department* (New York: Norton, 1969); and Forrest C. Pogue, *George C. Marshall: Statesman, 1945–1959* (New York: Viking, 1987).

On Churchill's second residence at 10 Downing Street beginning in 1951, see Martin Gilbert, *Never Despair: Winston S. Churchill, 1945–1965* (Boston: Houghton Mifflin, 1988), the final volume in Gilbert's masterful life of Churchill. Anthony Eden gives his version of events in *Full Circle: The Memoirs of Anthony Eden* (Boston: Houghton Mifflin, 1960). For other views of Eden see Robert Rhodes James, *Anthony Eden* (New York: McGraw-Hill, 1987), the official biography, and for an extremely unfavorable portrait, David Carlton, *Anthony Eden: A Biography* (London: Allen Lane, 1981). Evelyn Shuckburgh, *Descent to Suez: Diaries, 1951–1956*, ed. John Charmley (New York: Norton, 1987), opens a window into British thinking in the years before Suez. For Eisenhower consult Stephen E. Ambrose, *Eisenhower: The President* (New York: Simon & Schuster, 1984), as well as Eisenhower's own not particularly inspiring memoirs, *The White House Years*, 2 vols. (Garden City, N.Y.: Doubleday, 1963–65). For Dulles, see Townsend Hoopes, *The Devil and John Foster Dulles* (Boston: Little, Brown, 1973), and from a British perspective, Richard Goold-Adams, *John Foster Dulles: A Reappraisal* (New York: Appleton-Century-Crofts, 1962). R. B. Manderson-Jones, *The Special Relationship: Anglo–American Relations and Western European Unity, 1947–56* (London: Weidenfeld & Nicolson, 1972), is useful on the question of European unity. On the 1956 Suez crisis, see Hugh Thomas, *The Suez Affair* (London: Weidenfeld & Nicolson, 1967), for the British side; Herman Finer, *Dulles over Suez: The Theory and Practice of His Diplomacy* (Chicago: Quadrangle, 1964), intensely anti-Dulles and written before the materials at the Eisenhower Library became available; and Donald Neff, *Warriors at Suez: Eisenhower Takes America into the Middle East* (New York: Linden Press, 1981), probably the best general account of this most serious breach in Anglo–American ties. Richard E. Neustadt's *Alliance Politics* (New York: Columbia University Press, 1970) is an influential comparison of the Suez and Skybolt crises. As the title of Leon D. Epstein's *Britain—Uneasy Ally* (Chicago: University of Chicago Press, 1954) suggests, many Britons felt uncomfortable even before Suez with the extent to which their affairs had become entwined with the Americans.

Harold Macmillan's multivolume memoirs (London: Macmillan, 1966–73) contain a great deal on British–American relations. For his years as prime minister see *Riding the Storm, 1956–1959* (1971), *Pointing the Way, 1959–1961* (1972), and *At the End of the Day, 1961–1963* (1973). Studies of John

Kennedy's presidency include Arthur M. Schlesinger, Jr., *A Thousand Days: John F. Kennedy in the White House* (Boston: Houghton Mifflin, 1965); Herbert S. Parmet, *JFK: The Presidency of John F. Kennedy* (New York: Dial, 1983); and Henry Fairlie, *The Kennedy Promise: The Politics of Expectation* (Garden City, N.Y.: Doubleday, 1973), by a well-connected British journalist. David Nunnerley's *President Kennedy and Britain* (New York: St. Martin's, 1972) draws heavily on interviews with key decisionmakers in the two countries and remains extremely useful for Anglo–American relations in the early 1960s. A year after the Skybolt crisis, Henry Brandon published a long analysis of the affair in *The* (London) *Times* of 8 December 1963 (pp. 29–31), which more than a quarter century later remains an essential source for this episode in British–American relations. Frank Costigliola offers a very useful overview of relations between the United States and Europe during the Kennedy presidency in "The Failed Design: Kennedy, de Gaulle, and the Struggle for Europe," *Diplomatic History* 8 (Summer 1984): 227–51.

Lyndon Johnson's memoir *The Vantage Point: Perspectives of the Presidency, 1963–1969* (New York: Holt, Rinehart and Winston, 1971) gives little evidence of a special relationship between the two, or for that matter, of any relationship. George W. Ball, *The Discipline of Power: Essentials of a Modern World Structure* (London: Bodley Head, 1968), is an analysis of international affairs in the 1960s by the Kennedy and Johnson administrations' leading skeptic of the utility of close British–American ties, and may be supplemented by Ball's memoirs, *The Past Has Another Pattern* (New York: Norton, 1982). Harold Wilson's account of his first term as prime minister, *A Personal Record: The Labour Government, 1964–1970* (Boston: Little, Brown, 1971), remains a leading source for the British side, although it is more narrative and less analytical than one might have hoped for. The memoirs of one of Wilson's foreign secretaries, George Brown, *In My Way* (New York: St. Martin's, 1971), though otherwise thin, has a bit on Vietnam.

Richard Nixon, *RN: The Memoirs of Richard Nixon* (New York: Grosset & Dunlap, 1978), is singularly unhelpful on British–American relations. This is also true of Gerald Ford's account of his two and a half years in the White House, *A Time To Heal: The Autobiography of Gerald R. Ford* (New York: Harper & Row, 1979). Henry Kissinger, *White House Years* (Boston: Little, Brown, 1979), is essential for American foreign policy during Nixon's first term and devotes a fair amount of space to Anglo–American ties. The second volume of Kissinger's memoirs, *Years of Upheaval* (Boston: Little, Brown, 1982), covers the nineteen months of Nixon's second term in even more detail than is contained in the first volume. Frustration with Edward Heath's aloofness runs throughout. Kissinger's "Reflections on a Partnership: British and American Attitudes to Postwar Foreign Policy," *International Affairs* 58 (Autumn 1982): 571–87, displays a commitment to the special relationship not always apparent in the foreign policies he and Nixon pursued. Laslo V.

Boyd, *Britain's Search for a Role* (Lexington, Mass.: D. C. Heath, 1975), explores Britain's relationships with America and Europe in the 1960s and early 1970s and reflects the pessimism observers of the United Kingdom frequently displayed in the mid-1970s.

The principal history of American diplomacy under Jimmy Carter—Gaddis Smith's *Morality, Reason, and Power: American Diplomacy in the Carter Years* (New York: Hill and Wang, 1986)—does not deal with British–American ties at all and refers to the British only in the context of other international problems. The same is true of the leading study of Cyrus Vance's tenure as secretary of state, David S. McLellan's *Cyrus Vance* (Totowa, N.J.: Rowman & Allanheld, 1985). This is probably a more or less accurate reflection of the importance Washington accorded the bilateral relationship in the late 1970s (as always, the British had a far different perspective), although it may also simply reflect the fact that there was little controversy in Anglo–American ties in those years. Jimmy Carter, *Keeping Faith: Memoirs of a President* (New York: Bantam Books, 1982), mentions the United Kingdom only in passing. Also consult Zbigniew Brzezinski, *Power and Principle: Memoirs of the National Security Adviser, 1977–1981* (New York: Farrar, Straus & Giroux, 1983); and Cyrus Vance, *Hard Choices: Critical Years in America's Foreign Policy* (New York: Simon and Schuster, 1983). James Callaghan, *Time and Chance* (London: Collins, 1987), is perhaps most helpful for Callaghan's years as Chancellor of the Exchequer between 1964 and 1967, but also covers his period as foreign secretary and prime minister in the 1970s. Kenneth Harris, *David Owen* (London: Weidenfeld & Nicolson, 1987), is quite helpful for the first two years of the Carter administration.

There are as yet few useful studies of the Reagan–Thatcher relationship or of the renewal of British–American ties in the 1980s. One might, however, begin with Joel Krieger, *Reagan, Thatcher, and the Politics of Decline* (New York: Oxford University Press, 1986). Ronald Reagan has offered his own appreciation of Thatcher in "Margaret Thatcher and the Revival of the West," *National Review* 41 (19 May 1989): 21–22. Alexander M. Haig, Jr., has published an account of his stormy service as Reagan's first secretary of state in *Caveat: Realism, Reagan, and Foreign Policy* (New York: Macmillan, 1984). Also helpful is Martin Holmes, et al., *British Security Policy and the Atlantic Alliance: Prospects for the 1990s* (Washington, D.C.: Pergamon-Brassey's, 1987). On the Falklands war, Max Hastings and Simon Jenkins, *The Battle for the Falklands* (New York: Norton, 1983), is a good introduction. For the Anglo–American partnership in action, see the very helpful "America's Falklands War," *Economist*, 3 March 1984, 29–31.

Finally, those desiring further titles might do well to consult David A. Lincove and Gary R. Treadway, *The Anglo–American Relationship: An Annotated Bibliography of Scholarship, 1945–1985* (Westport, Conn.: Greenwood Press, 1988).

INDEX

ABOUT THE AUTHOR

Robert M. Hathaway serves on the professional staff of the Asian and Pacific Affairs Subcommittee of the U.S. House of Representatives, while also teaching part-time in the Department of History at George Washington University. He received his Ph.D. in American history from the University of North Carolina in 1976. His *Ambiguous Partnership: Britain and America, 1944–1947* won the Harry S. Truman Book Award for 1980–81.

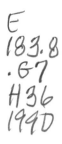